LUCKY BASTARD

Timothy Oliver

First published 2020
by Rowanvale Books Ltd
The Gate
Keppoch Street
Roath
Cardiff
CF24 3JW
www.rowanvalebooks.com

A CIP catalogue record for this book is available from the British Library.

ISBN: 978-1-913662-05-9

Dedicated to my amazing wife, Sue, and our children, Emily, Sam and Kate, for all their love and occasional understanding and making my life complete.

CONTENTS

Daoism is based on the *Dao De Jing*, the ancient book of philosophy by Lao Tsu:

If you remove ego from the process then there isn't much difference from success and failure. They're both just parts of a process. You shouldn't look at failure as something terrible, it just is what it is and you shouldn't look at success as great, it just is what it is.

MOCHDRE –
EARLY BEGINNINGS

I remember nothing of 4 February 1949, when I was born mid-morning in Smithdown Road, which had been an infamous part of Liverpool for many years. I did make an impression on the nurse attending, who told my birth mother that she'd never have another one like me—quite what she meant I'll never know, but my own family call me "different", and I never get a straight answer as to what they mean by that. Sue refers to me as "almost perfect", which is the epitaph for my tombstone—as everyone knows, a miss is as good as a mile, so she's left masses of room for interpretation.

My earliest memories are as a toddler in Mochdre, the most beautiful and friendliest of rural communities in the rolling hills and valleys of Montgomeryshire, Mid Wales, where the Vicarage had no running water or electricity—I still remember the comforting smell of oil lamps and the warnings to be very careful with the wicks as they could be easily damaged. There, I was christened Timothy Oliver on 9 November 1949.

I was unbelievably lucky to have the Rev. Oliver Jestyn and Enid Hill as parents: the most tender, caring, aware people, who exuded love and in turn were loved by the thousands of parishioners they served. Oliver was not only wise but one of the most enlightened people to have walked this earth, whose influence I benefited from greatly. Enid's family were millers and bakers, and she inherited the warmth of her father, John Davies, and radiated untold kindness, from which I also profited. Together, they set me on the path to the happiest of childhoods.

Mochdre was a magical place, full of friendly, smiling faces—just the same visiting sixty-eight years later, although the polecats, wild horses and red kites are no longer as abundant. These were post-war years, and rationing books were still in use; however, provided the government supplied the thick syrupy orange juice, it didn't matter whatsoever which other luxuries we were lacking. I remember being looked after by Miss Orells, who had a smallholding with ducks, cows, dogs and the smelliest of ponds in the farmyard. She told me the story about how I escaped from my cot, with Oliver and Enid content that I was fast asleep. I made it out of the Vicarage in my nightgown and down the road, only to be chased back by Merfyn Benbow, who lived in the nearest farm. I walked back in through the front door, much to the surprise of my loving parents. Another day, I came home and told Enid I had been across one field. The next day, two fields, and the following day, three — it seems I was destined to travel from an early age.

I had soon built total faith in the ability of my father to rescue any situation. The drive to the Vicarage was lined in springtime by a myriad of beautiful tulips. I thought I was doing a kindness for my mother by picking the heads off all the tulips—when I received a well-deserved telling off, I retorted, "Easy mend it; Daddy mend it."

One time, Oliver landed in severely hot water with Enid. He had taken me to Newtown, the nearest place with shops, and after the third person in a very short time told him what a beautiful little girl he had, I was taken straight to the nearest barbers to have all my golden curls shorn—not one saved. He redeemed himself many times over. One occasion was when he arrived home to find me with blood pouring from my mouth but with no idea whether it originated from my head or stomach. I had been standing on a bent wood chair, watching my mum make cakes, and I had fallen off and struck the floor. A quick dash to the local hospital, and Oliver carried me into the operating theatre in his arms—not something that could happen today. The surgeon soon discovered that the blood was pouring from my tongue, and a few stitches soon put that right; it didn't stop me from having my tongue between my teeth at times of concentration.

Another scare for my mum and dad came when a garden party was being hosted on the Vicarage lawn. All of a sudden, people realised the two-year-old had gone missing, only for me to be sighted waving from twenty-five feet up a tree. Another example of my "independence" was disappearing from Ffynnon-y-Cyff, Lixwm, Flintshire, after being unfairly put in the yard of Uncle Emlyn's farm by Aunt Gwyneth for making their youngest daughter cry. Even at the age of three I wasn't prepared to put up with injustice and had set off for my grandparents' in Nannerch Mill, some four miles away. I crossed the busy Mold Denbigh Road, up to Nannerch village, then walked the last mile along the narrow lanes to safety. I hadn't realised the scare I had created going missing, especially as my grandfather had been captured by gypsies as a young boy and kept for several days—he must have been equally as good looking and modest as me.

There was no better preacher than Oliver. I would crawl under the seats in church to be with my dad in the pulpit, and he delivered many a sermon with my legs dangling over the edge. Years later, Jim Malcolm, who I met in Hollywood in 1970, came to stay with us in Marford, North Wales, just after Emily, our first daughter, was born in May 1980. He was Dean of Colorado College and Head of Drama, and said he couldn't believe how well I projected my voice with no training—way better than many of his students who had studied for three years. My dad must have been the key to this.

Oliver's "rebel twin" was Bill Dickin. They had become firm friends at St Michael's College, Llandaff while training for the ministry; many hours, or rather days, they spent discussing where the Church was going wrong and how it should be put right. At the time, Bill lived with his lively family in rural Castle Caereinion, and the highlight of our visits would be to whoosh down the tyre zip-line in their garden.

It was a wonderful start in life, cocooned by so much love emanating from many different quarters.

LLANFYLLIN –
FORMATIVE YEARS

OJH was inducted as Rector of Llanfyllin on Tuesday 22 November 1952. There could not have been a more beautiful, friendly place to enjoy my formative years. A market town with a population of one thousand with a high proportion of Welsh speakers, nestled in rolling hills close to Lake Vyrnwy and the Berwyns, with the Cain River running through. The Rectory was massive with three pillars in the hallway, plenty large enough to ride a bike around. The drawing and dining rooms had the tallest ceilings and were oak-panelled top to bottom. The staircase was also made of oak with two gentle turns and was ideal for riding down using large cardboard boxes as bobsleds. There was a back staircase leading from the kitchen, which wasn't quite as grand, but had a series of bells on coiled springs, each one sounding a different note to indicate to the servants of yesteryear where their services were needed. There was an open fire to heat the smoothing irons and boil water in blackened pans, and a primitive cooker working off the old town gas, which would regularly catch fire.

The lavatory was like a throne room with the WC set on top of a series of pedestals; I imagine the helpers would have been expected to use the outside privy, which had three seats in a row to encourage communal spirit. We used them with squares of newspaper threaded with string to do the wiping business. In the yard was a pump that had to be primed before water could be drawn; Oliver had taken out the bolt that hinged the handle so little people couldn't drain the reservoir; however, a stick could be used instead, and my finger is still misshapen as a result of cousin David (Raglan) not following the safety rules.

Box hedges surrounded the various garden plots, and I'd take great delight diving into them from my speeding tricycle.

When the old Rectory was demolished, it appeared to be crying. One happy resolution was that OJH bid

Old Rectory Crying

Oak panels were installed in the chancel of St Myllin's Church

unopposed for the oak panels, which were installed in the chancel of St Myllin's.

The coronation of Queen Elizabeth II in 1953 caused great excitement in Llanfyllin, not least in the church, which for some reason had no flagpole. Oliver organised the making of the pole, and it was a moving sunny afternoon when the bell-ringers congregated on top of the tower and heaved the flagpole up the outside of St Myllin's church; no way could there be a coronation without a flag. The operation wasn't totally straightforward. The pole was heavy and its height was greater than the width of the tower. But with regimental precision, all went well, and most importantly, there were no injuries. The momentous day arrived, and after a service in church, there was a dash for the television. At the time there were only two in the town: a 9" screen in a tiny house in Narrow Street, and a 15" screen at the postmaster's, Mr Preece, both of course in black and white. The owner of the house in Narrow Street was regarded with a modicum of suspicion, partly because he had whippet dogs, which made him appear like Fagin from *Oliver Twist*, and of course because he could afford a television. The dogs took up a lot of space watching the scenes from Westminster Abbey. I was meant to be amongst the select few, with Oliver and Enid, above the post office, but even from the tender age of three, I was much more contented to be amongst roots people. (Later, in Jamaica, I'll relate how I was much happier with Cap, Tony, Owen and Steve, local Jamaicans from water-sports, than upstarts from the UK.) I was unaware of the great consternation that I was lost, not for the first time, but there was no fear of abduction or other belligerent behaviour in Llanfyllin.

Not only did Oliver deliver the most exciting sermons for people of all ages with wonderful delivery and command of the English language, he was also an amazing yarn teller. One lovely example of this is his Jacko stories, about a mischievous monkey who had wild adventures on trains, boats and journeys, which would inevitably involve getting lost and landing up in all kinds of trouble. I am pleased that I carried on the tradition with our children and wrote a couple of escapades involving the grandchildren.

Whenever I could, when I was old enough, I would accompany my dad while he visited hospitals in Oswestry, Gobowen and Shrewsbury, walking to Cwm Nany Y Meichiad when the snow was too deep to drive for the Sunday service. Also the Dolydd, which had been a horrendous workhouse until 1930, when it was turned into a care home run by the parents of Ryan Davies, who became one of Wales' finest entertainers. These experiences with OJH no doubt created the foundations for my social conscience. I also enjoyed watching *Muffin the Mule* and other children's programmes on television in the Dolydd as it would be several years before one arrived in the Rectory. I also learnt how to respond to people of all classes and states of health; one seemingly unimportant thing was to accept sweets or other small tokens you were offered, which made such a difference to the person giving and would bring a smile to their face as their gift was accepted.

Life seemed an endless flow of fun and adventure, including school. When I started in the church school, I felt six foot tall in my brand new pair of boots. The clip clop of the metal bands under the toes and heels would resonate off the walls of the houses as I ran down Narrow Street.

Gladys Mair Hughes, the headmistress of the church school, was a formidable lady—particularly in size—with a heart of gold which emanated through the music she created playing the harp. Mrs Owen, my delightful form teacher, was also kind and encouraging, but unfortunately this didn't filter through to me performing on stage in the Yrdd Eisteddfod. I had a lovely voice and enjoyed singing and reciting; however, my two performances in Llanwddyn, where the area's Urdd was being held, ended in tears, as I broke down in both. The only thing I could see in the crowd in front of me was the light reflecting from

Oliver's spectacles. It would be decades before I could stand in front of audiences and deliver with confidence.

Bill and Cynthia, my godparents, gave me a hand-me-down two-wheeler fairy cycle. Eventually I had the strength in my legs to go up Market Street unaided, and soon I was off—too far, Oliver thought, for a four year old. A friend of his reported seeing me heading

Cowboy Tie   *Bristol Channel*

past the Dolydd, a mile out of town, on the way towards Llanfechain; OJH's Morris 8 registration BAX 69 was soon in hot pursuit, the blue bicycle was bundled in the back and the front wheel taken off and hidden for what seemed an age.

Oliver kept a "Now and Then" diary, and these are entries from 1955:

I explained what happens at an election and T couldn't understand how we knew which candidate to vote for. T's last word to Mummy, "you look at their faces & vote for the one you like best"

When I wasn't well:

Bill & Cynthia Dickin & family cheered T up giving him 5 shilling in savings stamps & on his own initiative T went to the Post Office and opened an account with all the money he had & brought home a bank book with his own firm signature – it is something to have one member of the family on the credit side!

Being careful with money has always been part of my nature, most likely influenced by Oliver straightening nails and putting white sticky labels on to envelopes so he could recycle them to help keep expense down. Spending on large items, such as worldwide travel, has never been a problem, as Enid's influence led me to save up and buy quality. How true were Bernard Ruziewicz's words of wisdom in Miami: "What you regret in life is the money you don't spend."

From Oliver's Now and Then book:

T started wearing shirts instead of blouses & thinks himself no end of a feller

To Mummy: I've got a sweetheart in school and I have kissed her when Miss Hughes was out of the room – but don't tell Daddy

One of the fondest memories my dad relates was when I first bumped into Peggy, a dwarf lady, wobbling down the street and she remarked on the heartfelt smile I gave her, the like of which she'd never received before; we became firm friends from then on, exchanging happy beams whenever we passed each other.

A family of Pakistanis came to town, which caused a great stir. Ali Nazar, the father, opened a shop selling cloth, and as I spoke good English, Zacub, who was my age, was put to sit next to me at school. It caused much amusement for many that instead of him speaking like me, I began to squeak like him. We became good friends, and one of my joyous memories is when I walked to collect him to go to school at the beginning of his first winter. He was running around shouting and laughing, throwing snow in the air; he had never seen the white stuff before.

I remember the aromatic smells which hit me when I went into his house. I saw no difference between us despite his colour and language, and no doubt this, together with my enlightened parents, was the foundation of my enjoying the company of all races and creeds throughout my life.

The summers appeared an endless stream of sunshine, and the winters' falling snow provided excellent sledge runs down the steep hills, one conveniently above the Rectory.

I was the youngest of the "gang" by a few years, which meant I was always struggling to keep up and was the weakest when it came to fighting; however this stood me in good stead in later life, especially in rugby, swimming, cricket, tennis, fives and squash.

Summer meant days wandering over hills and down dales without a care in the world. My mum wasn't worried, as she knew I would come back when my sandwiches had run out and I was hungry. It took a lot of courage the first time I jumped into the River Cain at Bodfach Hall, not least because I couldn't swim.

One of the fun games we played was tick on bikes, and one ploy to get away was to time our runs across the "busy" road as close as possible in front of the cars travelling along, later called chicken. A little dangerous, but none of us were hurt; I do remember howls of laughter when the pursuer braked late and landed in the side of a car, only to receive a severe telling off from the driver.

Another great time for fearless fun was when the new Rectory was built in the grounds of the old one. Scaffolding was erected, and we had endless games chasing each other across the upstairs floor joists and around the outside; remarkably, I can't remember anyone tumbling off, but we did fall out of trees.

I fell out of my bedroom window, close to where I'd watched Dad painstakingly prepare the rough ground, sift the soil and plant seeds. When I looked out of the window after going upstairs to bed, I saw birds eating the vegetables. There was a supply of cotton reels I decided to scare them away with. Standing inside the bedroom or on the windowsill, I couldn't get a full swing, so on the outside ledge I stood. With great force, I threw the first reel in the direction of the vegetable plot, only to find myself falling through the air and landing with a thud on the ground. How long

I lay there I have no idea, but Oliver and Enid were well surprised when I walked back in through the open French windows.

I enjoyed helping Oliver with chores whenever I could, in the garden and especially collecting logs. I was delighted when I was tall enough and had the rhythm to go on the other end of the crosscut saw, standing on a box.

My dad wasn't amused when Richard Preece arrived on Bob a Job Week as a boy scout and chopped up his carefully tended bean poles as sticks for lighting the fire.

When the new Rectory had been built, there was a veranda on one of the bedrooms, and Oliver built a run by attaching a rope from the bars to the trees way below. A car tyre was attached to the rope via a pulley, and we would go crashing into the branches as there was no means of braking. This became dangerous after the car tyre was detached. We then hung from

Lych Gate St Myllin's

Chaplain to Lord Lieutenant Major Dugdale

the axle by both hands, which was fine, but the risk arose when we had to get off. As we let go, the spindle and pulley would fire high into the air. However, if both hands didn't let go at exactly the same time, there was a chance of being struck in the head—Oliver put a stop to this fairly rapidly.

Another opportunity for excitement arose from the long tarmac drive which was constructed for the new Rectory. Trucks were built using pram wheels, axles and a plank of wood; races took place on a regular basis, and a good run could get you down Market Street to the A490. As well as riding our trucks down the streets used by cars and lorries, we played games on the train from Llanfyllin to Oswestry, that the boys would take to go to the swimming baths, which chugged at a pace that enabled us to jump off while it was travelling along and clamber in the carriage behind.

Cricket was another regular pastime. The pitch went across the five roads to wickets drawn with chalk on the telegraph post at the bottom of Llwyn Drive. One evening, I came home and went straight to bed. Oliver and Enid knew something had gone wrong. My dad found out later as he was walking down Narrow Street and heard two ladies talking across from their upstairs windows, saying that the Rector's boy had only broken the stained glass windows of the bank

Footplate from Llanfyllin to Oswestry   Stilts

manager's house while he was away on holiday; it was an excellent leg sweep.

I had an ace day at the Llanwddyn annual fair when I cleaned up in the slow bicycle race, obstacle and fast race; the local boys weren't at all happy with me riding away with seven shillings and sixpence, a handsome afternoon's work.

Another great sport was to follow the fire engine on our bikes. The firemen were volunteers and called to action by the siren, dropping whatever they were doing and hurrying to the fire station; this was also the heads up for us to race there and follow the truck to wherever they were going. This must have been acceptable behaviour as I don't remember being told not to pursue. One distressing time was when the mountain around the Lonely Tree caught fire one hot summer. Over a series of weeks, the fire engine was called out on a regular basis as the fire would crop up some hundred yards away, having travelled underground.

Lake Vyrnwy was a favourite haunt and well within range of a good bike ride. One of the scariest times in my life was when Oliver drove us to Lake Vyrnwy soon after a cloudburst. Torrential rain had brought down trees from the surrounding hills, which were prevented from going through the arches of the dam because the water level had risen so high. The immense power of the water was only too apparent and I feared the dam might give way.

By contrast, there was a severe drought one summer, and the water sank so low that the stones outlining houses and the remains of the church could be seen. A stark reminder of the valley that had been artificially flooded to provide water for the Liverpool Corporation Waterworks, and of the resulting heartache for the villagers who had their tiny community destroyed.

Another reminder of the potency of nature and the ability of mankind to build homes in unsuitable places was reflected in the number of houses that were flooded each year in Bridge Street as the Cain burst its banks. Every house had slots in the doorways where boards could be fitted, and the severity of the floods was measured by how close to the A490 the river had risen. Sensibly, measures were eventually taken to erect flood barriers.

There were many interesting characters in Llanfyllin, amongst them Tom Jarvis, a solicitor, town clerk and church warden. He would get into trouble with his wife, a lovely Scottish lady, for over-drinking and overspending. Oliver would bail him out by buying from him the odd bit of furniture he couldn't afford, and we still have a couple of the pieces. Tom crashed one time this side of Llansantffraid, travelling back from a freemason's lodge in Wrexham. He was unhurt physically—just some ear-bashing from the usual source—and worried that the police might think the stench of wine wasn't from an unopened bottle that had smashed but his over-imbibing.

Betty Jones was my first love; I am sure she never knew. She had flowing auburn hair and the voice of an angel. I would often camp out at the top of the drive, and whenever Betty would come to practise singing with Oliver, I would lie about waiting; I don't think I ever dared go within ten feet of her. A press cutting from the *Express and Times*, January 1954, read:

"The Telephone" written and composed by Gian Carlo Menotti, was being given its first performance in Wales and was capably rendered by Miss Betty Jones as "Lucy" and the Rector, Oliver J Hill, as "Ben". It afforded the artistes much scope to display their stage ability and vocal power. The popular idea of the feminine long windedness when using the telephone and the associated importance of the masculine temperament – the themes of the opera – were well stressed.

Betty would later change her name to Elizabeth Vaughan and became the youngest person to play the lead role in *Madame Butterfly*. She was encouraged to pursue a career as an opera singer by Oliver and Mr Warner, against the will of her headmaster. Many years later in the early 1970s, she performed in William Aston Hall, Wrexham, and I took Oliver and Enid to see her. Also attending was Mrs Hywel Glynne Jones, who good-humouredly said, "If I'd had ten children, one of them would have been just as successful."

Church was a big part of my life, and I greatly enjoyed Sunday school. The fondest memories were of waking up early on Christmas morning and walking through deep snow for the 6:30 a.m. service. I learnt to chime the church bells and knew they were listened to when the local greengrocer asked Oliver, with a smile on his face, why I was playing "Now the Day is Over" at 8:00 in the morning.

Sitting on the wall at the bottom of the garden, chatting to the Wright brothers at a tender age, they asked me whether I was born or adopted; the parishioners must have been chatting. I went to Oliver and asked him, to which he replied, "You are our chosen child." A beautiful answer, although I didn't understand the question.

At a young age, I would help in the harvest at a local farm. Great fun was had sitting amongst the bales of hay and chatting with the farmer and his helpers. I was excited to see what animals would run for their lives as the harvester cut the final crops in the centre of the field. As they drank cider in the break, I proudly downed a glass of Adam's ale.

My mum liked a treat on Sunday evenings and her preference was sweets or chocolates; however, there were often occasions when she hadn't any. I would come to her rescue by raiding the stores I kept in safe-keeping behind the *London Town Crier* pictures up the stairs, much to Enid's delight.

The time came, at seven years of age, to move from the church school, where I had always been top of the class, to the Council school, where I was in the Welsh stream with natural Welsh speakers—competition toughened. Barbara and I would alternate being first in class. Another delightful friend was Haelwen and our families became close decades later in Wrexham; tragically, cancer took Haelwen away earlier in 2020.

We learnt Welsh history, and I profoundly felt Welsh blood was streaming through my veins.

One of my earliest memories of fishing with Oliver was on Bryngwyn Lake, Bwlch-y-Cibau, Llanfyllin, part of Ian Lawrie Mackeson-Sandbach's Estate. We took sandwiches and spent a delightful afternoon in peaceful wooded surroundings; there was much excitement when I hooked and landed a very big carp and was thrilled to take it home and show my mum.

This idyllic life of a romantic, sensitive little country boy who wore his heart on his sleeve, frolicking through the green pastures, was about to be shattered at the age of nine and a half, as I was sent away to school at Lawrence House in St Anne's on Sea, a million miles away in Lancashire.

Dungarees

Wilf and Mari Wedding

LAWRENCE HOUSE – A RUDE AWAKENING

It was done with the worthiest of intentions, to give me the best opportunities in life by providing the most beneficial education. Oliver and Enid made financial sacrifices as well as personal ones, losing me for thirteen weeks at a time, and Oliver was physically sick for days before I left Llanfyllin for the start of each new term at Lawrence House, St Anne's on Sea, Lancashire, which as far as I was concerned could have been the other side of the Pacific Ocean. Enid didn't have a notion about the hardships of boarding school and Oliver, no doubt familiar with *Tom Brown's School Days*, couldn't have imagined such behaviour still went on.

An entry in Now and Then:

John Dickin on his last year there & has been happy and well taught. Must try and find means to let Timothy go there. Have entered Tim at Lawrence House and now Mummy is getting his gear ready. School outfitters are a refined breed of extortioners.

Thursday 25 September 1958:

A brief farewell to Tim who looked rather bewildered; Enid and I, childless and too full to say much

Tuesday 16 December 1958:

Like children, we had both looked forward to home coming so Enid and I went to Shrewsbury to meet the train at 11:15. When we had almost decided that Tim and John Dickin were not on it there they came through the throng on the platform. We were glad they had managed to change from the Preston-London train at Crewe and Tim was travelling that way by himself next year.

I remember travelling to Lawrence House in the Morris 8 for the first time. The briefest of farewells—we were not touchy-feely people—a quick turnaround as I went through the doors to see my dearest Mum and Dad drive off with an empty luggage rack on the back of BAX 69. Oliver had made my tuck box, which neatly held my Meccano set in the top, had a postcard of Newquay (Cardigan) stuck inside the lid and tubes of condensed milk to sustain me.

Our letters home were vetted and didn't reflect any unhappiness, or no doubt Oliver and Enid would have pulled me straight out. They had no idea what a perverted, drunken sadist Dick Smith, the senior master, was, as he disguised it amazingly well to the outside world. He treated his wife, who I used to help in the kitchens, abominably; he should have been incarcerated for life for the loathsome physical and mental aggression towards his son who he brutalised more than any other child.

The matron was austere with not a glimmer of kindness in her visage. At lights out, the prefect in charge of our dorm asked, "Any bed-wetters?" I was too terrified to own up, and next morning was a walk of shame, as true to form, I'd wet my bed. I visited a consultant in Shrewsbury hospital, where I was prepared by two smiling nurses who did their best to put me at ease. Nothing was found physically wrong with me.

Every day started with a cold shower. Dick Smith shuffled down the corridors in his dressing gown and slippers, stinking of whisky. There were two rows of eight at either end of the bathroom with washbasins in between. He would call "on", count slowly to ten as he no doubt enjoyed watching the shivering bodies, then "off".

Our whole lives were regimented and controlled by bells. Strict rules such as no running in corridors, no wearing of outdoor shoes indoors, and never be late; any breach was punished by caning. Dick Smith had three lights over his study door. The first let you know you could knock, the second not to be interrupted and the third to let the world know that he was caning. One time fifteen little boys were caned one after the other for allegedly smoking. He would offer a choice of canes; his most popular was Benjamin, a long, thin, whiplashing inflictor of pain and discipline. Invariably, there were screams, the clack with resulting blue stripes lasting for days, but any bleeding would stop within hours. He had favourites who he took delight in caning more than others; one was Carr, who had an attractive mother, and another was Braithwick, who was bullied by all and sundry. Unfortunately for him, he would wet his short pants and worse during the day and would have toilet paper stuffed in and left dangling down. One time, this poor wretch was rolled up in the creosoted cricket nets which were then set alight; if it wasn't for the chance passing of a master, he'd likely have been burnt alive. There were other boys who would do runners and escape only to be brought back to custody; hardly in loco parentis. Birthdays were kept secret as rather than marking a happy day, your life was made as miserable as possible. Subconsciously, this may have created a barrier to my enjoying celebrations and walking out of a surprise 26th birthday party.

Saturday night was Dick Smith's time for serious drinking, invariably leading to a troublesome hangover the following morning, which sets the scene for my worst memory. On Sunday mornings, we were allowed an extra hour in bed for reading, strictly no talking. There were two dormitories directly above Smith's bedroom. His footsteps mounted the stairs; he may have been attracted by talking in our dorm—luckily for us he went into the one before ours. Carr had been playing chess in silence with another boy who was sitting on his bed. Before long, the air was penetrated by loud swishes followed by screams which echoed endlessly around the corridors. Carr, a young boy of twelve, had received six strokes wearing only thin pyjama bottoms which offered no protection, and the other boy four lashes.

Other marks of Smith's sadism could be seen on the inside flesh of children's legs, up to a dozen small circular bruises he called nips. These he inflicted by calling the culprits to the front of the class when the active tense was put instead of passive, or vice versa, in Latin lessons, and breathings were written the wrong way round in Greek.

Another teacher consumed with hatred was Turner, a fervent Roman Catholic, who was invariably found drunk on a Saturday night, lying in a bunker on the women's golf course, incapable of climbing out. He'd fall in while making his way back to the school from the club house of the Royal Lytham; only a narrow path separated the school from the golf course. He played the harmonium, and whenever he took the daily prayers, he would do his best to convert us to papism. There was a strong rumour that he was having an affair with Miss Kenyon, not necessarily because they were of the same faith. I later noticed I was regularly on the receiving end of their venom, most likely because my father was a Clerk in Holy Orders in the Church in Wales.

Mild Fracas   International boxing bout

There were lighter moments and I built some good friendships, especially with Peter Liver and Brian Wood. On the Friday before an exeat, the names of the few of us who weren't being taken out by our parents were called out in assembly and boys were asked if they could entertain an extra passenger; Oliver was taking Sunday services. The Livers were extremely kind and we would visit Fairhaven Lake and St Anne's Shore. Wood's family exuded wealth, and we were picked up in a smart Alvis and whisked off to their house in the country, throughout which odours of game bird pervaded. I was introduced to high tea, fat sausages at the centre of a feast of fried bread, baked beans, tomatoes, mushrooms; I was gutted when I threw up one time soon after getting back to school. Brian had a real live go-kart with a petrol engine, and we'd whizz round the driveways. His father would invariably work in the afternoon, and we would begin our journey back to school just as "Play Something Simple" started on the radio. First stop was a pillar box on the side of the road, where he'd lean out of the driver's window and post his letters.

One of my best friends was Rex Leyland, a Jewish boy from West Kirby. We'd travel on the train together at the end of term from Lytham St Anne's via Preston to Liverpool—by this time, Oliver had become Vicar of Shotton. Rex's parents stayed in the Norbreck Castle Hotel in Blackpool over exeats; I had never experienced such luxury, with its huge indoor swimming pool and fancy restaurant. I found it tough eating olives, which Rex's parents brought for him and his sister instead of sweets; his father owned pharmacies in Liverpool.

Escape from Colditz

Shotton Vicarage

There was sport every weekday, and "Spitter" was brought in from Blackpool FC to train us in football. Molloy, a more understanding teacher, was an excellent cricket coach, and various masters taught rugby. Members of the local cricket club would arrive from time to time to ensure Lawrence House fared well against other schools. I scored a six three years running, home and away, against one school, and the only time I bowled in a match, I caught the last batsman off my first ball, a perfect statistic—this feat wasn't placed on the noticeboard. I remember watching Michael Coxey representing Charnley Hall with his white-striped colours cap; a talented batsman. Much time was spent in the nets while up to six boys practised slip catching on the cradle. My fondness for cricket receded when my nose was splattered across my face misjudging a fast throw.

On Wednesdays, boys would cross the track to Royal Lytham to learn golf while the rest of us had cricket practice; no way would I ask Oliver and Enid if I could join the golfers, as I knew they couldn't afford the equipment, and I was left out of the cricket team to travel to King Williams on the Isle of Man most likely for the same reason.

Dick Smith tended the cricket square with more care than he'd treat boys, and he looked after the lawn tennis court with equal affection. There was a fives court, and I was thrilled when my very own gloves arrived. I fought one boxing match, which was billed as an international.

There was a boxing club with an imported coach, which I didn't attend. On the annual fight night, Garthwaite had no one to fight from the club, so non-boxers in the audience were asked if they'd step into the ring. I won on points, maybe because I was bleeding more heavily. The main bout was between Humble, by far the best boxer and a terrifying fast bowler with a face as fearsome as Fred Truman, against Langford, a gentle boy who had a stutter. Humble was way ahead after the first round and could have pulverised him. He eased off, and the fight was awarded to Langford.

There was an outdoor swimming pool, very cold, and I was given detention when I refused to get in, my pleas to avoid hypothermia ignored. We attended an athletics day at Stonyhurst College, and I—by some feat—won the all-comers high jump, beating Miller, the best in Lawrence House. My biggest sporting triumph was winning the table tennis trophy in a tournament which included the masters as competitors. In the final there was heckling and cheating, as Pimblett's supporters were determined he should win, but I overcame them all; a carpenter friend of Oliver's in Shotton had made a table for me one Christmas, which gave me countless pleasure and had honed my skills.

As a treat, a trip was arranged for the school football team to see the Blackpool Illuminations, and it was a huge joke that this country bumpkin from the Welsh Hills hadn't a clue what on earth they were. I couldn't believe my eyes when we drove through on the bus and saw the most amazing display of bright lights and animated cartoons. From the fateful dorm window, I used to watch the lift go up and down the Blackpool Tower, and I had no idea what other treasures that centre of show business would have in store for me over fifty years later.

It must have been through the school's connections with the entertainment world that well-known figures came to open the summer garden fete, including Adam Faith of "What Do You Want" fame and Ena Sharples from *Coronation Street*.

Every year the school put on a musical—and guess who would always play the lead, a monstrous giant amongst his little inmates? The performance took place in one of St Anne's main theatres, and the excitement rose as the grease paint was applied and the orchestra struck up. The hype continued throughout the show and in the dressing rooms as our makeup was removed.

Another extravaganza was bonfire night, when the best of firework displays, lasting seemingly forever, took place in the school grounds. Every effort was made to show parents what wonderful things were provided. They didn't hear about the necks of leverets being snapped by a pupil; I wondered whether the perpetrator landed in gaol for GBH or worse in a later stage of his life.

The acquisition of mini darts introduced a new sport into the school, and when these ran out, weapons were made by sellotaping drawing pins to the end of dip pens. The darts were thrown at each other, penetrating flesh on arms and legs and occasionally faces. The French teacher was an ex-colonel and ignored any bad tricks boys got up to, not adhering to the strict discipline regime. When darts were thrown at the blackboard as he was writing, he would just continue up and around. He had a quiet sense of humour and when asked for a translation of "au bord du ruisseau", up went my hand—"On the border of Russia" was my reply. He praised me for my brave attempt, whereas I would have received admonishment from others and possibly an excuse for a "nip" from the pervert.

Mercenary Mary

Petrol engine

At an early age, I found out my memory wasn't that good, as did Molloy the history teacher. Every Wednesday morning at the start of the lesson, there was a test comprising either ten or twenty questions, which always included something to do with the Gunpowder Plot: Year? 1605. Date? 5th November. Who was responsible? Guy Fawkes. This was to ensure I had at least one mark.

John Dickin was at the school with me for a year. He was extremely bright and was taken off all other subjects to concentrate on Greek and Latin, which Dick Smith taught. Cynthia, his mother, was vexed that his education was severely hampered by having such a narrow focus at a young age to satisfy Dick Smith's desire to produce a star.

The only similarity John and I had "academically" was the loudness of our voices. We must have picked up the ability to project our voices from years of listening to our respective fathers preaching from their pulpits, and our voices could be recognised above all others reverberating through the corridors; neither of us could or can whisper!

Great excitement arose in the autumn of 1961 when the Ryder Cup came to Royal Lytham and the school pole was adorned with flags of different nations. The final year students were to act as Stewards/Runners. I nearly missed the chance, as

I struggled in a Greek lesson the day before and Smith threatened that if I didn't get the translation right, I would be stopped from going. I managed to get through by the skin of my teeth and was able to watch Dai Rees, the Welsh captain, Bernard Hunt and Peter Alliss amongst others.

Ryder Cup

Dai Rees, Captain of the Ryder Cup Team

An enormously enjoyable experience was visiting Gometra, a small island off Ulva and the tip of Mull. The Schools Hebridean Society was formed by John Abbott, a master teaching at Lawrence House, with some of his cronies from St John's. I waited at Crewe Station in the early hours of the morning with my mum and dad, dressed in shorts because that was what all proper expedition campers should be wearing. The other reason could have been that cash was short; there was always good food on the table, but there was nothing spare for luxuries such as holiday clothes. The station was bleak and deserted, and eventually, several hours late, the train from London appeared with all the other campers, not one wearing short trousers. We had sleeper carriages, and by morning we were through Glasgow and heading to Oban. By Stirling, we discovered that the windows went fully down and bodies were running along the platform and diving back in.

Serious decisions had to be made at the Oban quayside. There were force eight/nine gales, and the captain of the fishing trawler stank of whisky. The choice was to set sail down the Sound of Mull in abominable weather or wait twelve hours until the next tide with nowhere to overnight. John Abbott decided to go for it, a decision he may have regretted a few hours later as the boat was tossed around in the Sound like a cork. Most of the twenty-two boys, together with the teachers, were battened down in the hold. Three of us occupied the captain's quarters at the rear of the trawler. I was queasy from the engines' diesel fumes but hugely relieved not to have been in the hold, as when it was opened, the stench of sick hit us. There was chaos—rucksacks, boxes and food had been hurled everywhere. We tied up at the dock on Gometra, sheltered from the wind in the small harbour, and farm trucks arrived to transport us, our tents and baggage. We waved goodbye to the trawler, and no doubt the captain had to glug more whisky to help him back to Oban.

Bell tents were erected to sleep in and a marquee as a general area, most importantly for eating. Clocks were changed to align with dawn and dusk, and no radios were allowed. We became part of nature, spotting golden eagles, sea otters, white-tailed sea eagles and puffins. The party gelled, which was just as well, because the gales returned, breaking the ridge pole of the marquee. We boys were evacuated for a couple of days to the granary in the nearby farmyard, where we sheltered amongst the sacks, waiting for the weather to abate. Meanwhile the leaders took the canvas down, spliced the ridge pole and re-erected the marquee. Teams were selected to watch during the nights. I found out my ability to stay awake was more or less non-existent, which hasn't changed throughout my life. We built benches hardly a foot wide to sit at the homemade tables, but they were adequate for me to lie on and sleep. Being one of the youngest, my conduct was tolerated.

Luckily the weather improved, the sun came out, the skies turned blue and "normal" activities resumed. The Lord Bishop of Norwich, Sir Lancelot Fleming, arrived in his kilt, helped re-establish the camp and organised the building of dry stone walls. I enjoyed several trips around the neighbouring islands in a small boat, including Fingal's Cave, Iona and most dramatically, Inch Kenneth, for tea with Lady Redesdale, mother of the Mitford sisters and mother-in-law to Oswald Mosely.

The raging seas throwing up white horses, the gusting winds, the wildlife and friendliness of the islanders inspired every essay I wrote in French, Spanish and English over the next five years.

Gometra

Steam boat

Back in Lawrence House, boys had recited the Lord's Prayer in Latin, Greek and French throughout the month, and now it was my turn in Welsh. A master was allotted to assist me in the days running up to the Sunday service, and he was satisfied with my performance. Unfortunately, I had learnt a shortened version, and the ogre's wrath descended on me. I felt lucky to have escaped being flogged black and blue, and the reward of a New Testament in Greek went begging.

Another terrifying moment was when the results of the Common Entrance Exams came through. Dick Smith's face at breakfast was thunder, bright red as if he was going to explode, and word shot round that it was opening the letter from St John's Leatherhead that was the cause. The temperature lowered when he realised that the marks weren't percentages and the totals possible for each paper ranged from between forty and one hundred; my name subsequently appeared in gold letters on the scholarship board. I have no doubt I would have succeeded far better academically if I had continued to Llanfyllin High School rather than been constantly inhibited in an environment which was hostile to my sensitive country-boy nature.

NANNERCH AND LLANDOUGH

My mother's family were millers and bakers, and their family home, Nannerch Mill, was in a small valley near Mold, surrounded by woods with a stream running through. One of my earliest memories is of being fed as an infant on the settle next to the black range in the living room, where the kettle was boiled on the open fire and food baked in the oven. This was the centre of all family activity, including the daily counting of money from the bread rounds. The yard opened directly onto it, and there was a door off to the parlour, which was used for special occasions, such as entertaining the Minister, who called on Sundays after the Calvinistic Methodist Chapel in Pentre Felin. A passage led to the back kitchen, and there was a door leading down the steps to the grocery shop.

Enid's father was John Davies, one of the kindest, gentlest people you could ever meet. There were tales of his generosity towards country folk who couldn't pay the bill for groceries and bread. Mary, her mother, was a totally different kettle of fish. Skinny, stern and a stickler for rules—no surprise, I suppose, as she had to bring up nine children, six of them boys.

Great Orme Llandudno   *Mochdre Welcome Back*

Pen y Lan cottage opposite Llandough Hospital, outside Cardiff, was where Oliver's parents, Emily and Gus, lived. This was the home of happy memories: helping mangle clothes, feeding hens, collecting eggs and jumping into the bomb craters when playing in the fields overlooking the Bristol Channel. A great day out was a trip to Penarth docks to look around the Royal Navy frigates, corvettes and destroyers that had been mothballed after the Second World War, and afterwards catching the ferry to Weston-super-Mare, past the lighthouse on Flat Holm Island.

Gran Llandough was a slight lady with a lilting South Wales accent and perpetual motion. I remember walking with her through Cardiff when she was fairly old, and she suddenly shot across the road, sidestepping through the busy traffic as if she was Barry John. Gus was a kindly man with a head that felt "just like ham", without a shred of hair on top. Oliver's love of the sea came from spending time on the boats in the Bristol Channel, and his excellent French was inspired by the lady teacher in Penarth Grammar he was charmed by.

Occasionally I'd go down with Oliver when Enid was helping out in Nannerch Mill. I have wonderful memories of Oliver preparing BAX 69 for the journey from Llanfyllin, through Welshpool, Newtown and up over hills with beautiful views looking down on Mochdre. Oliver told tales about ponies running wild on the hills, red kites and polecats, while we admired the red squirrels in the trees as we drove through the woods. We avoided potholes driving through Radnorshire, which Dad proclaimed had the worst roads in the country. When we spotted a car ahead and were catching up, Oliver would wind down his window, gently slap the side of the car as if he were a jockey riding a horse, and whistle to make BAX 69 go faster. The journey of four or more hours never seemed to take long.

When Enid was with us, we'd stop at one of our favourite spots on the banks of the River Wye outside Builth Wells, lay out a blanket and enjoy a picnic. No visit to a river was complete without skimming stones and much laughter; I invariably fell in. When I was young, Oliver wanted me to join Chester Cathedral choir school, and he was offered the parish of Ecclestone, a beautiful village close to the Dee; the main reason he decided not to take the appointment was the Vicarage was only a couple of hundred yards from the river and he was afraid my adventurous spirit might land me in deep and dangerous waters. Oliver stayed loyal to St Asaph diocese the whole of his life but was never properly rewarded for his ability as a priest as he was not prepared to kowtow before the powers that be. As a young curate in Penrhyn Bay he attended a meeting of the Missionary Committee in the British Hotel Bangor. The clergy were booked in for three nights; however, the business was finished after two. Oliver said they shouldn't be spending money on a "jolly" extra night from the hard-earned funds. He was outvoted, immediately resigned and returned home.

A week during the summer holidays was invariably spent in Nannerch or Llandough. Enid was taken advantage of by her brothers, especially Jed, the eldest, who went to Oxford before becoming a priest. He had five children, and the youngest boys, Philip and Alfan, would have their mouths roughly washed out with soapy water if they used bad language. Incredibly, they travelled together shut in the boot of the Standard Vanguard when the whole family went on a journey. Enid was called on to help in the mill shop when they were short, even though her life was full as wife of a parish priest. It was only as I grew older that I realised how much she was put upon and that Oliver obligingly drove her over; they disguised their displeasure well.

The only time we holidayed somewhere other than the grandparents' homes was in 1957, when we took a room in a boarding house in Newquay, Cardigan Bay. Mr Ford, the landlord, a delightful fellow, was an ex-seaman and had watched the Battle of the River Plate from Montevideo, when the *Graf Spee*, a German cruiser, was scuttled after a heavy battle. We watched the film with Mr Ford in the village hall, sitting on wooden benches. Newquay was a wonder-world for me. The prettiest of villages on the coast, with narrow roads leading down to a small sheltered harbour, clinker-built boats and a beautiful beach round the bay. I soon made friends, and we would disappear for hours on end climbing the rocks, playing by the water and learning how to row; this is where I caught Oliver's love of the sea. Once again, they were the happiest of times.

New Quay, Cardigan

John Davies, my grandfather, was an innovator and the first person in Flintshire to acquire a motorised van to replace the cart horses which were used to pull the bread wagons. One of Enid's earliest and saddest memories was of standing by the front door as their horses were commandeered by the government for the front lines in the First World War.

The bakery at the mill, run by Idwal and Huw, two of Enid's brothers, was self-contained, with electricity produced by a generator; the only advice my mum was given before getting married was to be careful of mains electricity because it was more powerful and dangerous. There was a mill pond, which Grandpa Nannerch stocked with rainbow trout especially for my dad, who was very proud of his Greenheart rod; I inherited his split cane. We used worms as bait with some success. Oliver had been taught to fish by someone who had been released from jail having completed his sentence for committing murder; unfortunately, he wasn't able to cope in society and landed back in prison.

The waterwheel in the mill was used to grind corn into flour, and there was a complicated system of belts to connect the shaft to the wheel axle through a series of gears and cogs to drive the machinery. I wasn't allowed to go near the mechanism, which could take your fingers off, especially when first loading the belts onto the rotating wheels.

Fish would congregate in the pool around the base of the waterwheel and my cousins would occasionally pour in flour to easily catch them—not a fair system of fishing. I was delighted when I caught an eel with my rod, and I learnt the art of tickling trout by standing with my feet astride the stream and slowly moving my fingers under a fish before scooping it out of the water.

John and Richard, my cousins, children of Idwal and Evelyn, were a few years older than me and were daring in their exploits. Oliver and Enid were worried when I went around with them, and Kelvin and Geraint, Huw and Ann's children, were totally banned from joining in their pranks. John wrote off his AJS 650 motorbike riding back from St Albans; the front wheel was shaped like a half moon and the speedometer stuck at 67 after colliding with a van which had pulled in front of him. The dashboard of the van was knocked out on impact, but as John was travelling so quickly, he cleared the accident landing up in a field.

A fun time of year to be at the mill was in the summer for the agricultural shows. It was all hands to the pump, and I'd join my older cousins the day before to erect the marquee and trestle tables, then sleep under canvas to safeguard the equipment. There were several shows each year, including Rhyl, Colwyn Bay, Denbigh and Flint. They were great community events with many food and craft stalls and rings where farmers would show off their fine animals, competing to win the highly prized rosettes. Nannerch Mill was famous for its bread, especially bara brith, and hundreds of ham salads would be served. I'd help with the collection of money, and to make things easier one time, I posted prices of lunches on a board for one to six people—a customer pointed out

I'd inadvertently given a discount on five and six plates by wrongly calculating the maths! Once the lunch crowds subsided, we'd wander about enjoying the happenings around the show fields, including motorbike stunts. I was worn out by the end of the day, and it was a real treat to stop on the way home for fish and chips.

There were plenty of wasps around the mill, especially in summer, and jam was mixed with warm water in jars to catch them so the bakers could work with little fear of being stung. My worst memory was foolishly poking a wasps' nest in a bank with a stick. Within seconds, they were swarming in my curly hair and sweater, stinging relentlessly. I ran screaming into the house, and people surrounded me trying to get them out of my locks and clothing. My legs swelled up, but luckily there was no need for me to be rushed to hospital.

St Ethelwolds

Nannerch Mill

ST JOHN'S –
A LESSON IN RESILIENCE

September 1962 arrived, my trunk was packed in readiness for my new school and sent PLA (Passenger's Luggage in Advance) from Chester station. All my clothes, including detached-collar shirts, had been name-taped by Enid with E328 (East House 328). A few days later, cousin Philip and I were waiting at Chester station for the steam train to take us to Euston. Philip knew the ropes as his two elder brothers had been at St John's a few years earlier; Huw had the questionable record of being the last boy to receive a public caning from the headmaster.

Tom Peacock was head of chemistry, a wonderful chap who taught his sixth formers how to make fireworks. This was great fun for the boys but caused a certain amount of mayhem in Leatherhead, the local town, so much so that the Chief Inspector of Police arrived one evening to make a formal complaint to Hereward Wake, the headmaster. Unsuspectingly, he left his wife sitting alone in his car on the driveway; an opportunity too good to miss. She was terrified by the bangs detonated beneath her, and the next day there was a school assembly where Wake asked those involved in the attempt to blow up the Chief Inspector's wife to step forward. Without further ado, Huw approached the stage, bent over and received six of the best.

Travelling to London and on to Leatherhead for the first time was a chilling experience, not knowing where I was going or what trolls might be waiting—I only hoped it wouldn't be as dastardly as Lawrence House. My first day, however, wasn't as traumatic as

John Dickin's three years earlier. His mother, Cynthia, had name-taped his clothes and packed them neatly in his trunk, which was sent PLA. On the morning of his departure, the household realised everything had been sent on ahead and John had no school uniform to wear. He was dressed in his father's clothes, and as the trousers were too big, they were tied with a length of string to stop them falling down.

We soon arrived in Euston station, and the underground ticket inspectors allowed us to travel on to Waterloo with no extra charge. We had two hours to spare, and we went into the free cinema in the station to watch cartoons and Pathé news; this became one of the few things to look forward to at the beginning of each term.

St. John's. Picture courtesy of St. John's School.

It was an austere arrival. There were six houses with roughly fifty-five boys in each, from thirteen to eighteen years of age. I was to discover later the houses had their own individual characters and I was lucky to have arrived in East, which was relatively friendly with its own ghost—a fireman who had been killed trying to put out a fire a few decades earlier. Other houses were much more strict, and two of them had approaching forty in their respective dormitories, so when gastroenteritis ran through the school, the sounds and stench of puking was unbearable.

East House had a junior common room for about twenty, covering the first two years, and it soon became apparent who the seniors were, immediately imposing their authority and making your rights, or rather lack of them, known.

In October 1962, shortly after I arrived, Oliver had an anxious time over the Cuban Missile Crisis, when there was a stand-off between Russia and the United States with a reasonable chance of nuclear war. He thought seriously about bringing me back to Wales, away from the environs of London, which was likely to be the first target. Luckily, everything passed peacefully and Khrushchev ordered the missiles back to Russia.

Meanwhile, I had other things to worry about. There were notices everywhere, and us new boys had a week to learn the contents of all of them: the names of prefects, different ties for each of the sports colours, the captains of the various teams and so much else. We were tested, and failure meant a beating. There is little doubt this is the primary reason for me ignoring noticeboards even now, whether it be at the golf club or library.

The psychological pressures were immense with no family to go home to for thirteen weeks and no mobile phones or email. Being "sent to Coventry"—completely ignored and not spoken to in the common room—was a severe punishment meted out by boys of a similar age, possibly more damaging than physical bullying. Two boys were taken away from East House in straitjackets in my first year.

The bullying centred around humiliation as much as physical cruelty, the opposite of Lawrence House. One of the milder punishments was to be made to stand on top of the lockers and sing while well-rotted oranges were thrown at you. This happened to me in my first year for making up a couple of verses of the song "In the Stores" about Lewis, Fowler and Woodburn on the bus returning from an away rugby match. One step up was "basing"; milk was saved for two weeks or more so that it was rancid, and you would stink for days when it was rubbed into your hair together with boot polish and Mycil foot powder to make sure it stuck. Again it was the same three who tried to inflict this on me. I was small for my age but, growing up with friends in Llanfyllin who were older than me, I knew how to look after myself. There were cellars in the basement of the building where we stored our games kit, shoes and boots, with wash basins in the adjoining room. On this occasion, the three grabbed hold of me and were dragging me to the basins by my feet when I took hold of the metal mesh of one of the lockers. There was stalemate for a while until I swung my right foot with all the force I could muster and it caught Lewis, a doctor's son from Cardiff, on the side of his head; I can still sense the sweet blow, similar to hitting a half-volley cricket ball over the top of the poplar trees. No one laid a finger on me from then on. On the contrary, my vengeance on Lewis continued year after year. On the rugby field, I would go for him as viciously as I could at any opportunity; high tackles weren't an offence in the '60s. On the fives courts—a game similar to squash using a hard ball and padded gloves—we were brought together each year on the same team. In the juniors and seniors, we represented East House, and Lewis knew that whenever we practised as a foursome in readiness for the competition against the other houses and I was in the out court and he in front, a ball would be aimed at his head.

The cruellest form of bullying was "wappering". This took place on a Saturday night, when there was a film which was compulsory for all to attend, and anyone found to be missing was caned. The victim was doubled up in a plastic waste-paper bin, and the curdled milk, boot polish, powder and anything else foul was spread all over him. The bin was then placed on top of the lockers, about six feet off the ground, and there the hapless quarry would remain until he was discovered at the end of the film. There was virtually no room for movement, and breathing was difficult.

Any attempt to climb out would cause the poor boy to fall six foot to the ground with potential injury to his head or spine.

It is a well-reported story that Leonard Wilson, who later became Bishop of Birmingham after spending two years in Changi Prison Camp, Singapore, following arrest by the Japanese in the Second World War, said he would prefer to repeat those two years than suffer his first year in St John's again. The trials boys had to suffer in his day must have been closer to the "warmings" in *Tom Brown's School Days*. However, there were lighter pranks; twenty years before I arrived, the toilets were in a line with a channel running beneath them which was flushed periodically by a strong stream of water. Fire boats were built in readiness with paper and flammable materials and launched with the flow of water, causing backsides to be singed.

Friendships and alliances were struck—although as a romantic soul from the hills and vales of Montgomeryshire who wore his heart on my sleeve, I felt like a fish out of water amongst the stiff-upper-lipped hardness of the majority of boys who came from Surrey. The feeling of not fitting in stayed with me during my years at St John's; although when Sue and I visited Dave Gee, one of my old schoolmates, in Spain in 2015, he maintained I was the most popular boy in the school.

There was an emphasis on helping in the community, and East House played its part, which included aiding old people in their gardens and carol-singing round Leatherhead, which I enjoyed immensely. Families knew we were coming and plied us with hot chocolate and mince pies, harder stuff for the older ones. It was soon recognised I had a good treble voice and I sang plenty of solos, as a result of which there was pressure on me to join the school choir, which I managed to avoid.

It was sport that enabled me to keep my sanity, abetted by Glyn John, who was head of games. He had excelled in each position down the back line for Cardiff RFC and played on the wing for Wales. At the time, he had been the only person allowed to appear as an amateur international, having played rugby league, and was given dispensation because he was serving in the RAF at the time. He stood out whenever the staff paraded wearing their gowns, which they did every lunch and dinner time, as the others had graduated from Oxbridge while he proudly represented St Luke's College, the foremost athletic establishment in Britain, together with Loughborough. He was in charge of swimming and especially keen on water polo. There was organised sport for two hours Monday to Thursday, CCF (Combined Cadet Force) Fridays, interschool matches every Saturday, and on Sundays we invariably played squash in the winter and tennis in the summer.

Schools in our circuit included Charterhouse, Epsom College and Whitgift, and some years later when I captained the first XV, I propped against Lord Llewellyn Mostyn on the playing fields of Eton. Needless to say we won, and I will never forget the cry of "Gladstone" as one of the prefects called "fag" back in one of the college houses and minutes later someone came running to find out what chores he was required to perform. We were amazed that there was a bar/mini-pub for sixth-formers.

Swimming Team

Rugby XV

I chose swimming as opposed to cricket after my nose had been splattered at Lawrence House, which remained fresh in my memory. I wasn't accepted into the club for crawl or breaststroke as I was too slow. Luckily, someone suggested backstroke, which I had rarely swum; they saw potential and I was accepted. Everyone had to swim naked in the swimming pool, other than members of the swimming club and prefects. The major bonus was that Glyn John took the club practices. Training was intense, up and down the 25-yard pool, length after length, day after day, measuring times and checking pulse recovery rate. John's love of water polo meant we had a session after every swimming practice. There was great rivalry between the sports coaches of each school, and when I was captain in my final year, we were undefeated at polo, much to Glyn John's delight.

I experienced a fantastic feeling of relief when we competed against Christ's Hospital in Sussex. The pool and surrounding area stank of urine, and I spent minimal time in the water. There were around a thousand pupils, and because of these large numbers, they lined up and marched into the dining room military style for every meal, and each pupil wore a cassock. There were many scholarships, especially for orphans and special circumstances, and a round badge exhibited their origin. Paul Dickin had gone there, and

Oliver had sought a sponsor for me; the relief was that he had been unable to find one!

For several years I competed in the medley relay team at Seymour Hall in London; this public school event was light relief amongst the Oxford and Cambridge varsity match. Twenty years after leaving St John's, my 100 yards backstroke record still stood.

There was inter-house competition in all sports, and rivalry was intense. In my first summer, I was chosen as the East House under-16 wicket-keeper, as there was no specialist and I was considered better than Bill Russell, the only other candidate. I made quite a lot of money as I was given cash incentives if I let through a minimum number of byes. The added bonus was I took some catches and was top scorer in the final when we defeated Churchill House. Everyone thought I would be awarded junior colours for my performances and playing a significant part in winning the cup. Others who had contributed little received the tie, but not me—another lesson in life not being fair.

However, a better bonus was that I struck up a friendship with Alasdair Forbes who captained the team. He was a fast bowler and our tactic was for him to bowl every fourth ball slower to give opportunity for stumping. The biggest weakness in my wicket-keeping was that I couldn't remain stood up to the stumps as when the batsman raised his bat I would move my head back. Alasdair's father was a judge and I visited their beautiful house and small holding in Uckfield, Sussex, which had a swimming pool. He had a sister my age who played the guitar, had the voice of an angel and was the spitting image of Francoise Hardy.

Tom Peacock was the housemaster of East when I arrived. A tremendous character—widely travelled and an excellent mountaineer and skier. He was chosen for the ascent of Everest in 1953 and trained with the team in Snowdonia. His signature is amongst the others on the ceiling of Pen-Y-Gwryd pub, close to the start of the Miners and Pyg tracks. He encouraged me to join the school mountaineering club, and we had days out at High Rocks and Harrison's Rocks on the sandstone near East Grinstead. Unfortunately, I didn't go on any of their annual ski trips because funds didn't allow. There was one memorable day on Box Hill when it was covered in deep snow—a rare occurrence. A few skied while the rest of us interchanged tea trays and sledges. I never lost the respect or fondness I had for Tom Peacock, despite the odd caning.

Robert Haymes came to St John's the term after me, and we soon become known as the terrible twins because of the pranks we carried out together. He spent his early years in Singapore, where his father had been manager of the Hong Kong and Shanghai Bank before retiring to Harcourt, Feock, in Cornwall, a beautiful property with gardens running down to the creek, where their sailboats were moored across from St Mawes. Robert could swim like a fish, having spent so much time in the waters around Singapore, and was a good diver. One of the most amazing coincidences happened when Robert's parents were being shown round the school at the same time as Tim Griffiths' father. They had all been held by the Japanese in a prisoner of war camp in Singapore during the Second World War. Single adults were being separated, so the Rev. Griffiths had married Robert's parents so they could remain together—this was the first time they had been in touch since the war.

Robert's social skills were way ahead of mine, and he had a much greater propensity for spending money. At a swimming dinner towards the end of my schooling, Robert and I were drinking vodka and limes—Glyn John said that I'd better start drinking pints or we'd be laughed out of any self-respecting rugby club. It was a new experience for me to visit restaurants, and I was introduced to this by Jo and Geoff Pitt, friends of Oliver and Enid for decades, who used to take me to their home on exeats. One notable occasion was with Sir William Robson Brown, MP for Esher, and his wife at the Mayflower outside Cobham. I ordered king prawns, and when they arrived I didn't have a clue how to start eating them. Luckily Jo was having the same starter, and I carefully watched and copied her breaking the shells.

I admired Oliver massively, for many different reasons. I had been waiting ages in anticipation of turning fourteen, when I would be old enough to tour John Summers Steelworks in Shotton, where my dad was vicar in the sixties and chaplain to the plant, which employed fourteen thousand people. John Norbury, the manager responsible for apprentices, showed us round, including the "secret" shop making Stelvatite, a new covering of coated steel for white goods. The most awesome experience was watching the blast furnace being tapped, feeling the immense heat, with sparks flying everywhere and up to three hundred tons of molten steel being carried in huge ladles. At lunch, we were escorted to the directors' dining room, which was oak panelled with high ceilings and cut glass. We were asked what we'd like to drink, and my dad chose a lager. I requested a rum and Coke; Oliver hadn't a clue I drank liquor but didn't bat an eyelid. A few minutes later, a flustered waiter came back apologising they didn't have any Coke. Would I like anything else? Gin and tonic, please! I had a lager to accompany the meal in the sumptuous dining room, and not a word was said. If I had thrown up, things might have been different. Rather, Oliver dined out on the story that I'd brought the steelworks to a halt because they didn't have any coke.

There was a system of fagging for boys in the first year at St John's, when they had to turn up to the prefects' studies at the sound of a bell and make coffee, toast or run errands to town. Fags also had to dust and clean the studies, and there were the usual beatings when these chores weren't done properly. In addition, there were personal fags, which meant waking the prefect up at their chosen time, washing and ironing their shirts, cleaning their shoes and rugby boots, as well as polishing their CCF webbing and brasses. Luckily, Humphrey Malins, who I ran errands for, was part of Civil Defence, which I later joined, and we would spend our Fridays in mufti building bridges across the River Mole or carrying wounded down fire escapes in stretchers, so appearing on parade spic and span wasn't necessary. Being a "shagger" in Civil Defence was one of the early points of conflict I had with Major DuPrez, who ran the CCF as well as teaching French and running the careers office.

The annual field day was enjoyable. We'd put our battle dress on, carry Lee Enfield 303 rifles, which we'd first clean with a 4x2, then receive a given number of blank cartridges. We'd be split into different platoons; some would be attacking and some defending a piece of land detailed by map references. One time, the day was cut short after an angry farmer complained a cow had been shot—one crazy boy had decided to put a pencil down the spout, which turned harmless wadding into a dangerous weapon.

There were visits to army camps at Wisley and Warminster, and one summer holiday, I spent a week in Warcop Cumbria playing proper soldiers. Two other boys and I had to camouflage ourselves and were given a two-hour start heading into the countryside. On the way, we came across burnt-out Panzer tanks about thirty foot apart—obviously a shooting range but with no flags flying signifying activity, we went to explore. All of a sudden—*voom voom bang!*—we were being fired at by Chieftain tanks. It didn't take us long to vacate the area. We continued on our way, eventually taking refuge in a bank around a lake, and after a while, we heard the voices of our pursuers. It was a good lesson in hiding, as several looked straight at me and no doubt the other two, but because our faces were broken up with mud and flora on our clothing it took some time to be discovered.

The facilities at St John's were excellent, in large part thanks to the generosity of Field Marshall Montgomery, chairman of the board of governors, and his friends, who financed a gymnasium, language laboratory, hot lab—Tom Peacock's nuclear pride and joy—and a beautiful modern chapel with copper roof. Mr Peacock experimented with microwave ovens but advised us not to go close to one as the insulation was poor and they could fry our gonads; this fear remained with me for decades to come, and we've never owned a microwave. Before speech day, certain boys would be assembled to listen to Monty's speech, which was the same every year. "At St Paul's School I was captain of rugby and cricket, and before each match, I would devise a plan and we would execute that plan and be victorious. The greatest general in history was Rommel. In my desert caravan, I studied his picture every night to know him and anticipate his tactics."

They opposed each other in the Second World War at Tobruk, which he regarded as his biggest triumph, and Alamein. "There was only one greater general than Rommel, and that was me. You know who won the war: I won the war."

He was knee-high to a grasshopper, and most of his men would do anything for him; many gave the ultimate sacrifice of their lives. Harry, my birth father, had a different opinion.

For speech day in summer 1965, Monty said nothing new. Lord Gardiner, High Chancellor of Great Britain, should have been more interesting, but Monty had told him to talk about his job, so we didn't experience any of his great oratory. Afterwards, I went back to Ely, to Jo and Geoff's home in Cobham, with their kids Viv and Philip. On Friday, I travelled up to London and watched the Changing of the Guard. A charming, attractive American girl asked what happened in Buckingham Palace, and I just froze. For lunch, I joined Geoff at the Charing Cross Hotel, where he was meeting with the two other members of the Skal Travel Committee, for steak, flambéed crepe suzette and excellent service in a fantastic environment. Afterwards, I walked to Whitehall, New Scotland Yard and the Houses of Parliament, which unfortunately were closed, so not even Sir William Robson Brown or Eirene White, East Flintshire MP, could show me around. Instead, I spent time in the Imperial War Museum. In the evening, I met Geoff at his Cunard offices in Pall Mall, then to the London Palladium to see Ken Dodd, the Kaye Sisters, Barron Knights and others. The following day, while Jo and Viv watched Trooping the Colour, Geoff, Phil and I went ten pin bowling by Heathrow Airport, then watched planes taking off and landing every three minutes. I spiked their lawn in the afternoon, then scampi and chips on the Thames for supper. On Sunday, we had Dublin Coddle on the South Downs before visiting Brighton. What started as a boring speech day landed up an action-packed weekend.

Not long after I arrived in St John's, a notice went out saying that boys were no longer to wear duffle coats. I never had one, but for many teenagers, it was the cool thing to wear. A scandal had arisen because of a considerable amount of theft taking place in the local record shop. The scam was that a few boys would attract the attention of the shopkeeper while others stole 45 rpm single records, which fitted perfectly into the duffle coat pockets.

The reputation of the school in the local community was of great concern to the headmaster, and that is one of the reasons why there were always some unfortunates from the local home employed in the kitchen—as well, of course, being cheap labour. I'm sure it wasn't intentional that strange objects were found in the food; scourers in the porridge weren't one-off events, but I only once remember a rat being found in a tea urn.

The first major concert I experienced was going with Robert Haymes and Dave Gee to watch Simon and Garfunkel in the Albert Hall, London, in 1965. Robert arranged it all, and we made our way to Leatherhead station and boarded the train, which consisted of individual carriages in three sections. We began to change out of our school uniforms, and straight away the carriage lights went on as it was beginning to get dark. Not wanting to be seen in this position, I put my hand up and removed the lightbulb, causing a huge blue flash; I had fused one third of the train. There was commotion on the platform and a guard put his head through the window, but fortunately I had already replaced the lightbulb. The train left the station and I could breathe again, to the great amusement of my best friends.

The excitement mounted as we travelled on the Underground and walked up to the grand Albert Hall. We were huge fans of Simon and Garfunkel; they were rising to the height of their popularity and enthralled the packed audience. When we boarded the train in Waterloo to head back to school, my trepidation grew and my imagination ran wild with the thought of public disgrace and humiliation. We discovered later that pupils from Epsom College had been fingered for the lightbulb, so the heat was off. Enid asked how come I'd lost so much weight when I arrived home the following week—I didn't tell her it was from worry. About the same time, a master driving round Piccadilly Circus noticed a pupil smoking, and he was caned the following day after arriving back at St John's; vandalising a train would have had much more severe consequences.

If you worked hard and studied, you were considered a swot, so it took little persuasion for me to do as little as possible. One of the few times I went to the library was to find out about Freemasonry. An appointment was to be made for the Chaplain General of the army, one of the two final candidates was a Freemason, the other wasn't, and both had sons at St John's. The whole school took interest and roughly divided down the middle. I sided with the one who wasn't on the square, probably because of my rebellious streak. However, I can't remember who was appointed or whether I ever found out.

Considering St John's had four chaplains, there was considerable lack of pastoral care. I was about fifteen years old when a teacher came in, interrupted a class and called out a boy named Peachey. He returned a few minutes later doing his best to hold back tears; he'd just been told his father had died. A similar thing happened to a good friend of mine, David from Gresford, who attended Epsom College, down the road from Leatherhead. His father died when he was fourteen and he wasn't allowed to go to the funeral, giving added credence to the saying that the Battle of Waterloo was won on the playing fields of English public schools.

At O Level, I was removed from the English Literature and Additional Maths classes, continuing with just English Language and Elementary Maths, no doubt to make sure I didn't pull down the overall school exam results. I landed up with seven O Levels, most on or around the pass mark, with French and Spanish being the strongest subjects. Uncle Jed, Vicar of Mold, phoned Shotton Vicarage the morning the results came through. I had done considerably better than his son Philip, who didn't return to St John's the following year and continued in the state system. He became a solicitor, was allegedly involved in a fraud, sold his assets, ran from his mortgages and debts and has been living in Thailand ever since, beyond the reaches of the Law Society. I've known four people who ended up in gaol at the same time in different parts of the world, and if the allegations were true, he narrowly avoided being yet another one of them.

John Dickin's academic progress was quite different from mine. John Davies, one of Jed's other sons, remembers him in the sixth form Latin class at the age of fifteen, knowing not only more than the other pupils but also the teacher, who had an Oxbridge degree. He won an Exhibition Scholarship to Jesus College Oxford to study greats, gave up after a year and married a French girl who wanted British citizenship, which his parents didn't discover during their lifetimes. He spent the money she paid him travelling Greece for a year learning the modern language, returned to Oxford and got a fourth—his father said it was harder to get a fourth than a first. He returned to Lindos in Rhodes and met the lovely, talented Mariana—half

Peruvian, half American. They got married and had two amazing sons.

Exciting things happened in London, which was less than an hour away by train. During term in later years we'd make our way on 5 November to Trafalgar Square, where plenty would jump in the fountains in drunken stupors. One time, we went up in cars. Dave Clayton had a 1936 Singer Le Mans, and the Fowler brothers each had Austin 7s. With the same cars, we joined the London to Brighton Veteran Car Run. The drive was fun enough, and one of the lads knew a girl in Roedean School, Brighton, and we proceeded up the long driveway to visit her. The headmistress, an enormous battle-axe, and her entourage had different ideas. After a begging discussion, by which time there must have been at least thirty nubile girls hanging out of the windows and waving, she marched behind us to see us off the premises.

Another friend had a flat in a mews behind Baker Street, and while I was visiting, I was surprised to see a large black Mercedes draw up diagonally opposite, a minder open the door and escort Christine Keeler of Profumo fame into her home. Despite the bromide in the tea, there was never so much testosterone running as in the queues for the Sunday papers in the passageway opposite the main school entrance when the scandal spread. Lord Astor and two-way mirrors, the deceiving of Harold Macmillan, a Russian diplomat and, of course, the defence secretary. In 2012, I was told by an ex-member of MI6 that Dr Stephen Ward, the main witness, hadn't taken an overdose but was murdered to prevent a trial taking place, enabling members of the aristocracy and high society to avoid disgrace.

How it happened I can't remember, but Clare Maddocks started turning up at swimming galas and I was told her eyes were for me. Over a number of years, we had a fumbling schoolboy romance. A couple of weeks before I left St John's, Steve Kohn and I went out with our respective dates. The weak and pathetic housemaster, Mr Kennedy, who took over from the characterful Mr Peacock would have given me permission, but Steve persuaded me not to ask because his housemaster wasn't so lenient. Off we went for an enjoyable evening, and I returned to school to be given an urgent message to see Mr Kennedy, who was somewhat angry. He'd received a phone call from Clare's mother asking where Tim Hill was because he'd run off with her daughter. He reeled off a list of possible punishments including being banned from the swimming club dinner; I assured him that without me it wouldn't take place. Then in frustration he threatened me with expulsion if the slightest misdemeanour happened before the end of term; quite an empty threat, as by this time I couldn't give a damn. There was still the matter of Steve Kohn, who was also in trouble as we had been linked. We cooked up a story with an alibi that we had been on the school grounds at all times, which saved his bacon— or rather pastrami.

After leaving St John's, the next time I saw Steve was walking down the Champs Elysées in Paris, dressed up to the nines. He had just flown in for the weekend to visit his girlfriend. I on the other hand had hitchhiked for the last three days and nights from Sitges, Barcelona, where I'd had the most amazing time with a bunch of almost unintelligible Glaswegians. I'd travelled to Le Havre a few weeks earlier on the second voyage of the *QE2* in 1968 and had the run of the ship thanks to Geoff Pitt, who was the sales and commercial director of Cunard. I didn't have a map of Northern France and thought I'd hitch a ride on a lorry that was going to Spain. First of all, they didn't understand my O Level French, "ou sont les camions qui vont a l'Espagne", and when I did make myself understood, they hadn't a clue where Spain was. Three days later, having spent one night in a car while the owner slept in an auberge, another night under a hedge, the last outside someone's tent, I arrived at the border of Spain. Having spent three days speaking nothing but French, my language skills had become proficient. The reason I was heading for Spain was that Clare had given me the name of a friend who ran a bar and said I'd be able to earn some money working there. I turned up at said bar, and all denied knowledge of her. I landed up at a posada where the Glaswegians were staying, and the owner gave me space to sleep on the floor of a room between two beds occupied by South African mercenaries of tremendous proportions who spoke in grunts. After a couple of days, they moved on and I had the room to myself. There were several drunken nights with my new-made friends, after one of which at two in the morning, three of us lay on the tracks of a six-lane main railway to Barcelona in an attempt to stop the next train. Luckily, none came. At the end of this adventure, I hitched back north via Montpellier and had some crazy lifts, the last being a tremendously long leg, and the kind driver dropped me in the gardens around the Eiffel Tower, where I spent the night in my sleeping bag. I wasn't robbed or murdered, and smelling badly after going without a shower or shave for three nights, I bumped into Steve. He bought me a Coke and said I could have any francs he had left when he flew back to London. Having said our goodbyes, I headed straight to the train station to get to Calais as quickly as I could.

Clare, in the meantime, attended Lucie Clayton's, became a model and then on to J. Walter Thompson's.

It is not surprising that exam results at St John's were generally good, as the teachers were under pressure to get results, and as well as lessons on Saturday mornings, every night there was prep (homework), overseen by prefects in classrooms, one session for juniors and two for the rest. The most memorable time was 22 November 1963, when the news rapidly spread that President Kennedy had been assassinated.

At the end of my first year in sixth, I was doing well in economics and British constitution, also Spanish, and my strongest subject was French. There was bad blood between me and Mr DuPrez, possibly over CCF, and that foolishly spread into his French classes. I can't remember what the deciding factor was, but I dropped French. I'm sure this was upsetting for Oliver and Enid, as although I had a scholarship reducing the fees, they were still a considerable burden on the stipend of a parish priest. Geoff Pitt arranged an interview in Café Royal, Regent Street, with a senior manager as I was contemplating a career in hospitality but was humiliated by the lift attendant when I asked for Mr Bottle—you mean Mr Bott*ell*. There was one very short advisory meeting with Mr DuPrez, where the only career he suggested was to work in a timber yard with the possibility of becoming a manager if I did well. I always remember Oliver's words from when I was about fifteen, standing by the car in Shotton Vicarage: "Whatever you do, make sure it's to the best of your ability, whether a dustman or anything else."

The deciding moment choosing a vocation happened when I was staying in Feock with Robert Haymes. His father was a pleasant but firm character, and a couple of years earlier took it out on Rob for losing against me at squash having just taught me how to play. He also let me know he didn't approve of feet dangling over the front of his sailboat as we headed across the creek to St Mawes. One evening, he asked what I was going to do about a career. "No idea," I said. He suggested accountancy and recommended I get in touch with Peat Marwick Mitchell (KPMG), who had been his auditors when he managed the branch of the Hong Kong and Shanghai Banking Corporation in Singapore. I did, and was offered a job by ex-Colonel Alan Pownall, the senior partner in Liverpool. Amazingly, I won a place at university, and Mr Pownall was happy for me to join them after I had a degree.

My housemaster, Mr Kennedy, did me no favours. Before leaving St John's, I applied for a management accountancy apprenticeship with a plant in Capenhurst on the Wirral, not far from Gresford. I attended one of the top twenty public schools in Britain, was captain of rugby and swimming and didn't even get an interview!

Leatherhead was occasionally affected by London smog, and when the yellow pea soup descended, visibility was reduced to a matter of feet. There was no heating in the dorms and we removed our clothes from the pegs hanging against the wall and placed them on our beds to prevent them getting soaking wet. The next morning, there'd be footprints across the grass quadrangle, which only masters and school prefects were allowed to walk on. However, the funniest prank during one of these lockdowns was Mr Rees' Bubble car being purloined from the staff car park by some daring pupils and placed on the high table in the dining room.

There was demarcation and privileges which came with various achievements. The enamel baths in the basement had marks scraped in them, measuring about a foot of water, and yes—if you had more water than that, you were punished. That is, except for school prefects and boys awarded 1st XV colours. We would let the water run to overflowing and keep the hot tap running to make sure the bath remained hot, with another advantage being that our permitted soak time was not restricted to ten minutes.

To play in the 1st XV was regarded as a huge honour. If there was a home match, it was compulsory for everybody not competing in one of the other school teams to watch, and it was a caning offence not to obey. The team was clapped back under the arches at the end of the game. My nose invariably bled in a rugby match and my face and shirt would be covered in blood, which gave the appearance that I had played really hard, which was mostly the case. Only a few were awarded colours each year, which again was an important event. At lunchtime, with everybody in the dining room standing, including the full array of masters at the top table in their gowns, the boy receiving the honour was clapped from the doorway all the way to his seat. Another quirk in my character was I didn't tell my parents I had achieved this. The regular school tie was black and the blazer blue with the crest sewn with white cotton stitching. The 1st XV and XI ties were one-inch green and white stripes distinguishable from afar; the blazer was green with a gold braided badge. I was the only pupil in the history of the school to decline asking their parents to fork out for a green jacket. I did, however, negotiate a price for the badge alone. I also didn't tell Oliver and Enid when *Songs of Praise* was being delivered live from St John's new chapel. Luckily, one of the astute parishioners in Shotton saw it advertised in the *Radio Times* in enough time for Evensong to be cancelled that Sunday.

An example of prejudice in the locker room was when, after we'd lost a house tie, one of my side said he refused to try hard with me as captain as I wasn't English. Even if he had worked his socks off, that spineless lump of lard's performance couldn't have been any better. It was also peculiar when twin brothers arrived from Hong Kong whose surnames were Wong. The headmaster decided that officially they would be called Wang, and their names appeared as such on all lists to avoid being mocked for being the Wong Wong.

For the last couple of years, I played for the school at seven-aside in the Richmond Sevens; a huge event, where the best rugby schools in the country were represented. For three years in a row, Llandovery College won the competition but were disqualified from entering the following year because they were too professional as they wore tracksuits; they didn't appreciate a Welsh school dominating.

Another privilege from being in the 1st XV was tickets to all the home games at Twickenham; rules were relaxed and accompanying masters would buy us a drink in a pub. The French were the best crowd to be amongst, as bands would play, cockerels were released onto the pitch, and they freely shared their whisky.

Another mark I made on, or rather off, the rugby field was when I accidentally sank my teeth into one of the opposition's forehead. After the match, I was taken to the dentist, who managed to save four front teeth by placing a silver splint over them. I visited my home dentist in Chester with a copy of *Rugby World* containing an article about mouthguards. He followed it up, and a week later, I went to be fitted with a large U-shaped plastic trough, into which was poured liquid until it hardened around my teeth.

This made an impression at Bangor University, as not only had no one seen a rugby mouthguard before but most had never heard of one.

It was fun sharing a study with Dave Gee and my terrible twin Haymes, where music sustained us: Bob Dylan, Joan Baez, Buddy Holly, Elvis Presley, Pink Floyd, Simon and Garfunkel, Francoise Hardy and, number one, The Rolling Stones. I had every track of theirs on my Peto Scott reel-to-reel tape recorder. Dave provided a balance with his classical music collection.

I couldn't wait to leave St John's. I'd had enough living in a regimented environment becoming cantankerous and rebellious. No one had my respect unless they earned it, and there was no doubt I had been taught resilience. The last speech day typified my mood. Guest of honour was the Duchess of Gloucester, and there were plenty of other high and mighty visitors. With a few mates, I climbed a fire escape and enjoyed some beers in the sunshine. The risk was that, because I had captained teams and was a member of the Gourmond Club, a select group who were allowed to wear the only non-school tie—white pigs on a brown background—I could have won an award. I guessed correctly, and luckily nothing came my way.

The happiest person appeared to be Vickers, who had been expelled for smoking and dealing dope. He turned up in front of the school in an open-topped Lotus Elan with three dolly birds, two sitting up on the back scantily dressed, displaying beautiful sets of legs.

I know I was a late developer, but my academic results didn't reflect my ability, rather the happiness rating. Becoming a chartered accountant and being the first to pass all three professional exams for the first time in three years in the Liverpool office of Peat Marwick Mitchell (KPMG) surpassed Mr Duprez's expectations of working in a timber yard.

Llanfyllin Report

St John's Report

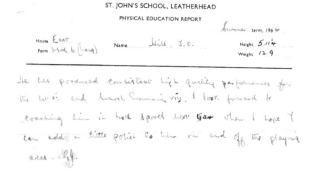

Measures of happiness

SHOTTON, GRESFORD, BANGOR

The summer of 1967 was the best of my life, partly because I had left school, but also because I had built up a good number of friends in Chester, largely thanks to the bishop, who, a couple of years previously, had arranged a gathering in the cathedral for young people who went away to public schools and as a consequence had few friends to muck around with in the holidays. There were various activities in the morning then a break for lunch in the palace. A good spread had been laid on, and drinks included cider and beer. David Clapham and I were getting along famously, and when time was called to return to the cathedral, we headed into town and had a few more drinks. A lifelong friendship, still strong after fifty years, began. David's father was a colonel in the army, which led to me being introduced to a larger sphere of his friends.

Another series of social events arose through the chaplain, the Rev. Metcalfe. He had four sons— the youngest was a couple of years behind me in St John's—and lived in a magnificent house in Upton Park with large grounds, including a lawn tennis court and bandstand. Through these army connections, the sons and daughters had been given a room in the basement of Chester Castle, and provided it was cleared and painted, we could use it for revelries in the year of Flower Power. More bashes happened in the Parrot Club, a private barn between Winsford and Northwich, mainly with pupils and ex-pupils of the King's and Queen's schools in Chester. The Wild Boar Hotel was another favourite last haunt for Saturday nights; there was a disco on the top floor, and provided we bought food, we could continue drinking after eleven, when pubs officially had to stop serving.

Life of a different kind continued in Shotton. Solid dependable people and several of my friends sang in the choir with me, but that didn't mean we behaved impeccably, especially me, as I wanted to fit in while attending a bastion of inequality and snobbery in Surrey. In August 2020, Jim Jones, one of my friends from the choir, contacted me out of the blue—we hadn't been in touch for over fifty years—and I learnt for the first time my Dad's nickname was Cheyenne, after the cowboy Bodie because of his ten-gallon hat. The following day Malcolm Williams, another chorister friend, called, and we reminisced about many terrific times, including playing with my air rifle in the Vicarage garden. I had persuaded Oliver to put his pipe through the study window, which I shot—out of his hand, not his mouth! Malcolm was amazed Oliver wasn't angry, just said, "Boys will be boys." Malcolm asked if any of my children had turned out as roguish as me, and I think he was referring to an infamous train trip to Rhyl in particular. Those conversations reminded me of the warmth and value of our friendships. Many fond memories with these friends were made in John Summers' Sports Club, where we played snooker and tennis. The manager, John Savage, was huge—a Commonwealth Games shot-putter who rode a 50cc motorbike, which was an amazing sight: a giant of a man with the tiniest wheels appearing below him.

It was a pleasure to visit Mr Boswell and his two sons Ned and Jim, who ran a haulage company transporting steel over the country for John Summers. From the moment my dad and I turned up at their yard in Connah's Quay, there was non-stop laughter as they told a never-ending stream of jokes and hilarious stories. There were three brothers in all, and they all became masters of their respective Freemason Lodges in the same year. Oliver was asked to join the fraternity many times and often attended Ladies' Nights with Enid. I'm sure he would have enjoyed the camaraderie, especially with his track record performing in plays as well as his gripping sermons.

A fond memory is of Oliver and myself being invited by a senior engineer to inspect the new Queensferry Bridge, which was being built over the River Dee. The traffic had become horrific with over thirteen thousand employees at Shotton Steelworks and an increasing number of visitors making for the North Wales coast. We should have become suspicious when we were asked to climb a thirty-foot ladder leaning against a concrete wall. I followed one of the men and stupidly was astonished to see at the top not a four-lane highway but a dozen or so girders, each less than three feet wide. There was no turning back. The dirty brown river swirled below and a breeze was blowing. By the time my dad reached the top of the ladder, I was twenty foot along. He said afterwards he was terrified because he didn't know how he would save me if I fell, but I was the one who could swim! Fifteen minutes later, we made it to a semi-made-up span covering the width of the bridge.

The summer continued in Chester, with parties in various locations: people's houses, rowboats and small motor launches on the Dee, plenty of evenings in the Bear and Billet on Lower Bridge Street and Boat House on the Dee. Each Sunday, I'd attend Sunday school with David Clapham in the best room in the Grosvenor that wasn't occupied. Martin Thompson was a trainee manager, and four of us would play bridge starting midday, with beef sandwiches, gin and tonics and F1 Grand Prix racing—no better way to spend a Sunday with excellent company.

I applied to six universities, and Bangor was the only one that offered me an interview—goodness knows what my housemaster, Kennedy, had written about me. The economics department interview didn't go well; however, psychology did. I completed a psychometric test, and the conversation afterwards flowed. I was offered a place and got the grades.

At the end of the summer, I started in Bangor—a wonderful feeling of freedom after the physical and mental restrictions of public school. Plenty of likeminded people happy to express themselves, a good living grant, no tuition fees, and I soon found out there was little responsibility to anyone other than myself. Some were more equal than others, but it was a great environment to discover who you were.

We had our introductory talk in the student union overlooking Bangor Mountain and were told if you couldn't see the mountain it was raining and if you could it was about to rain—at least everything was fresh and green. We quickly retired to a pub and were joined by some good people who heard us talking about stuff other than home and school; several friendships were made on day one.

The only fly in the ointment was my accommodation. I was a fifteen minute bus ride from town in the middle of a council estate, sharing a small room with not enough room to walk round the beds—it wasn't how I had pictured university life. I arranged a meeting with my tutor Llew Rees, who was the rugby coach, and within twenty-four hours he found me a place in Neuadd Reichel, a well-established hall of residence with lovely grounds and croquet lawn next to the rugby pitches and a fifteen minute walk to the arts buildings; how lucky was that! The rooms were individual, and soon the neighbouring students were welcoming me. A Persian undergraduate hadn't turned up, and they thought that was me arriving late. Friendships were forged and we started a bridge school, all of the same mediocre standard. I religiously attended all my economics, sociology and, best of all, psychology lectures; there were only a few compared to the huge amount those studying sciences had to go to in addition to their lab work.

The standard of rugby was high, the back row well established, and at twelve and a half stone, I was too light to prop at this level, so I enjoyed playing open rugby for the seconds with the occasional 1st XV run out if they had any injuries—no substitutes bench in those days. If I was prepared to play in the second row, there was a permanent position, but I preferred not to play rugby at all than clog about in that position; plenty would disagree and I was no Alun Wyn Jones.

There was a great camaraderie surrounding rugby, and I'm glad Glyn John weaned me off vodka and tonics and onto beer. The fixtures soon started, and there were matches every Wednesday and Saturday with training in between and nights with John, landlord of The Globe. I hadn't a big capacity for drinking, which meant after six pints I'd have to throw up if I wanted to continue. With my wild curly hair and large gumshield, some of the boys looked at me wondering what South Pacific island I was from, and being exceptionally quick over short distances added to the mystery. I was the only one wearing a gumshield, but I was mightily relieved to have it when we played Pilkington Recs, a half rugby league, half rugby union team from St Helens. They were a small side, tough looking, with one thing in common—no front teeth. The ground was still frozen and not very even. Untypically of me, when a thirty-year-old hardened prop charged through the lineout to scrag our scrum half, I tripped him up; there was a thud as he hit the ground. Next lineout as the ball was thrown in, from out of nowhere I was short-armed across the mouth, which dazed me, and if it hadn't been for the super-thick mouthguard I'd have been spitting out teeth. As it was, several of them were loose, but luckily none fell out.

Highlights of the calendar were the UW (University of Wales) highly competitive matches. The different colleges would play each other at all sports: rugby, soccer, men's and women's hockey and netball; badminton was a separate competition. A fleet of coaches would leave to invade the relatively small towns of Aberystwyth and Swansea. After the matches, there was food then copious amounts of ale and enthusiastic singing. The climax of the night would be Dai Collins standing on a table and leading the inebriated throng in "Alouette". The pub would shut and we'd stagger back to the coach park attended by police cars to ensure the drunken rabble left without too many stolen trophies.

The long journeys back to Bangor were epic. On the rugby coaches, there would be limited stops over the several hours when the throng would line up alongside the coach to relieve themselves; otherwise the journey would have lasted until the next midday stopping for individual toilet breaks. There were cars with windscreen wipers working on clear nights as they were sprayed from the emergency window at the back, opened to urinate through. Students would be held securely by the collar as they peed through the open door at the front of the bus. The same would happen if someone needed to be sick, and a sample was taken using the driver's pretty flower holder. Vivid descriptions of the most interesting pukes scraped from the side of the speeding coach were read out at the annual rugby dinner. The rugby coach was relatively clean inside. The soccer bus was an entirely different matter. There would be buckets on board to urinate and be sick into, and the bus would reek by the time it arrived back in Bangor in the early hours of the morning.

One rag week, the organisers arranged for a striptease to raise money, and us rugby players had to act as bouncers, both before the show and to stop people climbing onto the stage. When the stripper was down to a scanty pair of panties, she signalled me to take them off. I leapt to my feet and found a breast was close to my eye. My hands were sweating and I was unable to undo the safety pin—this did nothing to enhance my reputation.

In the second and third years, I shared a cottage in Port Dinorwic with Tom Vigus, up a hill with beautiful views over the Menai Straits. We were on the topside of the lane, and the garden on the other side had a fifteen foot drop into their long plots. If I hadn't been sick in town after a night out, I would put my fingers down my throat and there would be a few seconds' pause before the remaining contents of the evening splattered into the rhubarb and vegetables below— wonderful fertiliser, and the bathroom kept clean!

It was ideal being in Reichel for my first year for many reasons, the main one being the many friendships that were made, as well as the excellent daily breakfasts and dinners. There was a little formality, and every evening student gowns were worn for the meal. There was also inter-hall rivalry for each of the sports. I played in the Reichel seven-a-side rugby team, and we wiped the floor with all opposition. Being on a steep hill with the lecture rooms at the top and student union at the bottom, as well as the walk from hall and rugby training, I and most others were in good physical shape. A fellow rugby player, with notoriously short legs, who also lived in Reichel and became a lifelong friend was Stan Moore, a farmer's son from Llay. We met up again at Wrexham Rugby Club when I returned from Jamaica and he had married the lovely, scintillating Lyn. I was privileged to speak at her funeral in Ebeneser Chapel, one of the most difficult things I have ever done; MS took her life away much too soon. Lyn wouldn't hesitate in telling me to go and enjoy sex and travel when I needed to be brought into line, but she'd use just two words not six.

The weekly highlight on the social calendar was the Saturday night hop in PJ Hall, an awesome building in the main arts lecture complex. Unfortunately, I would invariably drink too much beer beforehand, which would make the chances of tapping on at the end of the night unlikely. The student who ran university entertainments was from Birmingham and managed to book great bands, many just starting out such as Faces, and the Pentangle's performance was epic. One of the best concerts was not there but in Liverpool Students' Union, where I drove with a couple of mates to see The Who. Their music was fantastic, the atmosphere pulsating, culminating with the instruments—the guitars and finally drums—being smashed violently.

Studying was never a top priority, and I only went to the library in emergencies to complete a long-overdue assignment. I greatly enjoyed psychology, but I dropped it after the first year because I was too lazy to get my head around the chemistry, which would be ramped up in the second and third years. The department had, and still does fifty years later, an excellent reputation throughout the UK as a leader in its field. Economics at the time wasn't impressive, under Professor Black, a dour Scotsman. I passed the exams at the end of the first year with no resits.

I put myself forward for Sports Secretary in Reichel the following year. I didn't do any campaigning, unlike the other main contender, and lost. My best friend outside rugby was Tom Vigus, who I'd met on the first night. We had similar interests, mainly having a good time and a light-hearted approach to life. He studied forestry, which meant he had an eclectic group of acquaintances including many from developing countries. Ray Tan and Yassin Bin Salleh became good friends of mine also. Ray was from Sabah and played number one in the Welsh badminton squad. My eyes were opened when we went to watch him, as previously I had considered it a pit-pat game not one of high speed with the shuttlecock flying at one hundred miles an hour. Yassin was from Brunei and would turn up with exquisite goods from the Far East, including a beautiful silk dressing gown I still wear. Both were amazing cooks, and Tom and I learnt how to make beautiful Malaysian curries. Although we followed their recipes, adding the same spices in the same order, they never reached the same deliciousness as when either of them produced a meal.

Tom and I arranged to share a flat together in the second year and thought what a wonderful idea it would be if our good friend Yassin joined us, as he enjoyed cooking and we enjoyed eating his dishes. Unfortunately, Yassin didn't appreciate our strategy and had no intention of being our live-in butler. Instead, we found a cottage in Port Dinorwic, five miles outside Bangor on the road to Caernarvon, a small village with a few pubs, a lovely harbour and the Working Men's Conservative Club; nothing to do with politics, but it was open on Sunday nights with entertainment, a bar and a very low membership fee while pubs were shut as Gwynedd remained a dry county at that time. We had thoughts of entertaining young ladies who would be obliged to stay over if they realised too late the last bus back to Bangor had gone. But the main reason was cost, as this little jewel was just £5 a week between us. I also earned money decorating it for the owner over the summer holidays with Rennie, a friend from Queensferry who was an odd-job builder and decorator, also a keen rock climber—we spent a couple of days on the crags of Ogwen Valley.

The summer of 1968 was another example of the broad-mindedness and generosity of Oliver and Enid when John Golding, my brother-in-law, was filming *Alfred the Great* in Ireland with Alex Thomson, his brother-in-law, a director of photography for MGM; John's sister incidentally stood in more than once for Sophia Loren, who wouldn't be filmed topless. My mum and dad drove across to Moycullen outside Galway on the West Coast of Ireland and had a fabulous time, including a garden party at the castle Gayle Hunnicutt and David Hemmings were renting. At the end of their stay, they drove back to Dun Lahogaire, where Jude the Prude, my girlfriend of twelve months who had just finished her first year sixth in the Queen's School, and I were waiting on the docks. How this trip arose I don't know; our relationship had started in the flower power summer of 1967 at the home of Brigadier Olivier, brother of Sir Lawrence.

Oliver handed me the keys to the VW Beetle, and my mum and dad went as passengers on the ferry back to Holyhead, caught the train to Shotton, and the Vicar had two weeks without a car.

We drove back to Moycullen, and I had a part as an extra, where I earned more each day than I made in the factory in Queensferry working for a week; I was paid even more if I wore a scar. Each lunchtime, John, Alex and I would play darts with David Hemmings, who starred in the film along with Michel York and Prunella Ransome. The Irish Army provided the Anglo-Saxons, and I was amongst the invading Vikings. I was in trouble in my first encounter as I went in wielding my sword attacking the shields and there was swift retaliation—it was acting and no one was meant to get hurt. The filming took place in Ireland partly because the government was sympathetic to movies and offered financial incentives—also the director wanted battle scenes with dark skies and heavy mud. There was a drought that summer, and not a cloud appeared in the sky. In those pre-digital days, the film in the can was sent to London and returned the next day as "Rushes" to see what had gone well and whether re-shoots were needed. Helicopters were expensive to hire, and one scene was scrapped as an extra was reading a book while marching along to fight! The lavish lifestyle was something to experience. The senior members of the set worked hard by day, played poker and drank whisky till late into the night. While they were working, they earned serious money and were happy to spend it. The poker pot was huge, and with the pile of notes on the table, no way could I consider joining in.

One day, Marianne Faithful turned up, and she and I had breakfast together. We had a good conversation, but what surprised me was the colour of her language as not many women swore heavily at the time. She invited us to a party in the mansion she was renting from the Guinnesses, as Mick Jagger, who she was dating at the time, had just turned up with Keith Richards. Jude and I landed up not going following a row with my sister, who was most likely concerned about the activities which would be taking place around a young girl from Chester and the stories that might leak back. We did go to the variety concert that David Hemmings hosted for the Mayor of Galway's Biafran Fund, a great night—though not quite the same as the one we missed out on. I still have the Irish £10 note I won in the raffle draw and haven't got round to putting it on their lottery. We had a lovely time driving around the Connemaras down the coast, where we saw what we thought was a bunch of penguins on the rocks but, as we got closer, turned out to be a bunch of nuns playing guitars and singing the sun down. Five of us hired a fishing trawler for the day, and the captain found a shoal of mackerel. It was slaughter as the lines went over with five hooks on each, which were full within seconds; we landed up giving many of the fish to Keoghs, the local store in Oughterard. That was an experience in itself, as the bar was attached to the supermarket and only vertical coloured ribbons divided the two. Men could be seen drinking at the bar in the morning and were still there in the evening, in the same seats but at totally different angles, hanging on for dear life. On the August bank holiday, we went to a beach on the Atlantic coast with white sand extending for miles and three donkeys as our only company. Another pleasurable day was rowing on Lough Corrib, where one of the film crew was renting a villa that included a boathouse.

West Coast of Ireland Shotton   *Ball*

Returning home, everyone was pleased we'd had such a fantastic holiday, including Jude's grandmother, a traditional lady from the Isle of Man. A couple of months later, she was threatening to cut Jude out of her will when she came to Bangor for the weekend to attend one of the balls, which was memorable not for that but for Joe Cocker, an amazing star act. I never understood the grandmother's diametrically opposed reactions.

A sequel to *Alfred the Great* came when the movie was showing in the Bangor cinema. Rugby friends came to watch it with me. They had put a line through David Hemmings on the poster outside and in large letters inserted 'Tim Hill' as top of the bill. After a while, they kept asking where I was, and in the end I pointed to every crowd scene but never saw myself once.

Rennie, who I painted the cottage with, was a grafter, qualified as a teacher, but became disillusioned and didn't want to join the family building company who I worked for over the summer vacation. The worst part of that was when I was assigned to a small team to go to Sealand, the RAF barracks, and carry out repair work on what I soon found out was the sewage works. Neither my head nor stomach had recovered from the weekend's revelries, and it wasn't long before I discovered the meaning of shit-stirring. As we started our work, the sluice gates opened and a huge flood of excrement, condoms and other indescribable ablutions poured in, complemented by the most disgusting odours. I immediately retired fifty paces, where I remained until I had a lift back at lunchtime, never to be employed by them again.

Rennie looked after me; I'd help him decorate, and I bought an antique rum barrel with my first week's wage. One job was refitting a house in Buckley, an insurance claim following a fire. This involved washing the walls down with a special solution to get rid of the acrid smell and smoke damage, replacing the sheets of wooden panels and wiring in a new electric fire—no checks by anyone with certification.

My main holiday earner was a factory in Queensferry that ran 24/7 turning wood pulp into boards for the building industry. Wagonloads of tree trunks were continually delivered, stored in fields and fed by belts into huge hoppers. Upwards of a hundred men were employed on shift work, and another student and I stood at the end of one of the lines stacking the two-metre-square boards as we took them off the rails at the end of the production line. We were allotted different tasks around the factory at the weekend. There was a relaxed air about the business and a friendly atmosphere, other than a Polish man, ex-coal miner, who spoke broken English. There were several Polish communities from Anglesey through to Wrexham who had settled in the area after the Second World War. At breaktime he would sit in his favourite seat in the cabin and use a large sheath knife to cut his food. He was very strong, said little, and no one would question or contradict him.

In good weather we'd take our breaks outside, and I became known as the philosopher, as I would sit on the stacked boxes and relax, just thinking. As students, we paid no income tax. For some reason we were allowed to clock on at the beginning of a Saturday shift, go home for an eight hour break and not clock off till we left on Sunday night. We took home up to eight pounds a week, at least one pound more than regular workers who were supporting families on this one wage packet. From time to time there were friendly disputes between me and my fellow student about whose turn it was to take off the next board. When we both refused to do it, they'd build up on the floor until the line was stopped and we sorted the backlog.

My worst offence was turning up drunk on the late shift one Saturday night. There was a cabin where we took turns sleeping on the night shift. I woke up with a bad head in the middle of the night, felt sick and thought I should not be in such a dangerous place in such a state and went home. When I returned at eight o'clock the following morning, not having clocked out, I was met with stony silence by my mates. They knew I'd arrived the night before, and I'd told no one I was going home; I'd just disappeared. They had searched for me around the factory and feared I'd fallen into one of the vast hoppers never to be recognised again amidst the wood pulp. Someone said the manager was going to fire me, quite rightly too. I went straight to his office, made profuse apologies for my stupidity, and to everyone's astonishment I was not disciplined, only got a severe warning! I heard the poor other student had gone to the pub on the way to the bank to lodge his summer's earnings, only to be robbed of every penny.

Ogwen Valley

Bangor Uni

The fantastic news at the beginning of the second year at Bangor was that Professor Revell had taken over the Economics department. A bright, fresh, friendly man who was a world authority on banking, writing papers and sitting on high-level committees. None of us knew why he'd left Cambridge University to take up a position in rural Wales; we didn't complain—Cambridge's loss was our gain. There were only eight of us on the banking module of my Economics degree—three came from Quarry Bank, now Calderstones School in Liverpool—and we were having private tuition from this great mind. Although I was interested in the subject, it didn't inspire me to up my studies.

Some years later, I asked Jack Revell if he'd act as my referee for the Organisation for Economic Co-operation and Development. There was a French family living in Burton, by Rossett, and the daughter worked for OECD in Paris and extolled the virtues of living in a fantastic city on an inflated salary with a generous expense account, and she fed me the job vacancies. I understood the merits and wrote to Professor Revell asking if he'd give me a reference. He was pleased to hear from me and that I'd asked his permission first. He said he had no problem doing what I'd asked; however, he didn't think my character was suited to working in a large bureaucracy—how right he was, and thank goodness he knew me well enough to point it out.

Tom and I moved into the cottage, and we had a good year. Despite not having a car, we were content hitching into Bangor or catching a bus. It was a beautiful location, and there were wonderful walks into the countryside and down along the Menai Straits. We did a reasonable amount of entertaining, and parties were helped along by the homemade beer we brewed. We used fresh hops boiled in girls' tights, and the mixture would sit in the airing cupboard above the fire with a tube into the hot water cylinder. We knew the beer was ready for bottling when the rate of bubbles slowed to one every thirty seconds. I thought I'd polluted the whole of the Port Dinorwic water system when the water turned turquoise when I washed my hands in the sink; luckily there was a valve in the way.

With my earnings from the summer vacation I bought a minivan in Bernie's auction in Queensferry. Oliver did the bidding, which stopped at £80. I insisted on paying, although my dad wanted to buy it for me; I hope the pleasure in me earning some money outweighed his disappointment in not paying.

This made travelling in and out of Bangor much easier in the third year, although the number of lectures was minimal. No Monday or Friday lectures, no nine o'clock lectures and only one lecture after two o'clock; there was ample time for me to read around the subject, but I wasn't that way inclined!

One morning I was late for one of the few lectures and was having trouble passing an elderly gentleman in a Triumph Vitesse until I eventually overtook him on a series of bands. His horn was sounding, lights flashing and fist clenched. I opened the hatch in the roof of the van and flashed him a V sign. His anger mounted and he followed me to where I parked for the lecture and came up to me, shaking with rage. I listened and said nothing as he told me that what I'd done to him was a total insult and that was what they did in the war. Just before I turned around, I apologised. I've never known anyone's demeanour change from rage to gratitude so quickly. "That is what I wanted to hear," he said, and we parted the best of friends, but by this time it was too late to attend the lecture.

My twenty-first birthday fell on a Saturday, and I had a couple of pints before the rugby match in the afternoon. I was sent off for only the second time in my career, as the referee was most likely protecting me for my own safety. In the student union bar that night, I performed a "Zumba" for the baying crowds. There were manic strippers such as David Lugg, who one time took his clothes off in the Odeon cinema and ran a circuit crossing the stage in front of the screen.

Time came to revise for the final exams. However, rather than spend time in the library or in the cottage with my head down in books, like many others I'd head to the beaches on Anglesey. The weather in May was often the best of the year and too good an opportunity to miss. If it was cloudy on the west of Anglesey it would be sunny on the east and vice versa, so the decision was easily made crossing the bridge whether it would be Aberffraw, which had grass cliffs as well as sand, or Benllech beach.

It was on a Saturday at the end of May that the party we were at was interrupted when someone spotted flames leaping into the sky and some took off to be close to the action. Sadly, the Britannia railway bridge had been set alight by lighted paper used as a torch being accidentally dropped, setting fire to the tar and wood. Luckily the structure was still standing after the fire had burnt itself out.

The week before the exams, I became ill and could hardly leave my bed. The doctor couldn't help, so I phoned the Professor, who told me I should turn up as I would get a better grade than if I was awarded an aegrotat degree. Economics is a subject where you can leave an exam knowing more than when you went in as theories can be developed supported by convincing arguments, but this was no substitute for hard study; a 2.2 with honours was all I deserved.

I enjoyed my years in Bangor, made many friends and loved the experience of learning to be responsible for myself. There is little doubt that the social side was the most important part and was welcome after years in a restrictive, male-only public school system. Drinking beer was a significant part, but not often beyond the Saturday and Wednesday rugby matches. There were mock elections in St John's, where I'd thought I was extremely left wing, but at university I found I was centre at best. I was pleased to have lived in such a pleasant environment out in the provinces at a leisurely pace and not in the chaos of a city, though I enjoyed my visits to London. I failed to take opportunities, including majoring in Psychology, studying harder and reading more widely round the subject. My track record since leaving Llanfyllin Council School was to do enough to get through.

In 1969, Oliver was appointed Vicar of Gresford, which was a delightful parish with a church that had roots in the thirteenth century, being one of the Thomas Stanley Churches. It was his brother, Sir William Stanley's, intervention at the Battle of Bosworth which won the battle for Henry Tudor and gained him the throne as Henry VII. There was a cross-section of parishioners, from Lady Jones to coal miners, ideal for my dad, who enjoyed people whoever and whatever they may be. Unfortunately, this appointment came several years too late, as he wasn't a well man, having flogged himself almost to death in Shotton for a number of years without a curate. At the institution and induction there were a couple of buses of his faithful flock who tried to take him back to Shotton. About twenty had travelled from Mochdre, a parish we left in 1952. On the previous Monday, Sir Richard Summers, A. B. Stobart and the rest of the board of John Summers entertained Oliver with lunch in the directors' dining room, and "all spoke very kindly" and said they would be pleased to see him visiting the works as in the past.

Oliver had a wonderful way with children of all ages, from those he christened as babies in the font, and especially young ones who attended Gresford Church School. He wore a long black cloak, and it was a regular sight to see them following behind as if he were the Pied Piper of Hamelin. My friends from Gresford and university enjoyed spending time with him.

The Vicarage was amazing: high ceilings, porch and entrance hall, large dining and drawing rooms with sash windows opening to the ground, enabling you to step out to the beautiful cedar of Lebanon in the garden, six bedrooms, two bathrooms and a back staircase. Parishioners invited Oliver and Enid to dinner and tea—Mr and Mrs Lewis Jones, Langshaw Rowlands, Dr and Mrs James, Colonel and Mrs Vivian, Judge and Mrs Seys Llewellyn, Tiny Toller and others. During the short visits home, I met various people who would become lifelong friends, including David Spalding, Richard, Geoff and Anthony Seys Llewellyn, and others who were a good part of my life before I left for the Caribbean: Mike James, Martin and Robert Nichols, Dave Mayers, Colin and Francis Glyn Jones, Nick and James Churton.

I had the opportunity of travelling round the United States for six weeks and took it with open arms, not giving a second thought to missing my graduation ceremony. John Spiegelberg, a rugby friend from Bangor and one of several acquaintances from around Chester who went to Marlborough College, had a party at his family home in Little Budworth on the Saturday night before. I went with Janet Lewis Jones, who kindly drove me to Chester Station early the following morning in time to get to Victoria terminal by midday Sunday 21 June 1970.

Oliver and Enid Gresford Vicarage

USA SUMMER 1970 – THREE MONTHS AND NO CAMERA

NEW YORK CITY

I checked in at Victoria terminal in London and met up with Geoff Pitt to catch the shuttle bus to Heathrow. I was excited to find out what sort of experience flying would be, and taking off was little different from travelling in an elevator. Geoff was sales director of Cunard and spent one week in four in New York; he tried to get an upgrade, which didn't happen, so we mixed our own champagne cocktails with brandy over a sugar cube. However, New York as a first air-travel destination felt pretty cool, even though I was twenty-one.

We were met at Kennedy Airport by the company Lincoln Continental and rode into New York City in style. NYC was fantastic; streets a bit dirty but no worse than London! It was full of super restaurants, huge skyscrapers and steam blowing out of pipes into streets filled with yellow cabs. My hotel looked over Central Park, where people played baseball and basketball, rowed boats and jogged during the day. It didn't take long to get used to the grid system of avenues running parallel north-south—other than Broadway, which cuts diagonally across—and streets running east-west, with buses sticking to one route, travelling backwards and forwards. The subway worked well, with carriages covered in art, as were many of the platform walls. The people in Cunard office were most helpful, arranging trips including a boat ride round Manhattan Bay and using their contacts to get me on tours for free, including Westpoint. Lots of suggestions were made concerning work, but I thought there was little point staying in New York for long after Geoff and Jo, his wife who joined us for the second week, left—no more $10 meals on an expense account (after all, I was using a book, *New York on $5/$10 Dollars a Day*, all in). NYC had the best and worst of everything: expensive apartments right next to poverty, Bleaker Street.

I spent the days hopping on and off buses, walking miles, visiting museums. I was especially bowled over by the Guggenheim, designed by Frank Lloyd Wright, a circular building with the most amazing collection of modern art. I strolled in and out of shops such as Macy's and Bloomingdale's, stores that hadn't yet arrived in the UK, and Tiffany. I watched people being duped by chase the ball, the three cup trick. I was particularly enthralled by Steuben glass, and I had an inner desire to sculpt with light; bunches of solid plastic straws with pin-point glows reflected on top had just arrived, and I imagined this on a large scale. The tour of the United Nations, where there was a feeling of power and hope, was fascinating. I rode on the Staten Island ferry—the best value for money in NYC—where for a few cents you travel the commuter boat with stunning views of Lower Manhattan, Ellis Island and the Statue of Liberty, and I strolled along Coney Island Boardwalk.

One of the restaurants Geoff and I ate in was Steak and Brew; $3 got a steak, unlimited salad and all the beer you could drink. We returned a couple of times, and I became friendly with one of the waitresses, Jackie Abrams, who was working to supplement her irregular income as a dancer. We went to shows, including *Oh Calcutta* which was quite an eye-opener, and Brendan Behan's *Borstal Boy*; it was interesting to see the different appreciation of humour between Brits and Americans, who laughed in different places.

I had been warned not to set foot in Central Park after dusk; however, one night there was music cascading from far inside. After a period of deliberation, Geoff and I plucked up the courage and went to find the source. After about a quarter of a mile, there was a bandstand with a couple of hundred people sitting around enjoying great sounds.

It was more interesting when Jo arrived, and she had simple tips for getting around comfortably, such as walking on the shady side of the sweltering streets. We went to Westpoint, a concert in the Lincoln Centre where everyone except me was smartly dressed— some in pinks—and a great show in the Rockefeller Centre. We went up the Empire State Building and in the fastest lifts to the top of the Twin Towers; I got a type of labyrinthitis which took a good twenty-four hours to recover from. Jo couldn't believe I'd never eaten pizza and she soon rectified that—delicious. We travelled to Salisbury, New England, to spend a weekend in the country with the president of Cunard, and I couldn't have imagined how beautiful the country was: old colonial wooden houses, secluded, miles and miles of forests and lakes—not what I expected America to be at all.

After Jo and Geoff left, I moved into Jackie's apartment on West 13th Street, and I became part of New York life. There was a mix of people sharing the apartment and lots of friends diving in and out. I was intrigued by the different American accents, one of which was the Southern drawl of a Texan girl in her twenties who had flown to NYC for her 3rd abortion. Another girl's parents had a French restaurant with the best food, which we were treated to one night. I experienced Buddhist chanting for the first time when we went to a meeting together—a wonderfully pleasant, positive experience. We went to a party and people turned up with a few bottles of spirits, not just a bottle of wine or couple of beers.

New Yorkers were amazingly friendly, and several times I was stopped on the street or in the subway and asked if I needed help when I was obviously looking lost. Waiting for Jackie to finish work, I'd spend hours wandering around Times Square, sitting in bars watching people of all shapes and sizes—including whores—imagining, in my tall leather boots with a strap across the instep, I was Jon Voight in *Midnight Cowboy*.

CONNECTICUT

I spent a weekend with Gilbert and Jean Meek Barker in their country house in Connecticut. Gilbert's mum and dad lived in Queensferry, North Wales; his mother sang in the choir of St Ethelwold's Church where Oliver was vicar, and his father never left the house as he was blind and most bitter that God had taken his sight away. I used to visit him from time to time, and he would feed me pearls of wisdom, such as "If you become a chartered accountant you will always be someone's servant," and when I spoke about going to California, he told me the memories looking at the Golden Gate Bridge would always remain and I could look up from my desk in the middle of a boring job back in the UK and relive the experience. They gave me Gil's address in Manhattan but didn't tell him I was going to knock on their door. *Clunk, clank,* security bolts and chains were removed, and when they understood who I was, I received a generous welcome and arrangements were made to visit their country retreat. I went with Gil to pick up his 1965 Rolls Royce Silver Cloud from underground storage, and off we set to Sherman.

It was a lovely drive over the bridges out of New York City and speeding into the open countryside. Their hunting lodge was in the most beautiful rural location with an Arabian horse stud farm as the nearest neighbour. There was a big living room, which was open to the roof, a stone fireplace and Romeo and Juliet balconies facing each other at either end upstairs, with the master bedroom, kitchen and snugs off the downstairs. It was full of

85

character yet simple, with all the comforts of life, a lot of land and a splendid little tractor for moving earth and old trees; it acted as a mower in summer and a snow blower in winter. The whole setup was just like a dream. Lots of wood to chop and machines to facilitate inside and outside work. Gil and Jean loved their time living in San Francisco and said that if I didn't visit the West Coast I'd wasted my time coming to America. However, I hadn't the money to extend the airplane ticket, which would cost more than I paid for the original round trip to New York, and I didn't see how I could earn enough to spend another six weeks travelling. Jean was fashion editor of *Redbook Magazine*, and when we were back in NYC, she arranged for me to visit Rafferty studios and introduced me to the owner. I didn't realise I was pitching for work as an assistant photographer and didn't do a very good job of selling myself.

Rafferty Studios Redbook Magazine Photoshoot

CHICAGO

I'd had the most fantastic introduction to America in general and New York in particular, and I was impressed with the mind-blowing amount of choice and the can-do attitude.

I went to the Port Authority terminal and caught a Greyhound bus to Chicago to visit my dad's sister, Myrtle. I enjoyed the journey; however, I had to wait an age at the other end for Roy, her husband, to turn up. He'd been a GI in the Second World War when they got together in South Wales. Eventually, he drove up and we started visiting bars, as if he was trying to delay as long as possible before I could meet my aunt and cousins, who had stayed with us a few years earlier in North Wales. There was little doubt he was an alcoholic, and my cousin Gareth suffered from a limp after a bad car crash on their way back from a wedding when Roy was allegedly driving drunk. He didn't use the compensation for an operation to put his leg right, instead investing it in a drug deal from Mexico which fell through; he sadly died an early death. It was a joy meeting Myrtle and her daughter Jane, a pretty young thing who decades later on Facebook said she would never forget how kind and supportive I was to her; she was being bullied in school at the time and I gave her words of wisdom to boost her confidence and improve her life.

We visited the fantastic Museum of Science and Industry, drove round the Windy City, rode the Loop

87

and visited some bars in the attractive Old Town with Gareth. I arranged to see Elspeth Lewis Jones from Gresford, who was working in the university, but couldn't find her apartment. It wasn't long before I started feeling sick and began to throw up. Myrtle, who was a walking medical encyclopaedia, tried to diagnose my ailment, which Roy put down to me not being able to hold my beer. I visited their medical surgery, and the receptionist told me I looked well and enquired whether I should be there at all. Dr Edward Bruchan was amazingly efficient and gave me blood tests and took stool samples. He quickly diagnosed I had salmonella, which I had most likely contracted in Steak and Brew, where the lowest-paid worker would have been responsible for washing the salad and not have the best sanitary habits. The doctor knew I wanted to go to California and that I couldn't afford the cost of changing my ticket, so he got in touch with BOAC and told them I was a public health hazard and wasn't fit to go on public transport; two dozen people had died of salmonella that week. They replied saying he must give me a note when I was well and I was to fly within seven days.

BACK TO NYC

The doctor was upset to have stuck his neck out to enable me to visit California, which he loved, when he discovered I was travelling back to New York. Jackie had been in touch and said she had two jobs lined up for me to earn money. When I arrived at her apartment, there was no job—it was wishful thinking and she wanted me back. I took my bags and went down to the nearest bar for happy hour, where buying a glass of beer enabled me to have a good feed of meatballs and chicken legs for "free". I sat there wondering how I could earn some bucks.

Mario Puzo had just released *The Godfather*, and I was soon involved in a conversation with a group of people discussing whether it was a mistake for the consiglieri to be Irish and not Italian. My new acquaintances turned out to be East Coast artists, a film producer amongst them who was putting together a movie with six hoods, one of whom was from Liverpool. He asked me to audition for the part, but I declined. The most famous painters there were Larry Poons, David Budd and David Prentice. David Prentice knew I wanted to earn the money to travel to the West Coast, and had promised the dean of his art college that he'd lay a garage floor for him. He called to see if it was convenient to start. It certainly was, and I arranged to go round to his apartment, on Broadway between Bleaker Street and Bond, the next day. I went back to Jackie's apartment with a smile on my face and was welcomed in.

The following day, I turned up at David's studio with an overnight bag and pulled the chain which operated the lift up to the second floor. I was met by dogs, cats and a monkey. He invited me to see his work, which at first appeared as if nothing was on the canvas. On closer inspection, there were the faintest of weakly coloured broad lines; I later discovered they became more visible when you were stoned. We set off with his girlfriend, who was my age, to beautiful New England and arrived at an old colonial house with lawns open to the street. The dean came out to the car and welcomed David by dropping his white trousers, bollock naked from the waist down, and giving him a big hug. We took our things inside and soon began laying the garage floor. While we were there we were offered unlimited beer and marijuana, which the dean kept in the old oven by the side of the fireplace to annoy his new mother-in-law. His wife taught history of art at Harvard, and the next day a colleague came down as a party had been arranged to celebrate his first divorce. A local judge arrived for dinner; plenty of alcohol was consumed and dope smoked. After the meal, the wife stripped off and was dancing on the table—I, the wide boy, who had been to university and thought I'd lived, had never felt so far out of my depth, and luckily David's girlfriend was in the same predicament. We finished the floor and they were happy with our work.

I was surprised when David said he was impressed that I had come to NYC and was travelling round the States by myself at such a relatively young age.

Meanwhile Suzanne Tobias turned up at Jackie's apartment as her dad had been commissioned by UCLA to produce a scale sculpture and was looking for someone to do the work under supervision; he'd had a serious heart attack while working on the sculpture piece. His girlfriend at the time—her parents were already divorced—had inadvertently called him during the episode. He didn't sound well, so she'd rushed over, made him drink black coffee and told him to relax. He didn't have surgery, and he later told Suzanne that his doctor was furious with him for that. He lived a very productive life, all the while with part of his heart dead.

Suzanne asked if anyone was able to work wood. Precociously, I jumped forward, and she took me to meet her dad, Julius Tobias, in Great Jones Street. He was anxious that I shouldn't injure myself, as even if I made my finger bleed it wasn't worth the pain.

Over a few days he instructed me in what he wanted, then would go to lie down for an hour or so, followed by his loads of kittens. Every so often, he'd return to check how I was getting on. We chatted about the Second World War, when he'd flown bombers over Europe, and how he had become a pacifist. He was disappointed that his influence on Martha Graham's dancing, who lived in the same apartment block, hadn't been recognised. What I didn't understand at the time was that it was the space in and around his sculptures he regarded as critical, not the sculpture itself. We'd go to the supermarket, and I'd carry his shopping as he was still weak.

I finished the sculpture, which was a three-sided box with a block of wood inside wrapped in rope. The last half hour was spent with us adjusting the rope in turn and improving how it stood, eventually cutting a chunk from the bottom to lower it further down the block. He said if I repeated the work when I returned to Wales, he would send me a letter to say it was a Julius Tobias original. Unfortunately I 'never got round to it' and other than sending a postcard, I lost contact.

Suzanne, who like Jackie was Jewish, related some decades later that she remembered the day her father had mentioned he needed help making the piece I worked on. He'd seemed tired and discouraged, and she had not liked seeing him that way. She heard a guy needed money and had just finished a floor job, so he probably wouldn't be interested, but walked over to Thirteenth Street. She remembered seeing me in her dad's loft and did not want to interfere with the work, so did not engage much. She said I seemed like a pretty cool dude and mentioned that to her dad, who told her I was heading off to California in a few days and to forget about nice cool dudes. Julius Tobias exuded kindness and a love of life, mingled with sadness, and meeting him was one of the most enlightening experiences of my life. The memory of those few days in his company fifty years ago has stayed with me ever since.

ROUTE 66

In a week, I had earned enough money to buy a Greyhound ticket—$30 for thirty days—and spend six more weeks in the States. After fond farewells to my New York friends, I headed back to the Port Authority terminal. I was there in plenty of time to catch a bus that would travel the whole way across the States down Route 66, with drivers changing every four hours. There was a rush for the terminal door as soon as it opened, but as I had a ticket I let people ahead of me. The ticket wasn't for a seat but for the journey, and there was no room for me on that bus. I spent the next twenty-four hours chasing the bus across the States on short-journey buses. Every couple of hours, I'd arrive at the next bus station as the main one was leaving. In St Louis I saw my opportunity and, without going into the bus station, leapt straight onto the bus before the station door opened, much to the annoyance of the waiting passengers.

I headed for Santa Fe, a lovely town in New Mexico with pueblo-style architecture, where there was a conglomeration of artists and a lovely feel to the place. The bus arrived late in the evening, and I went into a hotel and persuaded the night porter to let me sleep on a settee in the lobby at no cost. I woke early in the morning, as requested, and wandered around the town, looking through shop windows at paintings and artefacts. I started chatting to a middle-aged Texan gentleman with cowboy boots and a Stetson who had come to buy property. He invited me back to his hotel for breakfast together with his wife. He and I sat at the table and drank coffee until she arrived: a beautiful tall lady, blonde hair and a Southern drawl. We talked for a while, then she placed a large case on the table, opened it up, and maybe forty lights came on all around the edges—it was a portable makeup stand and she proceeded to do the business. Her husband and I ordered steak and eggs, and the meat hung over the edge of the plate. Another example of the kindness and hospitality I was receiving all over the country.

I visited Santa Fe Chapel, the oldest church in the USA, built in 1610, then went on to a live Indian reservation. I spent time in a sweat lodge and observed a ceremony for prayer and healing. If it wasn't so isolated, Santa Fe is somewhere I'd like to have lived.

Back on a bus to Gallup, where I overnighted. It seemed a rough town, and I passed sheds where lots of Mexicans were sleeping if not living. I went to a bar for dinner and down the steps to the cellar for a drink. I was happily enjoying a beer, doing my best to talk to a Mexican in Spanish. I don't know what I said to upset him, but he pulled a large knife and chased me out of the building. Luckily he was drunk; I was sober and had no trouble leaving him behind, but it could have been nasty.

The next morning I headed through the Petrified Forest National Park and on to Flagstaff. I had met three others in Santa Fe who also were going to the Grand Canyon; we teamed up with two more and hired a station wagon for the day.

The Grand Canyon was an awesome, beautiful sight. The enormity of the canyon, through which the Colorado River flowed, was totally impressive. At sunset, the colours of the rocks continually changed; it was a magnificent spectacle, and a group of Native Americans performed a dance. It would have been good to have taken a three-day trip to the bottom but time didn't allow.

From Flagstaff, we headed to Las Vegas, the city with no clocks. There was only one strip in 1970 and four main casinos—Caesar's Palace, Stardust, Flamingo and Sahara—with twee wedding chapels dotted in between. I felt like James Bond as I wandered around the Caesar's Palace swimming pool late at night with no one else around and rode a glass elevator up the side of the hotel—not the one I was staying in! Whilst the main casinos were disappointing, with row upon row of slot machines, the entertainment was excellent and free once you'd bought a drink. I was thrilled watching Rowan and Martin's Laugh In with Goldie Hawn and other quality shows.

The day trip to see the Hoover Dam was amazing and included an excellent film recording the huge construction and tales of lives lost in its building.

Then on to Los Angeles. When I alighted from the Greyhound Bus in what turned out to be a bad part of town, two cops were chasing a man down the street, firing shots at him. I wasted no time leaving LA and heading to the Tammages' in Park View Drive, La Jolla. They'd moved out of the UK a couple of years earlier and lived in one of the most beautiful places in California. David, their son, took me surfing at the famous beach, but I wasn't able to get going and the experts showed no mercy. I sailed with Cyril Tammage in a fifteen-foot boat across the bay to San Antonio, a famous fish restaurant in San Diego. All was going well with me at the helm until I saw an aircraft carrier appear round the headland. The ship got bigger, and I checked if we would pass comfortably in front of it. "No way," says Cyril, at which point I handed over to him. The craft seemed so big that the *Ark Royal* could have been one of its lifeboats. It passed within a couple of hundred yards, and I had to strain my neck upwards to see the deck and waving sailors.

LA TO TIJUANA

After a most enjoyable couple of days, I crossed the border into Mexico and headed for Tijuana. A grubby town with lots of bars and beauties standing outside seedy establishments enticing people in; I had no difficulty resisting. I found a sports hall and watched an exciting game of pelota. There were plenty of shops selling trinkets, and after a beer in a quiet bar, I set off for Hollywood.

HOLLYWOOD

Gus and Jean Ryden had received a call from Gil and Jean and kindly offered to have me stay. They were two of the most friendly, unassuming people I'd ever met. Jean had been the top secretary in Paramount and Gus, following time in the Navy, arrived in Los Angeles as a coach for the Swedish Olympic Team in 1932. They were ahead of their time and lived together for ten years before getting married. Gus became a leading cameraman; Bob Hope and the Marx Brothers demanded him as their first choice when filming. Gus took me around Paramount Studios, introduced me to his old friends who used to be leading lights in the industry, took me to meals in the Spaghetti Factory and Victoria Station, an authentic railway car, and I went for a dip in Mae West's swimming pool. She didn't ask me whether "I had a gun in my pocket or was just happy to see her".

One day, Gus dropped me off at Universal Studios, which was a fascinating and eye-opening experience. I learnt the cowboy sets were built at 7/8ths size to make the likes of John Wayne appear even bigger. I was enthralled by Disney—what kid of any age wouldn't be?—however, for one of the few times in my life, I walked out of a film, which was *Winnie the Pooh*, because I couldn't abide the characters' American accents and I didn't want my fantasy spoiled. I saw the Chinese theatre and did the Walk of Fame down Hollywood and Vine, looking at the five-pointed terrazzo and brass stars names embedded in the sidewalks.

Gus and Jean tried to persuade me to stay as they were sure they could get me a break in movies. When I protested I had no acting experience, they said I had the height, looks and voice and they could make it happen. I told them I had a contract for articles with Peat Marwick Mitchell (KPMG) at £600 a year.

Jim Malcolm was staying with them at the same time. He had an interesting career and was dean of an art college in Colorado; he visited Sue and me in

Marford shortly after Emily's birth in 1980. He lived with his partner in the mountains overlooking the Cheyanne Mountain Complex, a military base and defensive bunker. One of his visions during the Cold War with Russia was that when they dropped a nuclear bomb on Cheyanne, their house would be in the cool area of the mushroom cloud and avoid the devastation all around. He had been involved in boxing and reckoned that, with the corruption involved in the sport, I could be heavy-weight champion of a minor state such as Wyoming with minimal ability—New York was possible but would require serious skills.

SAN FRANCISCO

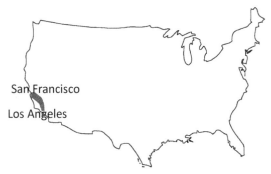

I left my Hollywood dreams behind and caught a Greyhound bus to San Francisco, where I was met by Bob Gilmore who took me to his beautiful Spanish-style house in San Mateo with thick walls and shaped arches. Rita, his wife, gave me a warm welcome and asked how long I wanted to stay—a day, week or month, it didn't matter; she just wanted me to let her know how long. Her next instruction was where to head in the event of an earthquake, the doorways being safest. They were a delightful family with four children, Alisanne being the eldest, a young teenager, visited us in Wales and another time with her mother; fifty years later, I'm still in touch with Alisanne and her sister Barbara.

Bob was highly intelligent, qualified as an attorney and CPA in more than one state, and was experimenting with seaweed for various medical cures. He had single-wing copters, designed like sycamore seeds, flying around a laboratory and had recently offered the White House a contract to end the Vietnam War within six months at a third of the spend the government were making. One of his pearls of wisdom that has stayed with me is that to be happy in a regularly ordered society you need self-discipline, and that isn't possible without experiencing discipline. This I combined with Enid's saying of "You can't give a child too much love" to create for me the two most important aspects of bringing up children.

Needless to say they had interesting friends who they introduced me to, including one memorable dinner with highflying bankers and professionals at their home where they presented this kid from the Old Country. We went to Mass in the SF Roman Catholic Cathedral, where I exchanged Peace for the first time and was moved by the experience.

A tremendous event was a BBQ for the Gilmore family and me at their friend Mousse's hacienda, where he owned a third of the mountain overlooking San Francisco. He was on his third stunning wife, and two girls were brought along to keep me company: Wendy and Sally. Wendy insisted I join her community social call to an old lady she regularly visited the next day. Wendy and Sally both visited Gresford Vicarage, and Wendy reads Dylan Thomas's *A Child's Christmas in Wales* to her family every year as a memento of the first of her visits. Emily and Mark stayed with Sally in Lake Tahoe, and Sam and Kate with Wendy in California. Kate babysat for Wendy and Larry in Paris when she was fifteen.

A reflection of the litigious fears of Americans happened when we went to the Gilmore's neighbours to swim in their pool, and I foolishly stepped on a rusty nail and was rushed to hospital for a tetanus injection. They were amazed, but very pleased, that I had no intention of suing them for the accident.

I fell in love with San Francisco—the fog rolling around Golden Gate Bridge, beautiful views from Coit Tower, Fisherman's Wharf with fantastic sea food, delicious chocolate in Ghirardelli Square, Alcatraz Island, Union Square, riding the trams, China Town with its typical herbal apothecaries. I walked through Haight Ashbury to soak up the hippie vibe and sent a card to Jude, as in 1967, the year of flower power, we had vowed we would visit San Francisco together. Sausalito, across the Bay Bridge, was special, with sailboats, lovely shores and the most delicious ice cream. The redwoods in Muir Woods were awe-inspiring, especially Cathedral Walk, where the majestic trees grew straight up to the sky, as imposing as the high arches in Liverpool Anglican Cathedral.

I was wandering around San Francisco Bus Station looking at the posters, trying to decide where I should visit for the day, when two people walked up to me and said hello; suddenly, I recognised them as friends from Bangor. I hadn't known they were travelling to America, let alone that they'd be in San Francisco at the same time. They were off to the Napa Wine Valley, and what better way to celebrate our chance meeting? It was a great day. We visited several wineries that were generous with their tastings and arrived back in the evening mellow and happy.

VANCOUVER

I headed north from San Francisco on a Greyhound bus even more effusive about the kindness, hospitality, generosity and friendliness of the remarkable people I had met, several of whom became friends for life.

I arrived in Vancouver, the starting point for my trip through the Rockies. I searched out a boat trip that would take me around the islands and fjords and found a day cruise to Granite Falls. The scenery was out of this world: mountains, rocks, valleys and beautiful waterways. On the way out, I exchanged smiles with two sisters but didn't engage in conversation because of their young age. However, over lunch we chatted. They were in their twenties, from Latvia, one of them was a nurse, and I was invited back to the beautiful apartment they shared with their mother, overlooking English Bay. Their kindness was incredible and created most favourable impressions of Latvians, who I was meeting for the first time.

Marite, one of the sisters, later visited Gresford Vicarage and possibly saved my father's life. She looked at the tablets Oliver was taking for his heart and arteries and asked Enid where a certain pill was that should always accompany one of the ones sitting there. My mum and dad had just spent a month in a beautiful retreat in Locarno, Switzerland, linked to the Church in Wales, to convalesce and improve Oliver's health. However, he'd returned home much the worse for wear, without a doubt because of the missing medication which, thanks to Marite, was immediately sorted.

ROCKIES

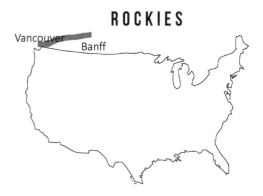

I was dropped off at the bus station early in the morning to catch the 6:30 to Banff. I shared the front seat of the bus with a lovely mature lady carefully holding a beautiful bunch of flowers she was taking to her daughter in Kamloops who had just had a baby. She was delightful and by coincidence Latvian—what a lovely country that would be to visit one day. I sat on the step so I'd have a better view of the Rockies, and fortuitously it began to snow. I received a tap on my shoulder, and two girls I knew from St Mary's College, Bangor, were travelling on that same early bus.

Lake Louise was another magnificent sight, with the valley glacier feeding the lake with beautiful blue-green meltwater, and soaring mountains and a palatial hotel at the other end. The water was stunning but too cold even to dip a toe in. While wandering around, I was lucky to meet a couple of the hotel staff. We got chatting and they asked if I'd like to see grizzly bears—are you kidding! We waited until nightfall then drove in a VW caravanette to where the hotel disposed of their meat and waste. No bears. We went back to their apartment and drank grizzly juice—white wine—for a couple of hours then returned to see one of the most exciting spectacles of my life. There was a huge male grizzly with the largest of teeth pulling a slab of meat from the pit with a mother and cubs watching on. A jackal joined the party and tried to nip the heel of the male to make him drop the meat. Up till then I'd imagined bears to be powerful but clumsy. Not a bit. His movement was graceful and feline, he'd just have to turn his head slightly and the jackal would jump away because it knew one blow from the paw would part his body in two. The mother and cubs joined in the feed. We watched this spectacle unfold from twenty feet away in the caravanette—not in safety, because the grizzly could have flattened the vehicle and eaten us for dessert. The headlights swept down the hill as we turned to leave and there were a dozen or more grizzlies coming up between the trees, which meant food must be plentiful.

The next morning, I continued to Banff, a pretty town with wooden buildings in the mountains. I made my way up to the springs, and luckily I was able to hire a bathing costume and sit with two others in hot sulphur waters looking across the valley to Mount Rundle as the snow fell around us.

BACK TO CHICAGO

At Calgary bus station, I met two more friends from Bangor. The trip was nearly at an end, and so to Chicago I went to pick up my doctor's note to say I was now fit to travel on public transport. I managed to visit Enid's cousin, Ernie Bellis, a university lecturer, and his wife in Milwaukee. We had a lovely evening and drank cocktails. Buffy, one daughter, was with them, and Mary, the other daughter, picked me up the following day. I spent a great time with her family, including a visit to the powerful Niagara Falls, where I met yet another friend from Bangor. Mary was involved in setting up Welsh American Youth, and we have kept in touch ever since. She's stayed with us in Wales several times, and more recently we visited her and Mike in Baton Rouge.

I went to a BBQ in Hamilton with Roy and Haidee Wood, who were close friends of Oliver and Enid in Penrhyn Bay, North Wales. Oliver proposed the toast to Dawn, Roy and Haidee's daughter, when she married in 1966 on a reel to reel tape and sent it over to be played at the wedding breakfast; I listened to the toast for inspiration for my father of the bride speeches for Emily and Kate's respective weddings.

One last night out with Gareth in Old Town Chicago, then a final Greyhound bus to J F Kennedy to complete my tour of the States. Around eight thousand miles at a cost of $30, sometimes sleeping but mostly watching the ever-changing dramatic scenery or driving through mile after mile of desert on Greyhound buses, for which I can't have enough praise.

Before I arrived in America, I'd expected cars flying everywhere at a hundred miles an hour, factories belching smoke and people loud, bombastic and self-centred. Those impressions couldn't have been further from the truth. You could lose the UK in one of their Great Lakes, while the population's just four times the size, with most living in a dozen or so cities dotted about. Driving, for the most part, was a great deal more sedate than in the UK. The people I met were genuine, helpful and kind, and I was surprised how together the country was, considering it was only a couple of hundred years old with the biggest mixture of nationalities and religions and the fastest economic growth to create the largest GDP in the world.

Not surprisingly, all was not perfect, and there were regions with intolerant rednecks and strong prejudices against women in general and non-white races in particular. It is certainly a land of opportunity and people talk each other up rather than down. I was sure the UK would benefit if everyone spent a month there to grasp the concept of Positive Mental Attitude.

PEAT MARWICK MITCHELL (KPMG) AND GRESFORD

I learnt more in the three months travelling round America than in the whole of my education, experiencing many different peoples in totally different circumstances and accepting diverse cultures. Whilst having many wonderful encounters, I was regularly out of my comfort zone and at times hungry with almost no money in my pocket, and I came to the conclusion that one of the main goals in life is to know yourself.

Luckily, Alan Pownall, the senior partner of Peats in Liverpool, was happy for me to take up articles despite arriving back from the States much later than expected. I started with a week training in the Manchester office, where double entry totally confused me, and I didn't get past the first question in the final test, not realising the sensible thing to have done would have been to struggle for a short time then just move on. I spent the first two days in the Liverpool office, just round the corner from James Street station, reading the Hawker Siddeley Permanent file. It consisted of two beefy lever-arch files containing the organisational background of the company, structures, authorities and legalities. After half an hour I was totally bored, and things didn't get much better for the first year. I'd arrive home each evening with a long face and rant at my mother, telling her how demoralised I was and that if I failed my first year exams, I was off. As ever, she was understanding, loving and solid as a rock, telling me things would work out.

My working life consisted of carrying out payroll and petty cash audits. Checking rates of pay, tax calculations and that posting to the ledgers was in order. Petty cash was no better, verifying there were authorised signatures, according to the Permanent File, and the amounts were within those stipulated for travel, meals and minor expenses.

The futility of what I was spending my life doing was brought home to me whilst I was looking at insignificant and repetitive sums at Provincial Insurance Company in Kendal; the company had taken massive hits through adverse movements in the exchange rate and a bad year for reinsurance inwards. Studying economics and enjoying reading the quarterly Bank of England reports, I relished arguing about broad concepts and overall effects on GDP and Balance of Payments, the way banks were controlled and lending policies. I'm sure the discipline must have been doing me some good after the profligate life I'd been leading.

Because I was unhappy in what I was doing, I had minimal enthusiasm, and my superiors had the impression I was pretty thick and were surprised when I was placed in the top two hundred in the country in my first professional exam—so was I. This was due to the tutoring skills at Caer Rhun Hall in the Conwy Valley, where a few dozen of us disappeared to for six weeks cramming. Before they allowed me to go, Peats wanted evidence I had completed my correspondence course of twenty papers. I had done the first two before giving up, thinking that was more than enough. Panic set in, and luckily I turned to my good friend David Clapham, who was a year ahead of me, working for Harmood Banner, and had diligently finished the course. He gave me all his past papers. I copied the answers, including a few mistakes, and sent them to Fred Wood, the training manager, who released the time and money for me to go to "Ronnie Anderson's", as Caer Rhun was referred to. Flintshire County Council also contributed to the fees, so I was quids in. The days were rigorous but fun, working into the evenings, and once again I met a lot of good people from all over the country.

As I was apprehensive about the unreliability of my minivan, we decided that on the morning of the exams

I should drive to Chester and travel to Liverpool with David Clapham in his reliable Renault. We only got as far as the Roodee Bridge into Chester when there was a clanging sound coming from the back of the car. We got out to investigate and a tyre had punctured—no problem, we had plenty of time. However, the toolbox was rusted and David couldn't get the jack out. I headed for the town hall and got a taxi to the railway station, boarding the train only to hear there was an unspecified delay. David appeared at the carriage window, hands covered in dirt and oil, and I joined him in his car and we sped to Birkenhead, where he dropped me at the station to catch the underground into Liverpool. I ran down the stairs just as the train was coming in; it turned out to be the same one I had been sitting on in Chester half an hour previously. I sat next to a student I knew who was on the way to the beautiful theatre where the exam was taking place. She ran ahead to the venue while I walked at a steady pace, and everyone had started by the time I arrived. I asked where my seat was, only to be told I was late. I stomped up and down until a kind-hearted invigilator showed me my place. The exams took place over three days, and at lunchtimes I'd wander around the Anglican Cathedral, which was only a few chains away, looking for divine inspiration.

Enid remembers me coming home one day with a smile on my face and she asked me what had made the difference. I had met John Davies from Llansantffraid when I was assisting him carrying out an audit in a quarry. We had similar backgrounds, and he went to the Llanfyllin comprehensive school, which I would have attended if I hadn't been sent away to Lawrence House. As well as having a kindred spirit, he gave me a much better perspective on working life, and I started enjoying not only my work colleagues but also the people in the companies we were auditing; years later I was his best man when he married Heather.

What better environment to be working in than the Lake District. I often stayed in the Blue Bell at

Heversham, a short drive from Kendal, where they served the most delicious dinners and breakfasts, run by a charismatic Irish woman called Shelagh, who after 10:30 at night would wander around in her nightdress. The main job was at the Provincial Insurance Company. On a separate occasion, we stayed at the Blue Bell whilst I worked at a solicitor's practice with James Vernon, having travelled up in his MGB. Auditing Hawker Siddeley, we used the Pack Horse in Bolton and enjoyed nightlife round the local pubs and clubs, but we had to keep our wits about us because they could be rough and someone had been murdered in a nightclub the year before.

There were two jobs in Wrexham I was assigned to each year. The knicker factory, a public limited company under the name of Universal Underwear, which made lingerie for the major retailers; Gordon Taylor was the production director and became a lifelong friend. It was always a cause of amusement that one of the major expenses for their Christmas parties was the cost of security, including dogs, to ensure there was not too much bloodshed. Border Breweries was well renowned for its many pubs and excellent beers. There was a taproom for sampling, which Richard Llewellyn, a friend from Gresford who introduced me to the hilarious Blaster Bates, took me to. There was always a barrel available under the stairs for general consumption. One memorable time there was a drinking challenge between the carpet layers and auditors. I have no idea who won, but not much work happened that day.

Ames Mills outside Bolton was another interesting job, especially seeing the working of the textile-weaving machines, which totally baffled me; the engineers who created them must have been geniuses. They had a factory in Ballymoney, Northern Ireland, and the partners were surprised when I refused to travel there because I didn't think I was being paid enough to fly into Belfast and onwards in the middle of the Troubles.

I understood, too late, that the main purpose of taking on articled clerks was to select those who were partnership material, which they recognised within the first year. Every eighteen months there was a lavish dinner for the North West, and in my first few months one of these happened in the Midland Hotel, Manchester; dinner jackets and plenty of booze. Towards the end of the evening, it was decided we would retire to Tim Beer's room, one of the partners. Peggy, his wife, and I went on and were innocently chatting on the bed about her adventures in North America with American Indians, when the rest came in and immediately came to the wrong conclusions. At the time, I drove a minivan with a sleeping bag in the back, and confirmation that I was not partnership material happened when Miss Ross, the senior secretary, came to me the following week and said I needn't have slept in my van after the dinner and I could have had a room.

There was an active student association, and a favourite venue was a trip on the fish and chip boat the *Royal Iris*, which we'd join at the Liverpool Pier Head. They were inevitably drunken affairs, and it was years before I learnt the boat just cruised up and down and didn't go to one single destination. One memorable night, David Clapham and I arrived in separate cars, and after a heavy night I drove John, his brother, home to Chester. There was great commotion in the Mersey Tunnel, with plenty of blue flashing lights and police directing traffic around some civil engineering works; possibly they had discovered a leak. John relates how he couldn't believe we weren't stopped as I crab-hopped all the way through; we arrived safely back in Chester.

I was enjoying living in Gresford Vicarage with Oliver and Enid. None of my friends who had left home could have dreamt of moving back in with their parents; I was incredibly lucky they were so understanding. I had my own back staircase with two adjoining rooms—one I used as a snug, the other as a workshop—an en suite bathroom and a bedroom. The Vicarage had once been even larger but part had been knocked down because of dry rot and a courtyard left in its place.

Bedroom showing one speaker   *Courtyard wearing Mexican hat*

I was enjoying building new relationships with friends in Gresford. Geoff was a keen musician and was the inspiration for building my bass reflex speakers with 12" axioms and 40 foot of battening in each; we still have them in our rec room today, properly covered, and Sue thinks it would be a good idea for me to be buried in them adjoined together. David Spalding and David Parry were training to become solicitors, and Rob Nichols a surveyor. All three were struggling with the accountancy module in their professional exams, and I'm pleased to say I successfully helped them to pass. Mike James and his brothers were good swimmers and athletes. Janet and Catherine Lewis Jones were still speaking to me after I missed Elspeth in Chicago. Anthony, Geoff's brother, was at Jesus College Oxford with my cousin David Raglan, and we enjoyed games of squash when he was home. I spent many a happy hour in Terry Moore's pub, The Red Lion, at the top of Marford Hill; he was a lively character. I turned down a ski trip with Martin Nichols because I was sure I would love it and I wouldn't want to wait twelve months before I went again and was certain I'd soon be living in a country where I could ski at weekends. Down Vicarage Hill were the Churtons, who threw amazing parties, and we had memorable lock-ins with Nick, Kate and Elen Roberts in the Cock O'Barton. Great parties happened at Julia Whitehouse's, who married Mike James, one of the few private homes with a swimming pool. There was a wider circle of friends linked to Gresford, and they intertwined with budding accountants and solicitors, also ex-pupils of King's and Queen's schools and Cheshire farmers. The Easter Gold Cup at Oulton Park was part of our calendar, and we'd often acquire paddock tickets and be close to the likes of Graham Hill, Jack Brabham and Jim Clark; I didn't lack for social life.

However, I wasn't playing any sport for the first time in my life, and had climbed to over sixteen stone reading Dostoevsky, Tolstoy and Chekov, fighting with my inner turmoil. David Clapham was an excellent friend throughout; we suffered the same lack of income, and we made one pint of beer last a long time. I helped him put a new gearbox into his Bullnose Morris; David was the brain and I the brawn. There was a rope holding the engine and gearbox and I was in the back of the car, taking the weight and guiding it into the drive shaft. I made loud lewd noises as the one entered the other; David panicked and yanked on the rope because he thought my fingers were caught. Much to my embarrassment, Colonel and Mrs Clapham were watching the whole palaver. David Spalding was happy to buy that car from him at a later date.

By the time my second year at Peats came round, my head was in a much better place. I was enjoying spending time with work colleagues and those employed by client companies, and seeing the inside of various businesses, even though the work was monotonous and certainly not challenging. Another kindred spirit had arrived in Peats in the form of Chris Statham, who was my best man when I married Sue. His claim to fame was that in the Rugby XV photo at Ellesmere College he was sitting while Bill Beaumont, the ex England captain, stood at the back. His earliest memory of me was in the Egerton Arms, Broxton, when I proclaimed that Positive Mental Attitude was what life was all about.

Chris was an accomplished rally driver, especially in the Welsh with Dave Richards, who later became

World Champion as co-driver to Ari Vatanen, as navigator. Both did well, Chris in the City and Dave with F1 and Prodrive, leading me to conclude that to be successful in business it was best to dip out of chartered accountancy before qualifying. We had fun at Brands Hatch with Chris and Bob Ellis, who built his own successful accountancy practice in Chester, and I'm pleased I helped him acquire an initial bunch of clients when he came from London.

Chris's parents lived in a lovely cottage on the banks of the Dee in Llangollen, and he invited me and John Davies back for coffee one night after a few pints in the Royal. Chris was showing us round outside when he and I looked at each other and without saying a word realised we had the same thought in mind. Somehow, John clocked on to what we were thinking: to throw him in the river. John bolted; we took a few paces after him then retired to the house. Half an hour later, John came back, his suit covered in mud; it would have been easier and much more fun if he'd let us throw him in. Chris's mother got out of bed and made us bacon sandwiches—what a star.

An interesting job was the acquisition of Meccano by Airfix from Lines Brothers in 1972. I was the junior to Tony Jacques, and I learned a different angle to work when we were together in Edge Lane, Liverpool. They had a great canteen where we'd have sausage on toast for breakfast and bacon sandwiches as a morning break. It was the year Bobby Fischer of the United States was playing Boris Spassky the Russian for the World Chess Championship. That week, Tony and I played thirty games of chess. We'd play when we went into the canteen; each lunchtime we'd take a rowing boat on Sefton Lake and play more. It was a great week and Fischer won; I can't remember who was victorious between me and Tony.

Status was important in industry during the '70s, and a parking space with your name on it was a sign you'd arrived. John Holt, part of the Tiny Rowland empire, was an interesting experience, with different bands on the tea cups depending on seniority. The tea lady was very cross one time when we lifted ones from her trolley with a thin gold line around the top which were for directors only. There were prints of the West African slave trade on the walls and excuses for non-compliance included 'documents have been eaten by ants'.

There was nearly always alcohol at lunchtime, and Hattersley Newman Hender, a foundry in Ormskirk casting valves that were shipped all over the world including Cuba, was no exception. They provided an excellent lunch—sherry first, then beer or wine with the meal and a range of cheeses. At the time, my car was out of action and I was travelling by train to Liverpool, then on foot to Lime Street station to catch the Preston train to Ormskirk; it was a good two hours each way, and I was allowed to arrive at 10:00 and leave at 4:00.

The larger jobs, such as Hawker Siddeley and Universal Underwear, were controlled from London, and seniors would come for reviews; the distinguishing factor was people from the London office could drink up to four pints at lunchtime while two was more than enough for the majority of us in the Liverpool office.

Tim Johnston, who became a national partner, was recently complimentary about the guidance I gave him as his senior at Bear Brand and reminded me of the time we spent a day purely speaking Spanish. After a build-up over a couple weeks, we had a swimming race one lunchtime, which he tells me I won.

To say that some of our driving was unruly is an understatement. A pattern came about whereby if a friend in front waited too long at a road junction, the person behind would sidle up and slowly shunt them out. One notorious evening in Liverpool, four of us were in Chris's Cooper S when the person behind him put their hands over his eyes, the other called accelerator instructions while I steered the car, which would turn on a sixpence, from the passenger seat. How we missed a string of cars when I unexpectedly turned right down a narrow road behind James Street station is a mystery, as the car was accelerating to continue in a straight line.

Close by was the Corn Market, a favourite drinking haunt for Peats' staff, and on 4 February 1972, my birthday, we celebrated Maurice Griffiths passing his final exams. My sister had flown up from London and had plenty to drink on the aeroplane. John Davies, who might have drunk eight pints, gave us a lift through the tunnel to pick up the VW Beetle, Dad's old car. I turned it round, then there was a tremendous argument with me being told I was too drunk to drive, which I lost, as usual.

Going round the bends past Cheshire Brothers, my sister lost the back end on Mount Road, Bebbington, and slammed into the stone wall, ejecting the engine on impact. As the car swung round the other way, she and I were flung out of the driver's door onto the road whilst an Alfa Romeo smashed into the side of the VW. Miraculously, the cars behind avoided us, the second of which was driven by John Davies. He relates how there were several police cars with blue lights flashing and we were carefully picked off the road, suspecting our injuries were grave, and put into an ambulance. John rode with us, and when he left Clatterbridge Hospital an hour later at 2:00 in the morning, a policeman was standing at the door and handed him the keys to his Mini Countryman; no breathalyser, even though he and his car must have stank of ale! I was kept in overnight as it turned out I had a hairline fracture of my pelvis. My head had been covered in blood and the back of my suit jacket ripped as I slid down the road. Lucky I'd landed on my head, my friends later joked, or else I could have done some real damage.

I was feeling much the worse for wear the following morning, as if I'd received a severe beating—which in a way I had. It was a Saturday and Wales were playing Scotland in the Five Nations. I asked the nurse if I could watch it on the TV. She helped me get out of bed, and doubled up, I slowly shuffled down the ward, not understanding why the other patients were all laughing—surely it couldn't be at the pain I was suffering? No, I was wearing a hospital gown, and my bottom was protruding from the rear.

A few days later, Bill Dickin picked me up and took me back to Gresford to my much-relieved mum and dad, who only a few days ago thought I might be dead. David Clapham took me to see the wrecked VW and every side, except for the passenger's, had been flattened.

I had time off work, and by the second week, I was able to walk with minimal pain. Terry Finchett, who was living with his parents at the bottom of Vicarage Hill, was out of work, and Derek Crewe, a children's TV actor from Llay, was between jobs. We started meeting at Terry's at lunchtime on a daily basis, and would walk along the bottom road to the Trevor Arms, Marford, where we spent a merry couple of hours laughing and joking, drank a few beers and had a couple of games of table football. Back to Terry's for a coffee, and Derek and I would leave for our respective homes; great restorative therapy.

Enid quite rightly questioned that if I was well enough to go to the pub I must be well enough to work. I went back, which was a mistake. Each week that had gone by I felt much better than the previous one, and every time I thought I was better. When I was back at Peats, I realised I wasn't 100%, but it was too late; they expected maximum performance, which I wasn't capable of.

I was driving Oliver's Beetle as I had sold the minivan to twelve-year-old Cousin Edward for £25, provided I delivered it to Ffynnon y Cyff, Emlyn, his father, stipulated. I was driving back from Manchester in the early hours one morning when the minivan's brakes failed as I approached a roundabout, which luckily I manged to get round—brilliant mini road holding with front wheel drive. The handbrake didn't work properly, so I went carefully in second gear—no problem, no traffic—third then fourth, and I was able to arrive home using the engine to slow the car. I got up early one Sunday morning to deliver the car to Lixwm with no brakes. Everything was going well until I was driving through Mold and there were two policemen at the side of the road waiting to stop cars, at 7:00 on a Sunday morning! Luckily, they didn't step out in front of me and the mini was delivered in one piece.

I acquired my next car from a parishioner, a Hillman Minx with twin carburettors so it went quickly for a tank. I bought it even though a cog was missing on the ring gear around the flywheel, and occasionally you had to get out and rock the car to engage the starter motor; the driver's quarter glass didn't have a catch to lock it either. David Raglan was a car ace, and we went together to Prees Heath outside Whitchurch and bought a scrapped engine with the gearbox attached. We rigged a block and tackle in the Vicarage shed, and in no time with me passing spanners, David had it up and running, and I no longer had the embarrassment of having to rock.

The Hillman made it to London a few times. The most aggravating was when I met a friend from Cheshire who was living there and after a meal took her to the cinema in Leicester Square. The car was parked on yellow lines amongst Jaguars, Range Rovers and other smart vehicles. When we came out, mine was missing but the rest were still there. After a few phone calls we discovered that mine, which couldn't be locked, had been towed away to the Hyde Park compound, and it cost an arm and a leg in a taxi and paying to retrieve it; all passion was lost.

The most memorable ride was to the North West dinner in Manchester, Chris Statham's first, and we each had a passenger, Nick Lunt and Maurice Griffiths. Quite out of the blue, it developed into a race against the Cooper S. The roads were busy, which meant Chris was handicapped but not by pavements, red lights or speed limits. When we parked up outside the hotel, both Nick and Maurice were white as sheets, shaking, and had to disappear to the toilets; it took quite a while for me and Chris to stop laughing.

Another episode of pure madness was when I went down to Raglan for Cousin Sarah's eighteenth birthday, and after a few drinks, we drove with me in the passenger seat to pick her up from Abergavenny station. We were travelling quickly, and for some reason, I was dared to climb out of the front passenger's window and through the rear window into the back. Halfway through this manoeuvre, the car went into a spin, but amazingly I landed up on the back seat.

From Oliver's Now and Then book, July 3rd 1972: *Tim took us to Manchester airport in his car, bought us magazines and papers to read on the plane and after a short stay with us in the airport hall went off with his dimpled smile as delightful as it was when only a few months old.*

Oliver and Enid had a wonderful time in Locarno for a month, saw plenty of the beautiful sights and made good friends from Europe, east and west, including Bishop John Herbert of North India. Some could speak French, and the Yugoslavs and Hungarians could manage German, but Italian was the official language of Ticino Province.

All wasn't as quiet back in Gresford. On the Friday night, I left the Peats crowd in the Corn Market early, drove home to the large, empty Vicarage and went to bed. I was woken from a deep sleep by pounding on the front door, smashing of glass and shouting. I immediately thought the house was being attacked by some drunks on their way back to Llay who knew the Vicar and his wife were away. I quickly went into my folks' bedroom, which had the only upstairs phone, got under the bed and dialled 999. I was put through to the police, who took some convincing that I was being attacked. I went back to my bedroom and heard a ladder being put against the wall, which was the only one with an open window, took down my cavalry sabre, which was hanging from the picture rail, and waited, hands above my head. Just then, I thought I recognised one of the voices. I went downstairs and opened the front door to let John Davies, David Williams and

John Traynor in. They had continued drinking in the Corn Market and decided they were much too drunk to go back to their respective homes. I warned John, who'd downed about ten pints, that the police were on their way, and he hid his car in the bushes. I was expecting at least three cars with sirens blazing and dogs straining at the leash; however, it was just good old PC Lloyd, who had been called away from a late drink in the Red Lion. "Is everything alright, Tim?" He came in for a quick drink and was on his way. It wasn't long before he had flagged David Spalding down for speeding, but let him go when David pointed out he wasn't in the thirty mile an hour area.

There was never much alcohol in the Vicarage, but whilst we played cards and John and I fleeced the other two, we finished what was left in a bottle of whisky and sherry then opened the communion wine. By this time it was gone two in the morning, and John Traynor, who luckily still had his head between his shoulders, challenged us to a swimming race across the River Dee; the other two declined and John took the keys to my car. We sped to Chester and parked just above the Weir. John jumped in fully clothed, then screamed out that he needed help and couldn't swim; I rescued him, which others in the office thought was a bad move.

I was up before anyone else, had a bath and did my best to get them going. Eventually, we left in two cars and headed for Liverpool very late. David Williams, a senior manager, was called into Mike Jebson, a partner's, office, and fifteen minutes later I was asked to go in. There was a period of silence then a shriek as I flipped. David had told Mike I had taken them back to mine against their wishes and refused to bring them to work on time. The reason for my violent reaction with hindsight was a couple of months earlier I had watched *Straw Dogs* at the Odeon Cinema in Chester, which was a thriller starring Dustin Hoffman. The action took place in a remote part of Cornwall, where a bunch of locals took revenge on an American for marrying one of their own. They attacked the farmhouse and each was killed in a different way—blown away by a shotgun, pouring of boiling oil, and one's head taken off in a man trap. I was shaken watching the film and had a large whisky in the Dublin Packet straight afterwards. The only thing missing that night at the vicarage was Susan George in my bed.

I had hardly slept that night, emotionally disturbed from the flashback, and Mike Jebson gave me a week's holiday to recuperate. I headed for Shoreham, seven miles from Brighton on the south coast, where friends of friends were leaving for Morocco. They were travelling on a motor cruiser, and I was to fly back from Gibraltar. I spent a couple of nights on the boat, but it didn't seem as if they were going to leave, so I was given the keys to Dennis, the photographer's, flat, returned to London and met up with the filmmakers from *Alfred the Great* in the French House, Dean Street, Soho, run by Gaston. I found out later that it was a drugs run to buy hash from Morocco. The engine had failed in the Bay of Biscay in a bad storm; the boat was taken on board a Russian vessel and repaired. That was one trip I was glad to have missed.

Now and Then book, 31st July 1972: *It was raining when we landed in Manchester to find Tim awaiting us with a great smile. What a happy home-coming! And his car did the journey without a squeeze!*

The time came for Final Part I professional exams, and once more there was not enough evidence I had completed the correspondence course, so Peats wrote to Caer Rhun Hall, and they once more confirmed that I should be allowed to attend the course, which was taking place in the Ormscliffe Hotel on the front in Llandudno. This was an inspirational venue, as each day I walked along the promenade, took in the sea air, admired the beautiful views of the Great Orme and threw stones into the sea. It was six weeks of constant work going through into the evenings. During the day we found various pastimes for distraction; one was to see how many cream crackers could be eaten in a minute without drinking any liquid. Some bright spark thought the seagulls should join in, and one gull caught four cream crackers in the air before landing; quite a feat.

The last night of the course was a celebration before we disappeared for the vital few days' revision before the exams. I was sitting on a stool at the bar, fairly inebriated, when somehow I fell off and banged my head and was carried upstairs to bed; I may have been concussed and woke up with a thumping head in the morning. The headache continued over the next few days and I couldn't do any revision, so I just went for walks and spent time in Gresford Church. Kindly, Richard Arkle's parents let me stay with them on the Wirral during the exams, which I took purely on autopilot as my head didn't get better. The morning of the exam results, nothing came through the post. I made my way to Llay to hitch into Liverpool as once again I had car problems. By chance, John Davies came by but there were no results when we arrived at the office. I phoned Clare in London, and she went to Chartered Accountants' Hall at lunchtime, and incredibly my name was on the list of those who had passed; when she phoned back, she first said she couldn't see it! The seniors were encouraging me to take the Final Part II exams within six months because of my successes, but I needed time to mend.

Squash had become an integral part of my life, having joined the section at Wrexham Rugby Club. There was a good crowd of people: Geoff, Ian, Glyn, Pat, Viv, Linda and several others. As well as leagues, there were weekly interclub matches. I also played in Liverpool with Tony Jacques at the Aigburth Cricket Club, and Chris at the Racquets Club, which was burnt down in the Toxteth Riots 1981. On Saturday afternoons, eight of us would book double courts at the Queensferry Leisure Centre for two hours then retire to the Fox and Grapes or Glynne Arms in Hawarden. Some decades later, it was a relief to recall that although I knew these friends well, there were always one or two names I couldn't remember on my return; my poor memory was already established.

Drugs played a negligible part in my life. The psychology campus at Bangor University was one of the leading departments in the country and one of the lecturers was carrying out research into LSD, but I stayed well clear of any trials. Marijuana was on hand amongst my friends in London, and I remember Chris, son of Robert Mitchum, being at one of the parties and relating stories about drug busts he'd been on the wrong end of back in the States. Hash was kept amongst the cornflakes in one of the flats in Bayswater, and when there was an unexpected knock on the door, I was commissioned to empty the contents out of the window if the visitors turned out to be the Feds. While I was living in Gresford Vicarage, I was given some seeds to grow, which I discovered much later had come from Jamaica, courtesy of Maxine via John Golding. I grew them in the coal hatch to the cellar, but they became too long and scraggly so I transferred them to the greenhouse. However, one wet and blustery night they were flattened as there were a number of panes missing from the roof.

Aunt Lil, Gran Llandough and Enid in front of greenhouse

Enid, Vicarage yard

Another momentous occasion was John Bell's 21st party in Marchwiel Hall, when there were over a hundred guests in dinner jackets and gowns. The atmosphere was astounding, and it is the only time I've danced on a sprung floor, which rose and fell over a foot so there was no choice but to be in rhythm. Bacon, eggs and sausages were served about 3:00 in the morning from silver salvers. It wasn't long afterwards I attended a dinner party in Wynnstay Lane, once more dolled up in dinner jackets and formal dresses. Afterwards Leonora, Gerald Grosvenor's sister, Jimmy France Hayhurst, Mary Bowen and I went to the midnight double horror billing in the Odeon, Brook Street, Wrexham, totally overdressed for the occasion! We watched *The Day of the Triffids* and Alfred Hitchcock's *The Birds* and returned to Marford without incident.

Every New Year's Eve there was an amazing party in the Churtons'. Barry would take me to Liverpool on occasions when my car had broken down, which is where they operated their whisky business, and Nick was training to be an accountant at the same time as me. One year I left at 11:00 a little worse for wear to help prepare the church for the midnight service, which was always well attended, and was asked to light the candles in the chandeliers; there were two in the centre aisle about twelve feet off the ground. The stepladders were wobbly, and it is a miracle that I succeeded in lighting all seventy-two without incident.

In the summer of 1973, I had the opportunity of a £10 return ticket to California through Geoff Pitt, who was now working for Overseas National Airlines. However, I could only fly provided there was space on the airplane after all paying customers were accommodated. I spent forty-eight hours hanging around Gatwick before I eventually boarded a flight to New York. We arrived late in the evening, and all passengers disembarked at John F Kennedy. The plane was deadheading to San Francisco that night, and I would be able to fly providing there was one extra crew member in addition to the flight deck. I waited several hours, then not only did the pilot, co-pilot and engineer turn up but ten stewardesses as well. It was a stretched DC 8, and I've never received better attention. I spent a lot of the time in the cockpit, and it was a wonderful experience flying over the Colorado Mountains with clear blue skies and lakes down below. I was told I couldn't stay on the flight deck for landing, but no one asked me to leave. In hindsight I'm sure I could have remained; another opportunity missed, but no complaints!

The plane was going to Hawaii, which was tempting, but the main purpose of the trip was to spend time with Wendy and Sally. I stayed the first few days at Sally's in Portola Valley. Her grandparents had built the house. Each room was a different colour, constructed from different redwood trees, and her brother introduced me to Grateful Dead. We spent time enjoying San Francisco, including the Japanese Gardens, back to Muir Woods which had enchanted me, and Sausalito. We made a road trip and took in the garlic festival in Gilroy. Sally's parents took us to see *Oliver* in the Performing Arts Theatre starring Ron Moody, one of the best shows I've ever seen. We spent an afternoon in Stanford University where Wendy's father was a professor. I visited the Peats offices to see what opportunities there were for transferring, and they greeted me well and gave me a tour. I already had a tan, but nearly everyone there appeared tense and ghostly white—it wasn't a working atmosphere that appealed.

We drove to Tahoe, where Sally's family had a beautiful wooden house on the North Shore within yards of the water. We went for lovely walks around the lakes in Squaw Valley and explored the area. Wendy's brother arrived from Costa Rica and couldn't speak highly enough of the country and everything it offered. Gil lent me his Alfa Romeo Spider to drive through the mountains to Reno, a fantastic experience. The town was much older and not as glitzy as Las Vegas. I visited Harrah's car museum, which had the best collection of cars, possibly in the world. I would have liked to stay in Tahoe longer, but I'd arranged to visit Barbara Tammage in San Diego, where she was living with Harry Wegerforth III, whose grandfather had founded San Diego Zoo, the only zoo I've seen on a par with Chester, with plenty of space for the animals. Harry had a Triumph Bonneville, which I rode on the back of round San Diego with no headgear and a great feeling of freedom. They had an enormous Doberman who sensed my fear, and it was two days before we could be in the same room together; the ice was finally broken by me feeding him chocolate brownies.

Late one evening we left for Yuma on the Colorado River, where the temperature was over a hundred degrees when we arrived after midnight. The next day, we joined Cyril and his new wife with their powerful speedboat for water-skiing. The water was the temperature of a warm bath. It took me several attempts before I eventually managed to stay up for a reasonable distance. Then back to their hotel, where I experienced drinking cold duck pink champagne in a Jacuzzi for the first time.

We left late in the evening with towels soaked with cold water and the windows fully open as the car had no air conditioning. The temperature and humidity were stifling and the towels were soon hot. We were treated to the most spectacular electric storm as lightning of all shapes and sizes lit the sky and shot towards Earth; the light show must have lasted for at least half an hour.

The next day, Barbara and I drove to visit the Lion Country Park where those beautiful animals roamed freely. Frasier, an old lion, was being feted, and his face appeared on tee shirts everywhere. He had been put out to rest, but the young lions had failed to get the lionesses pregnant, so as a last resort Frasier was set free. Very quickly, plenty of lionesses had caught and he became a local hero.

We drove to Laguna Beach and toured the *Queen Mary*, which was berthed there and had been turned into a hotel.

I had a call from Jean Meek Barker, who was staying with Gus and Jean Ryden, and they invited me up to dinner. Another first—flying into Burbank for an evening with actors intensely looking at scripts. They invited me to stay over for a few days, which I happily accepted.

I woke about 6:00, heard noises of someone moving about and went to see what was going on. Gus was sitting in a sun lounger eating ice cream, and he invited me to join him. I had never had more than a cone or wafer before, and he introduced me to eating a pint at a time. We chatted for hours about Hollywood and his adventures before the ladies, who had drunk heavily the night before, appeared. He threatened that, unless the UK behaved itself, they would cut off the Gulf Stream. I would stroll down with Gus to have lunch in his regular deli, owned by an Indian who some years later called to let me know Gus, the most gentle and friendly person, had died. It was a very sad moment and I felt privileged and humbled he had left instructions to let me know when he passed.

I went to catch the flight back to London, only to be told ONA hadn't renewed its licence and no plane could land in the UK with any passengers for whom it was the final destination even if it was en route to a different European country. Luckily I was able to stay in Hollywood with Gus and Jean until I eventually caught a flight to Frankfurt. I hitchhiked as far as Aachen before catching a train to Calais then a ferry across to Dover. It had been a fantastic holiday but not as relaxing as I had intended in the run up to my final exams.

The cramming course was in Hafodunos, an old school in Llangernyw close to Abergele in beautiful grounds, formerly owned by the Mackeson Sandbach Estate. I no longer had any problem persuading the managers that I stood a good chance of passing the exams before I went. The standard of teaching was excellent as ever, and I went back to Gresford for the few days between the end of the course and the exams, which were being sat where we studied. I played squash, studied, went for walks and looked as fresh as a daisy when I returned, compared to the others who had remained and worked through to the exams. That night, I didn't sleep and heard every hour chime on the old clock. Once again I was on autopilot, and the majority of the management paper I answered with the knowledge I'd gained studying for my economics degree. Cousin Edward, from Ffynnon-y-Cyff, drove me to the exams as once again I had car problems, and he wouldn't accept any money; however, I said I'd pay him a tidy sum if I passed. I was staying in South Wales when the results were published on my birthday. I decided that, if I got through, February 4th was a lucky day for me in that I didn't die in the car crash two years earlier, and if I failed it was unlucky—it was a lucky day, and Edward was delighted when a cheque unexpectedly arrived through the post. I drove to London singing and smiling most of the way and celebrated with David Clapham and other friends with a splendid meal in a French restaurant.

I immediately started looking for jobs. Although I had learnt a tremendous amount about business and systems at Peats, for the most part we dealt with historical events and it was future challenges that interested me. At the time, you were paid handsomely for expenses to go to interviews, and I had an opportunity with Uniroyal in London to be in charge of Internal Management Audit in Europe following three months training in Connecticut and three months experience in Australia. Before I went in, I had been given a set of their accounts to review, and the first question was whether I had any commitments afterwards, making sure we could overrun the two hours allotted time! Then came the interrogation about the accounts, which I think sealed the deal, as instead of talking about debt ratios and return on capital, I asked how on earth they controlled a company so diverse and large. The interview lasted fifteen minutes short of four hours, having spoken about motor racing, travel and how the interviewer had a best friend as a lad who was the son of a preacher man and Uniroyal needed any help they could get from above, knowing Oliver was a clergyman. They offered me the job, which I declined.

I wanted to work in California or Vancouver, both of which I really liked, and most importantly, I wanted to go skiing at weekends. I tried to discover what opportunities there were through my connections, but nothing turned up. I'd met David Rickham a few years previously, whose father was a world-renowned paediatrician, and had worked in hotel management at the Grosvenor Hotel in London, when he was talking about opening a hotel in Jamaica with Richard Salm. I had a call from Richard when he learnt I was fully qualified, asking if I'd like to work in Jamaica. By this time I'd decided I was going to travel round South America and told him I wasn't interested. He phoned back a week later to say they were interviewing over three days in St George's Hotel opposite Lime Street station in Liverpool, and I was given a choice of times before, during or after working hours.

Nothing to lose, I turned up. I knocked on the door of the room and was told to come in; it was locked, which they realised after a few loud shouts inviting me in, which I was unable to oblige. There were four spotlights on the interview chair—Richard Salm, Michael Seligman and Simon Marsh, all Oxbridge, together with David Rickham. They gave me a brief background and asked me what I thought the turnover was, then some more spiel before Richard asked me if I had any questions. I didn't want the job as financial comptroller of Club Caribbean, so on my high horse I asked why they needed a chartered accountant to run such a small outfit. Some months later, I was told I took over the meeting from then on. They offered me the job; I turned it down. It is likely my background at St John's had an influence on their decision. Some days later, Richard phoned and said they would pay my fare to Jamaica, if I liked it, I could travel South America for six months—I accepted.

I had brochures for Club Caribbean, and several of the accountants in client companies would readily have changed places, leaving me in no doubt I'd made the right decision.

Another adventure was my introduction to motorbike riding with the help of Dave Mayers. He had a series of bikes, including a Honda 750, which I enjoyed riding pillion. He also had an Ossa, which we took to Gresford Quarry, and I plucked up the courage to drive directly down the steep slopes. The biggest challenge was to let go, rather than hang on to the handlebars, when I fell off.

Eventually my confidence increased, as did the thrill of handling a trials bike. Not quite as exciting was the BSA Bantam I bought to get a motorbike licence in anticipation of travelling abroad! I enjoyed riding it to Liverpool during my last weeks at Peats and taking it across the Mersey on the ferry boats.

There was a big going-away party in the cellars of the Vicarage which started early in the evening and went on till 3:00 in the morning. Oliver and Enid went to bed early and assured me they hadn't heard a thing the next morning. The crowd from Peats started it off by turning up after work, then the Gresford friends merged in, followed by my squash mates who were the last to leave; Glyn Evans DJed through the night. David Clapham had helped me prepare the cellars, and Dave Gee came from London.

It was a tough decision to leave the UK, with Oliver not well and Enid under pressure looking after him. He was still Vicar of Gresford but needed help dressing. Enid was as strong as ever and said they'd be alright. Decades earlier, a friend of theirs who had been an officer on the *Titanic* offered to take them on a ship up the St Lawrence River to Montreal to stay in the Chien D'or, whose motto was "I gnaw my bone and bide my time". Whilst their parents were alive, they decided that they shouldn't travel, and they didn't want to take this opportunity away from me.

The last service was heartbreaking. In the church crypt after the service, Oliver broke down in tears and Eric Nichols, a church warden, ushered me out. Two days later Bill Dickin, Oliver's good friend and my godfather, drove me to Chester station. I caught the train to London and I was soon flying out of Heathrow to start a new life the other side of the Atlantic.

A few days before I left, two French guys I had made friends with the year before returned to Gresford and were camping on the green next to the church. I invited them back to the Vicarage for something to eat and introduced them to Oliver when he came into the kitchen after conducting a marriage ceremony; too late, they were the best of friends talking away in fluent French—my dad had met them on the way to the church and invited them to the wedding. The day after I left, the heavens opened, and late at night, the two Frenchies, looking like drowned rats, knocked on the front door and asked if they could camp in the garden. Enid invited them in and gave them my rooms—I felt better when I heard that story as at least they temporarily filled the gap I'd left. It also demonstrates the openness of Oliver and Enid, looking after friends from all over the world. Another example of this is the inscription in the front of their copy of John Steinbeck's *The Moon is Down*—"With grateful recollections of a dark night in September 1942. Peggy Lea Carlops."—from a lady they'd put up who'd had nowhere to stay that night. Oliver thought she might have been a German spy.

Oliver wrote on the back "His Holiness Himself"

Oliver and Bill Dickin Righting the World

BSA Bantam

SOUTH AMERICA

I left for Jamaica intending to spend six months in South America then return to work as financial comptroller in Club Caribbean. If I didn't think I'd enjoy the wonders of living on a tropical island, I would seek a life in Argentina or Chile. You have to put yourself in positions outside your comfort zone if you want to make things happen.

Dave Gee came to Heathrow to see me off, which was really good of him. The flight from London was long, and we landed in Nassau, which appeared to be scrubland and didn't look appealing at all. What was Jamaica going to be like? I had done no research whatsoever—exactly where it was, how big, what the climate was like… all I knew was that it was in the tropics.

The Caribbean Sea was a beautiful deep blue, and looking from the sky, I was tempted to open the window and dive in. We landed in Kingston at nightfall and after refuelling continued to Montego Bay. I had an anxious moment when no one was there to meet me.

The next day, I rested on the beach and soon forgot how cold and wet the English weather was until I realised I was frying in the sun; you don't need to remember an umbrella in Jamaica, only to carry some shade. I was introduced to good people and quickly made up my mind that I would like to work in Jamaica, but it took a couple of days to agree a price for my labour as Club Caribbean first offered me a quarter of what Uniroyal did, who in the meantime had been in touch with Enid to ask if I'd reconsider. However, there was no comparison between a life in Jamaica and one in Europe, and I agreed to work there for a year.

Jamaica was a stunning island: miles of empty beaches with white sand, cliffs, sun, offshore breeze to stay cool during the day and warm winds from the hills in the evening, mountains up to 8,000 feet and plenty of rich green vegetation, which I wasn't expecting.

I stayed at David and Ele Rickham's house in the cane fields. In their garden was a grapefruit tree—freshly squeezed juice every morning!—an avocado pear tree with the thickest, creamiest pulp, a custard apple tree: a weird fruit which comes ready in dishes (called chiri moya tree in Peru), bread fruit trees and plenty more. At the weekend, we travelled to Negril, northwest of the island, with lovely beaches and cliffs where we visited Rick's Café, a famous haunt for sunset drinks. Richard Salm taught me to play backgammon and I beat David Rickham in the first game I played solo, and they thought they'd made a good choice for financial comptroller. We went into the mountains—quite like Wales in parts, especially Fern Gully, which is similar to the Nant Y Garth Pass between Llandegla and Ruthin. David and Richard showed me a really good time, and I was greatly looking forward to life in Jamaica.

I flew to Lima via Guayaquil, Ecuador, and arrived at midnight to find all the hotels were full because there was a mining conference, nor was there room in the pensions. I eventually managed to find space thanks to the tourist board—two girls manning a desk at the airport; Lima is a big city and I didn't want to risk some bandit taxi driver taking me on a wild goose chase to find John Dickin's Lima address in San Isidro, as I thought John would be in Huancayo, 10,500 feet up in the Andes. The pension was a beautiful Spanish-type house with friendly people running it. I hadn't contacted John, and he had no idea I was travelling to Peru. The next day I set out for San Isidro, a lovely area of Lima, where he and Mariana lived. I knocked on the door; no answer. I came back an hour later, and a neighbour appeared and told me John was around and would be back in a couple of hours, and so he was. He came to Lima from the mountains for three days each month to collect rent from Mariana's family properties; they had been wealthy, but the communist government had taken the lion's share away. We visited relations of Mariana who resided in a mansion: grandparents living with children and grandchildren and two families of servants. Initially I was unable to converse in Spanish, although I had studied A-Level and had a wide vocabulary, whereas John spoke like a native.

Pension

Lima

In Lima, I had a lovely dinner with Bruce and Angela, a girl from Denbigh, North Wales, which she prepared at short notice, and John came to join us. There were lots of interesting museums, especially the Anthropological Museum, which had beautiful woven clothes, amazing pottery, skeletons and skulls from Incan and pre-Incan periods; there was evidence of brain surgery having been carried out on the skulls and second procedures as the first had healed, leaving just a hole, so they must not have died on the slab.

There were many attractive parades and buildings, those in the main square appeared to have been built from stone, but it was a very good imitation layer of plaster. There were people everywhere, and the traffic was chaotic: cars, buses and lorries going different directions at incredible speeds with apparently few collisions. The centre of the city had suffered major earthquakes, and there were cracks down the outside of many of the buildings, which still continued to function. We visited some friends of John who had serious cracks in the outside of their building. Inside, there were two lift shafts next to one another; one was working, the other wasn't because of quake damage! Lima is the centre of the city, and I visited the Basilica Cathedral; what sickened me was the body of Pizarro, the persecutor who despicably wiped out the Incas in the name of the Roman Catholic Church, displayed in a glass cabinet for people to revere. John's small, attractive flat was quite a way from the centre, close to the sea. Mariana and their son David were in Florida, which meant John had the opportunity to make the trip to parts of Peru he hadn't previously visited, including Machu Picchu, the Lost City of the Incas.

Before we left Lima, we went to the Inkari, an annual festival where peoples from all over Peru bring their artefacts, beautiful clothes, ponchos, rugs, wooden and leather work. Folk groups played; there were dancers and singers from the mountains and jungles, and plays performed which didn't hold back on how badly the native Indians had been treated by the government. An amazing atmosphere of colour and sound, not far removed from Llangollen International Eisteddfod.

In Lima, I had a second shot of gamma globulin so I would hopefully not get ill from eating local dishes, street food and drinks—very tasty, but not so clean. The nurse took a look at how big I was and added an extra dose as I was off her scale.

The day before leaving Lima, we toured the city, buying many kilos of rice and sugar to take to John's village, Mito. By this time, my Spanish was fluent and I came to the conclusion that listening to a foreign language was the key to learning.

The morning we left for the Andes, there was an earthquake—6.6 on the Richter scale. I was wakened thinking I was in a flat I used to stay in in London above the reverberating tube trains. I dashed across the room and tried to open the door. It had jammed, so I went back to bed and listened to the deep rumbling from the belly of the earth until it stopped. People were shouting in the streets, dogs howling, cats screaming and telephone lines jammed for hours while families and friends checked whether they had survived.

The journey out of Lima in the Toyota Jeep was fantastic, the ideal means of transport for the terrain. The road rapidly deteriorated to a dirt track with stones and potholes, but in a strong vehicle we could travel amazingly quickly given the conditions. The road climbed rapidly to 10,000 feet; luckily I didn't suffer from headaches and altitude sickness, which could have been trouble. There were incredible views all the way: steep valleys, mountains, crags with only a little snow, way up on the peaks.

At too frequent intervals there were altars commemorating people who had died driving over the edge.

Mito is situated in a beautiful valley, fifteen miles away from a dirty town, Huancayo, with a river flowing through and surrounded by rolling mountains with high peaks in the distance—stunning.

Andes

Mito

Unfortunately, soon after this shot, my camera broke, after I'd already sent two back to Hanimex because the lenses had curvature of field, so I decided to buy postcards and missed shooting hundreds of rolls of film to capture this staggering country. On the bright side, it saved money and alleviated the worry of having a camera stolen—in places, theft and picking pockets was a fine art: straps slashed with razor blades to steal cameras, and the bottoms of bags slit and their contents extracted!

John's house was attractive with thatched rooves, a large courtyard and outhouses, a vegetable garden and lots of animals: dogs, cats, ducks, hamsters, rabbits, etc. A lovely set up, other than the outside privy, which needed careful balance.

The villagers were extremely friendly, a setting quite like Mochdre. One house in particular reminded me of my early days in Mochdre with an enclosed courtyard, as nearly all the houses had a woodpile, chickens running around, an adjoining small yard where the bull and a couple of cows were kept, a kitchen where all the cooking was done in ancient smoke-blackened pots on a wood fire by an old lady whose husband still drove his cows to the fields—very much like Arthur, the old guy at Pen-y-Graig farm. Once you fought your way through the flies, the food was tasty: bread, potatoes and rice, of course, and beautiful rich soups like cawl. The insides of the houses were simple with earth floors, and part of the kitchens were boarded off, from which emanated squeaking sounds of the cuy—guinea pigs—dozens of them running round. They were part of the staple diet, the flesh looking and tasting much like chicken. In need of a meal, the villagers would lean over, grab two, off with their heads and straight into the pot. John took me to the fields where the farmers grew their crops. There was a river running close by and irrigation ditches passing through each of the areas owned by different people. Democratically, the water was shared by diverting the channels on a daily basis.

The food was delightful, with plenty of people cooking and selling on the streets. It was unbelievable the different things that could be done with potatoes. All fruits, avocados and vegetables were dirt cheap; fresh pineapples and papaya were a dream, but apples and tomatoes didn't compare with those in the UK.

I climbed the hill at Mito to look at the tremendous views over the village and valley but was soon out of breath and had to lie down.

From Mito we visited Huancayo market, one of the biggest in Peru, where everything was sold, from cheap tourist goods to beautiful clothes, ponchos, gourds, food, drink, frying pans and junk; the market seemed to fill the streets for miles. There were markets in most towns; the main ones opened on Sundays, when people came from miles around to sell their goods.

Gourds

Ponchos

I learnt how to haggle, and in one small town it took me a morning to buy a poncho from a good-looking Quechua lady with a lovely smile, bulging cheeks and black lips from chewing coca leaves. We drank manzana tea, chatted, mentioned the price, chatted some more, then John and I walked away to look round the town before returning and starting over.

I bought gourds distinguished by small, fine carvings, each of which told a story about life in the fields, love, fights and any number of different happenings.

After a couple of days in Mito, we left for Huancavelica Ayacucho, Andahuaylas and Cusco. The trip was incredible, and it was unbelievable where roads have been built—single tracks clinging to the sides of mountains above thousands of feet of sheer drops. I was more than a little frightened, especially on the corners where the rain had washed away much of the road. The other worrying times were when I was next to the hillside and could see John looking over the steep cliffs—more than once I had to tell him to look straight ahead. One time he was driving too fast and he spun the Jeep 180 degrees; luckily, nothing was coming the other way and he didn't roll it—I received a big apology.

The colours were spectacular, all shades of brown, and the mountains countless shapes and sizes; poor old Snowdon would be completely out of its depth but nevertheless attractive in its own right. At times the road climbed to over sixteen thousand feet with only traces of snow. The peaks we passed through were indescribably beautiful: blue lakes, condors, eagles, buzzards, horses, cows, sheep and all kinds of mammals. The llamas, alpacas and vicunas were gorgeous, proud animals.

In Huancavelica, we met a couple who were working for the American Peace Corps and had been told to leave supposedly because the Ministry of Agriculture could handle the immense farming and crop growing problems. The real reason was the suspicion that they were linked with the CIA in Peru. They were anxious because the time limit to get out was short and were worried that hostile feelings towards them could have leaked out. We drove fifty-odd miles to their hacienda to pick up their belongings; the inbred kind-heartedness of sons of clergy! The hacienda was miles away on the side of a steeply sloping valley with spectacular views. It had previously been owned by a rich "farmer" who had built a small palace to live in and rule the farm from. David, the current farmer, was a typical mid-western American overflowing with life and character and was able to face hardship provided his Jack Daniels was at hand, which he shared generously. After a pleasant night we continued our trip through the incredible sierras, which were overflowing with minerals of every description.

There were mines everywhere, which meant the roads were more reasonable, but unforgivably, the once-beautiful rivers were badly polluted and great scars of filth and waste were distributed all over the mountains. A relatively small area of the vast mountain range was ruined, but still painful to observe and to think of the natural, outdoor mountain people and farmers being forced down the mines.

Apparently over six million African slaves were shipped across the Atlantic to Peru; a third of them died at sea, a third in the climb to the Andes, and the remaining third mined silver till they died without seeing the light of day, all to enrich the Holy Roman Empire.

It was amazing to see the places where land had been cultivated on the sides of steep mountains seemingly miles from any village. It made the slopes outside Llanfyllin seem like flat ground; they were growing some of the four thousand varieties of native potatoes.

Most of the ploughing was done by pairs of bulls; a lovely sight to see a field full of these powerful animals working away surrounded by continually changing colours of earth. The mountain people worked hard, dressed in attractive clothing: some bright and others in natural colours.

The sierras were a mixture of the Scottish Highlands, Welsh Berwyns, Snowdonia, Rockies, Alps and any other mountains you can think of.

The Jeep went tremendously well, except for a few punctures—or rather one reoccurring one, because of the crude method of mending them: heating a block of metal above the patch with petrol until the tyre moulds, oblivious to any flames which spread around the tube.

Along the road, especially in the highest narrowest places, there were once again crosses marking the spots where cars and buses had ploughed over the edge. An encouragement to drive carefully!

From heights of fifteen thousand feet, the road fell to six thousand and rose again rapidly. One of the valleys we passed through was just like entering a different world: a wide, fast-flowing river bordered by orange trees, cacti and other tropical trees and fruits. The houses/huts were no longer dobby huts but made of cane and reeds. It was an amazing contrast to the high mountains we had been travelling through. Fortunately, it was afternoon and the flies and insects were elsewhere. I'd been very lucky and had few bites up to then.

The whole country was one of extreme change: sun, rain (little so far), desert, sierras and jungle, which I'd not yet seen but hoped to if there was time. Most of our travelling we had managed by day, sleeping in the back of the truck at night. John's first duty each morning was to wash and replenish his natural yoghurt plant. We had covered 1,500 miles of rugged road— another world. We were able to stay alert and not feel hungry by chewing coca leaves. All markets had a wide variety of leaves to choose from and *cal*, lime, to speed up the effect, which we didn't use as it could contain unpleasant formula. It was an art acquired with practice to have a bunch of the leaves sit in between your teeth and cheek and let the juice slowly flow out; in the beginning I would land up with a mouth full of tiny leaves—not very pleasant.

Village band

There were fiestas in several of the towns we came across; the country folk really enjoyed celebrating.

The fun started in the morning with the band getting together, warming up and having their first gulps of chicha (fermented alcohol). We didn't see any looking as organised as in the picture above. They played as they went round and round the streets, getting more and more drunk and the music less coordinated. Everybody seemed to be having a great time.

We passed groups of Quechua Indians, brightly dressed with beautifully braided hair, on the roads travelling to the fiestas and markets. We discovered the ladies travelled commando as they squatted and peed whenever and wherever.

We arrived in Cusco at night and were hit by a massive blaze of light, as great as that of any metropolis. Next day we woke up to a beautifully clean city, with an open central square, narrow streets and lovely stone buildings, many with Incan walls as their basis. The streets, for the most part, were smooth to drive on, and there were the first examples I saw of some of Peru's incredible stonework: stone walls fitting exactly, without mortar of any sort, and it was impossible to pass even a razor blade between them.

From Cusco we visited Pisac, a small village beneath Inca ruins way up above in the mountains. The steep slopes were terraced up to thirty feet wide so otherwise impossibly difficult, almost vertical inclines could be tilled and planted with maize etc. The stonework there was unbelievable: rocks weighing hundreds of pounds and fashioned as smoothly as if the sides were slate. Although the vertical and horizontal lines were not at ninety degrees, each side of every rock fitted perfectly. The walls were angled inwards slightly and the doorways narrowed towards the top. The outside rocks would keep the rounded appearance—the total effect was beautiful. Pisac had been rebuilt around 1,400 A.D. by the Incas. There were older, rougher buildings around, but all remaining walls were still perfectly in place. It appears the only reason the walls of the buildings were not complete is that people in following years had removed rocks to build houses, churches and other buildings.

Another amazing ruin was Saqsaywaman, an Incan fortress just above Cusco. There were stones weighing up to three hundred tons used in the construction; how they were moved is difficult to surmise, and each stone was fashioned perfectly so that a knife blade could not be put between the rocks—and this after hundreds of years.

The other incredible citadel is Machu Picchu, Lost City of the Incas, rediscovered by Hiram Bingham in 1911—what a place! A five-hour train ride from Cusco down to 6,500 feet. Whenever the train stopped at villages, people rushed to the windows to sell food and drink; there were several stoves cooking at each station. We travelled on the local train rather than the tourist train, partly for cost but more importantly for the experience. There were people selling food on the train and others playing musical instruments. We arrived at the station in the heat of the day and I was in no condition to climb the 5,000 metres to the Incan city, so we travelled by bus up the roads, which wound back on themselves because of the steepness. The city was situated on the top of a mountain which in turn was surrounded by taller, precipitous peaks, well hidden from potential enemies. Although the stonework was not the same quality as Pisac, the location was astounding and many slaves must have died carrying the thousands of stones needed to build the city, which had been inhabited and augmented by pre-Incas as well as the Incas themselves.

Machu Picchu

The Incas worshipped the sun, moon and stars and employed precise calendars and sundials. The temples were fascinating and simple. That evening, we walked down the mountain and a couple of miles back along the railway track to Aguas Calientes, natural hot springs, and it was sheer ecstasy to relax in the steaming pools.

The next day, John and I were going to climb Waynu Picchu, the narrow mountain 1,400 feet directly above the city. However, in the morning there was heavy cloud and, what's more, there was a train strike and we thought we'd have an eighteen-mile walk to the nearest road to catch a bus! The clouds lifted and we walked to the railway station below the city and set off up the mountain at a tremendous pace and were whacked by the time we arrived in Machu Picchu. We learnt there was a train coming for the tourists who had stayed the night at the hotel, so after a quarter hour rest, we set off for Waynu. The drop was thousands of feet from a path cut into the side of the mountain with no rails—fearsome if you were to step one foot to the right of the two-foot wide path! We rested every ten paces towards the top because the air was so thin, the mountain was so steep—and because we'd climbed a long way very quickly! The view from the peak of Waynu over the city and valleys made the hike more than worthwhile (the view from the hill on the other side of the city we climbed the day before was out of this world). The rocks seemed to be vibrating as we lay recovering on them; I don't know whether it was because it was a magical place on a ley line or my senses were confused. I would have loved to have spent hours gathering the sensation from the rocks, admiring the beautiful views of the surrounding mountains, valleys and river while imagining the lives of the rulers, workers and slaves in Machu Picchu below. But within minutes, we heard the train whistle and saw buses leaving the city, so we ran down, oblivious to the rock face! How mad, huh!

We then ran through the trees, crossing the winding road up to Machu Picchu, only to find that the train had brought a load of passengers and was not returning till the evening. Totally shattered, we sat amongst the soldiers who had travelled on the tourist train to prevent any locals climbing aboard and watched them play at target practice with their rifles.

Another interesting walk the previous day was to the Inca "bridge" consisting of five logs thrown together, fifteen feet long, on a trail along the side of a cliff with a steep drop off a very narrow path. Almost as dangerous as crossing the Queensferry Bridge, but not as frightening as Waynu.

We visited various other ruins around Pisac and Cusco, each with different styles and incredibly accurate fashioning of the rock using natural hollows for caves and tombs. The beauty of the Jeep was that we could travel when and where we wanted without the discomfort and slowness of local buses, and the great cost of taxis; petrol in Bolivia and Peru was 10p a gallon!

From Cusco we travelled to Puno on the edge of Lake Titicaca. A beautiful lake with Indian villages floating on reeds and settlements all around. We visited a peninsula and saw houses made of reeds and beautiful boats; it was a family from Titicaca that built the *Ra II* in Egypt, the boat which sailed to the West Indies in better shape than the *Kon Tiki*. Puno itself was an uninteresting place, despite being one of the major lake ports.

I left John in Puno on Tuesday 26 November saying I would return on the Thursday unless anything unforeseen happened. The journey to La Paz took eight hours in a very shaky bus full of dust for a large part of the journey; the trip around Lake Titicaca took a couple of hours and was very beautiful.

I travelled on the back seat with a journalist and discussed the precarious state the world was in, with troubles in Ireland, Israel, South Africa and Russia.

At the border between Peru and Bolivia was a hick town, Otovalo. The streets once again were full of people selling everything from food to furniture. The customs on the Peruvian side was closed so I walked round the town eating bits and pieces of the delicacies the street vendors were offering. The origin of some was dubious, but the bananas and oranges were always a safe and tasty bet. After an hour or so, the customs officials must have decided that they had siestaed sufficiently after their lunch and condescended to stamp our passports in their shanty offices.

There were pictures and busts of Che Guevara, whose picture was everywhere in Peru including on the wing-mirrors and windscreens of nearly every lorry. The Bolivian customs were surprisingly easy, but everywhere the police and officials carried machine guns and rifles. Eventually we set off, handing in a passenger list at each checkpoint at the start and end of every village—we must have given out twenty copies in total, and possibly three people got on or left the bus during the whole of the journey. At the second control point, twenty miles into Bolivia, two soldiers climbed on the bus with machine guns and tried to check the numbers of passengers against the lists. After several attempts, each of them counting the passengers then the lists and not being able to agree, they eventually gave up and left the bus in less military fashion than when they had entered.

An hour or so after entering Bolivia, we climbed a steep hill at zero miles an hour, and on reaching the top there was a spectacular view of the snow-capped Andes behind La Paz, overlooking sixty or so miles of plains. Then followed two hours during which the bus was completely filled with fine dust from the road, which was flat with few potholes. It was getting towards dusk when we came upon La Paz. After turning a bend, we saw the city way down in a valley, hundreds of lights, really pretty and not the blaze that hits you entering Cusco. We zigzagged, falling five hundred metres through some of the poor districts of La Paz into the centre of the city. There was not the poverty that there was in the outskirts of the Peruvian cities. La Paz appeared clean and tidy, and luckily I didn't suffer from altitude sickness despite being at twelve thousand feet. That night I stayed at the house of a friend we had met in Cusco. The following morning came the tragedy! I phoned Lorna De La Prudencio, the sister of Gilbert Barker, who I'd spent time with in NYC, and received an incredible welcome and arranged to meet Sara, her daughter, in the centre of town at midday. I then discovered that the ticket I was going to trade in and use to amply cover a flight to Caracas was only worth $20—the return flight Lima – La Paz normally costs $142. So there I was in La Paz with a ticket I could have used to fly to Lima after spending a week with the Prudencios but no way to get in touch with John in Puno—he was going to phone a hotel in La Paz if I didn't turn up on Thursday night. In Puno, I couldn't find Lorna's telephone number as I had only her mailbox number in the Central Post Office and not her actual address! Mad I was, and after much deliberation I decided that I could not let John down after he had waited three days in that lousy place Puno with the possibility of two days' drive to Lima by himself. So the following day I decided to take that terrible dusty journey back—ugh!

In the meantime I had a delightful lunch with Juan and Lorna Prudencio in their beautiful house five hundred metres from the city in a residential area. Their home was full of colourful flowers with a splendid view of the mountains all around. They had built a self-contained flat separate from the main house, which led straight onto the garden at the higher level for Mr Barker Senior, Lorna's blind father from Queensferry, North Wales. I was sure the altitude would not affect him if he took it easy for the first couple of weeks. I stayed the afternoon at their house then went with Sara, their daughter, to a university class, which carried on well into the evening. The teacher spoke the most beautiful classical Spanish and I was able to join in with the discussions. The subject was language, compulsory but basic. Sara was majoring in medicine, which included the sciences and mathematics. Apparently there was a surplus of doctors in La Paz and fierce competition to attend the university courses. However, there were only a few good physicians, who shared most of the work between them. Juan Prudencio was outstanding amongst them as an orthopaedic surgeon—a really nice guy and most interesting. The government changed about every six months as the capitalists and communists fought it out, and many were killed in the process. Both sides looked after Juan as they desperately needed him to operate; his leanings were towards the communists. I had dinner at their house before returning to where I was staying in the city. I was very sad to be leaving such good people.

I managed to survive the bus journey back to Puno, and John was grateful for my sacrifice, but he had already found company back to Lima!

We sped back and soon hit the desert, which lasts for hundreds of miles, passing through Arequipa, a beautiful city with white rock in abundance and a lovely central square.

From there, we drove to Nazca and could see the tracks Daniken made famous with his theory that pre-Christian astronauts had used it as a landing strip, further evidenced by the rocks, which had melted in the heat from their engines.

Then back to Lima. By that time I had decided to use my return ticket to get the aeroplane meals! Or rather see the Andes from the air, spend a night with the Prudencios and hopefully see the pre-Incan ruins of Tiahuanaco. While in Lima, we went to John's neighbourhood fair, a bi-annual fiesta akin to a garden fete where the locals drank beer and danced. A really friendly gathering, mainly Peruvians, about two to three hundred good people from a pleasant area. We left in the afternoon whilst the feria was in full swing to see the Lima beaches, which had sections for the Peruvian Indians interspersed with expensive beach clubs for the rich Peruvians, walled and topped with glass! There were beautiful birds flying around, some with bright red beaks and feet, and lots of pelicans, which looked like flying elephants as they appeared so clumsy. When we returned to the fair about 7:00, it had mostly cleared away except for a handful of helpers who were finishing the remaining booze. Tired, we visited a "hippy" market in the centre of Lima—not people selling hippies but hippies selling all sorts of handicrafts: skins, leather, beads, jewellery, etc.

Next morning, I left for La Paz! An enjoyable trip, mostly over desert. It was great to see Lake Titicaca from the air—it looked like a prancing panther! How did the ancients know to call it Rock of the Puma? And it was amazing to see the islands of the sun and moon.

The landing at La Paz airport was particularly worrying. The plane, an old DC4, seemed to take forever to stop; the runway was extra-long because of the thin air at 12,500 feet. I called Lorna from the airport and spoke to Sara; they must have thought I was crazy but gave me a really warm welcome again and an excellent dinner. We talked a whole lot more and played backgammon. Snr Prudencio arranged a trip for Sara and me to Tiahuanaco. In the morning, a taxi and guide picked us up and we travelled in style; one hundred times better than the bus. It was more comfortable than the Jeep— quite a treat!

The ruins were extremely interesting, especially the huge Gate of the Sun. I saw stone monoliths for the first time, resembling astronauts, and once more stones of amazing size and weight but not standing perfectly as the Incan ruins in Peru. Not surprising, as one scientist reckoned that the buildings were from 10,000 B.C.! There is a whole city to be excavated deep below the surface. These ruins are at about thirteen thousand feet, and theory is that the sea might have surrounded the city as fossils had been found in the area!

Another lovely dinner that evening, and we talked about many things, including the jungles of Bolivia, the Yungas. Juan owned a thousand acres and offered to take a week off work and go camping. Foolishly I said, quite truthfully, I had to get back to Jamaica to start work. In life you have to take opportunities because they could well not happen again; a lesson I've passed to my children, which Kate benefited from by travelling the world after university.

Juan Prudencio gave me a beautiful stone monolith which was discovered in Tiahuanaco, also two stone arrow/spear heads that might have been thousands of years old. I asked if I could give him anything in return; he refused and said, "Just think of us when you look at them."

Inca belt

Monolith

Spear head

That night I flew back to Lima, where John met me, and we drank a bottle of wine and played dice in the airport till 3:00 am. I slept till 5:00, and at 6:00 I discovered the plane had been delayed until the afternoon because of a mechanical problem.

I was transported to the Gran Hotel Bolivar in the centre of Lima. I went to my room and lay on the bed, looked up at the ceiling only to see there was a massive crack all round the room, six inches in from the walls. I prayed there wouldn't be a quake, as the upstairs floor could neatly press down, as in *The Murders in the Rue Morgue* by Edgar Alan Poe—I didn't need drugs to imagine that!

Still, there was soap, hot water and a shower. I slept, showered, ate a huge breakfast and sat in the entrance hall of that palace under a beautiful glass dome, and the strong pillars gave me confidence.

The plane left for Quito that afternoon. It was amazing to see how much desert there was in Peru, along the whole coastline and well into the mountains. It was hard to believe there was desert at eight thousand feet; I associated desert with the sea. The sand in the mountains was more like a finely polished dust. Near the border with Ecuador, the jungle started. I couldn't see any lions, tigers or elephants, but then again I suppose they do not grow on the tops of trees—also it was not India or Africa. My regret, or rather big incentive to return to South America, was that I didn't explore the jungles. In Quito, they were celebrating the week that the city was founded, 6 December 1534. There were bull fights every day—I didn't attend any, as I'd come round to thinking it was a cruel pastime and not a source of pleasure. On Friday 5 December there was a grand procession through the streets, with many colleges from Ecuador entering floats and dance teams. The colours, flowers and music were awesome, and it took over two hours for all to parade by. On the way I met a group of local young people who invited me back to eat in their most pleasant and comfortable home.

Quito was a clean city, and it was very nice not to feel overawed by armed police. There was an old part with narrow streets and attractive, small, white terraced houses. The city was surrounded by beautiful mountains, which I could admire from the smart hotel I was staying in:

1.   As most hotels were full with Ecuadorians and foreigners enjoying the celebrations

2.   To clean myself up after Peru!

The night after the parade, there was dancing in the streets, which we joined about 11:00 pm and left at 4:00 am when it was still in full swing. The people I was with were related to the drummer of one of the bands, Klan 5—a rock/folk group.

On the Thursday night, I caught a local bus to Otavalo, a market two and a half hours outside Quito, through the mountains and fertile valleys. I stayed at a lovely hotel in Otavalo for $2 and went out to dinner, which cost 30p! The next morning, I got up about 6:00 to get to the market early. It was busy by the time I arrived. The textile market was a spray of colour; the ponchos were made of many bright shades; however, I preferred the natural colours of the ones I'd bought in Peru. There were birds woven on cloth and beautiful blankets. I could have bought so much, if only I'd had a truck to ship it. The atmosphere in the market wasn't as gleeful as in Peru. There was a large food/vegetable market which had more local atmosphere.

That afternoon I continued to San Antonio de Ibarra—a small village steeped with beautiful wood carvings from a couple of inches to several feet in height. The quality was unbelievable and prices so low I could have bought hundreds. The figures were mainly of beggars, some playing musical instruments, and animals. I have never seen so many thousands of beautiful carvings as in the main square of the small village and in every house along the side streets.

I was given a lift from Ibarro to Quito by an evangelical preacher who had spent thirty-five years in the jungles of Ecuador among the Indians, including head hunters—Billy Graham had nothing on him—as he preached the Glory of God and his wonderful works to me all the way back. I was disgusted that his wonderful works included converting Indians who were enjoying a simple jungle life centred around happiness and sadness, while introducing modern diseases. He was proud he had taken young boys and schooled and converted them to his Christianity. It was a really interesting journey, and I think he was more than a little disappointed when we arrived that I didn't "give myself to God" there and then. He drove a large van covered with speakers which he used for showing films of Jesus Christ. In the back of the van was a library, which is where his wife and daughter spent the four-hour journey—I don't know whether there were any windows!

Sunday I flew to Bogota and received an invitation to go to Panama. There were so many stories about thieves in Bogota that I was almost afraid to step off the plane. A few years previously, they had called Scotland Yard to help clean up crime, but they'd had their luggage and equipment ripped off on the way to their hotels. Later, the Columbians brought in the FBI. These agents handed over their passports at the airport for inspection, and never saw them again! They had to fly back to the U.S.

Monserrate is the mountain overlooking the city. There is a funicular railway to the top as well as footpaths. It's known as the mountain of thieves, and I heard several stories to back that up—one about a guy who had his camera and money stolen on the way up, then returned down thinking he was safe as everything had been stolen, only to have his sweater taken.

I heard that a woman was jumped in broad daylight by four men who stole her jewellery and money while passers-by looked on. I didn't go there; Bishop William Franklin advised me not to. I got in touch with him, as someone we'd picked up in our Jeep in Peru knew him. He took me for an excellent lunch and would have had me stay if he and his wife had not been flying out the next day. It turned out I knew his son who was at St John's the same time as me and worked for the British Tourist Board in New York. The Bishop was really interesting and enlightened me about Bogota, the Church and South America in general. Archbishop Ramsey had recently stayed with him; it appeared the Episcopal Church in Colombia was getting quite a boost from the Holy Spirit.

I visited the Gold Museum in Bogota. Four of us entered a secure lift which took us up, and the doors opened into pitch darkness. The lights were slowly raised, and hundreds of pieces of gold jewellery, pectorals, ornaments and carvings slowly appeared behind thick glass cabinets—an awesome experience. The National Museum was interesting, with much anthropology and early carvings.

The rest of my time in Bogota was spent charging round looking for leather goods, bags in particular. It was a clean city, without the obvious military pressures of Lima and La Paz. I was relieved to leave Bogota completely intact with my Incan belts and stone monolith. I met some interesting people, including Dixie, who was a guitarist and Mormon and had spent time in Manaus, which was on my six-month itinerary.

As I passed through customs at the airport, I was taken aside and strip-searched; presumably they were looking for cocaine. Luckily, none had been planted on me.

I left Bogota bound for Panama. It was a fascinating flight through green mountains, and we were soon over the Pacific. We landed, then had a half an hour's drive to the city through pouring rain—very hot and unbearably sticky. It had the most unfriendly people in South America, Ecuadorians being the friendliest. My invitation fell through, so I was glad to be leaving in a couple of days. To cheer myself up, I spent the day hunting for a camera. I bought a Pentax Spotmatic 1.4 with a 50mm lens! I delayed buying a watch till the airport, but there wasn't the same choice as in the town and I couldn't find one I liked for under £200 so I didn't get one. Thursday afternoon, I went to Miraflores Locks and watched a ship travel through the Panama Canal, which was exciting, especially the mules: diesel engines that tow and guide the ships from the banks with minimal room to spare. That evening, I found myself in a sordid club and talked in Spanish at length to a Chilean girl behind the bar who had fled the country because so many of her friends had been killed—desaparecidos. Augusto Pinochet assumed power in 1973 following a United States backed coup d'état, and years of unspeakable atrocities followed.

I boarded my flight to Jamaica on Friday 13 December, leaving a wonderful part of the world, very much hoping I'd have the opportunity to return some time

JAMAICA ABRIDGED PART 1

Club Caribbean (CC) came about as a result of the
Oxbridge ski team training in Chile during the summer.
Simon Marsh had a place in Jamaica where a few stayed
on the way back to the UK. Richard Salm (RPS) fell in
love with the island, moved to Ironshore and persuaded
the Founding Fathers—Michael Seligman, Simon Marsh,
Martin Vincent, Ken and John Hamilton—to put money
in and buy ten acres of land, which included a thousand
feet of sandy beach frontage opposite Salem village. A
team was soon put together to bush out the mangrove
swamps from Beverley, Mines and Salem, and the hotel
opened in 1968 with the swimming pool half-finished and
guests putting their hands to the grindstone; several of
the initial visitors returned year after year.

When I came back from South America in December 1974, RPS had taken over from David Rickham as MD; Herman Chin, a Chini Jamaican, was resident manager and Peter MacDonald, the chef, was from the UK while all others were black Jamaicans. The previous financial comptroller was an Englishman and had been relieved of his post because of excess alcohol, drugs and sex, island fever, which must have been ginormous considering the mores of the island. Harvey was the accountant, with a staff of ten; altogether, I was managing about forty people including cashiers and stores. The accounts were a total shambles, nothing balanced other than the bank accounts, which thank goodness were reconciled, and despite being a chartered accountant I had never prepared a set of accounts in my life other than the Queen's Institute of District Nursing, a tiny operation in Liverpool, and those I screwed up. Harvey came to our wedding in 1979 when we were married in Wiltshire and arrived just as the speeches were ending. The main purpose of his trip was to watch the West Indies play at Lords—he missed that as well.

I soon discovered CC had been insolvent from the time they'd started building, and it wasn't until we went all inclusive in 1993 that we made our first profit. Creditors were screaming for money and the bank was regularly threatening closure. Until then, I had never heard of "kiting". A cheque would be drawn by "A" and deposited in the CC bank account; "A" had no funds, so "B", who had no money either, drew a cheque which was deposited in "A's" bank account, likewise with C and D, by which time a travel agent would have paid some money and all the cheques cleared in turn.

My work permit hadn't come through, so I lived in one of the Rondavel cottages and was told not to exert authority, i.e. not do much work. The cottage was a stone's throw from the swimming pool and a few strides from the beach.

Livingstone Harvey

The festive season soon arrived, and it was peculiar to be spending Christmas Day in the hot sunshine with Mummy Christmas arriving along the beach on a donkey. There was much merriment, plenty of dancing and John Canoe troupes providing entertainment. The real partying took place in the New Year's celebrations. Friends of RPS and Rickham came down from Miami: Lester Lesavoy, Joel Happy Rich Magazine, a very large drugs lawyer, together with their entourage. Locals included Ele, Rickham's wife; Maxine, her sister; Bernard Ruziewicz and Evan Williams, who were partners with Rickham in Epiphany, a successful night club in Kingston, and plenty more. I hadn't experienced partying quite like it.

It wasn't long before I was feeling quite at home. The majority of staff were extremely friendly and freely smiled, laughed and joked despite the tough life most were living with each wage supporting at least five people; they left their cares outside. In January, I went with RPS to Miami to meet some people and look about importing various goods into Jamaica, as hardware was limited on the island. We visited a friend of his who had a connection with Million Dollar Baby, a clothing company financed by using mules to import cocaine from Columbia, controlled by a telex machine in his bedroom and a pistol under his pillow for safety. I was introduced to Lulabelle and her friend, who lived in Coconut Grove, whilst RPS was off on other business. Suddenly, the door shot open and two young South Americans came into the room laughing—apparently a shipment of cocaine had successfully got through and they'd come to celebrate. Lulabelle and her friend tried to teach me to snort cocaine from a mirror through a $100 bill—those two girls didn't do a very good job. Miami was an exciting city, which I'd visit regularly.

Back in Jamaica, Joe James became a friend from early days. He owned an art gallery for his paintings and sculptures, and the Lobster Bowl restaurant in Rio Bueno. A larger-than-life character with a wonderful smile, we'd have long conversations over several beers when I'd call in on my way from Montego Bay. A strong feeling of his, that I didn't understand initially, was his opposition to the growing tourism market and the effect it would have on the Jamaican way of life. He was proved to be right with the subsequent growth of all-inclusive hotels and the demise of local restaurants as tourists were persuaded to stay within their compounds unless they took organised tours. Jamaica was an expensive holiday destination in the '70s, and the staff supporting families on a basic wage could see what they might describe as the "obscene wealth" of foreigners, which made their lives seem inadequate and made them think they should get out of Jamaica as quickly as possible and go to a country where the streets were paved with gold. Joe had the opportunity to experience lavish hospitality in the UK to watch his son, David James, play for England in goal—he raised two fingers to this. He recognised the value of life in Jamaica and was not enticed by false materialism. He said he had other children and he didn't favour any one of them over the others. He had two houses either side of his yard, each with a different wife and separate family.

On February 4, a surprise lunchtime birthday celebration was arranged for me by the MD's secretary, Jennifer B., who resembled Diana Ross. I was determined I was not going to get involved with any of the staff, but in the end I succumbed. There were a dozen people waiting for me, including RPS and David Rickham, to enjoy champagne, lobster and other delicacies; I'm ashamed to say I turned round and walked out—maybe a flashback to Lawrence House.

The relationship developed, and I remembered a conversation with Tom Vigus, my cottage mate in Port Dinorwic, who was going out with an attractive Rhodesian nurse in Bangor who would regularly visit. He said being in love with someone black was no different from anyone else; this was in 1968, the time of Enoch Powell's Rivers of Blood speech. What tickled me was that, with her dark skin, Jennifer still had a bikini line. Tom eventually married an aboriginal from the Highlands of New Guinea.

At last, towards the end of February, my work permit came through and I was able to move into accommodation off the premises. It was a pleasant, semi-detached house, the other half occupied by Herman Chin, but it backed onto the main road from Runaway Bay with considerable traffic noise. The final straw was finding out in an emergency I was unable to get into the bathroom as it was locked from the other side; it was shared. The next morning I went to RPS and said I was leaving and that I hadn't come to Jamaica to live like that. He asked me to hang on for a day, phoned Jim Pringle, a property agent, and that evening I moved into Encore, a beautiful property in Cardiff Hall, with a thirty-foot lounge that opened onto a large patio area with a swimming pool and extensive gardens overlooking the golf course and the Caribbean beyond—I was staying. There were two en suite bedrooms on my side of the house, and a bedroom the size of a football pitch, dressing room and bathroom which RPS occupied on the other. The two years we lived in Encore RPS said were the best two years of his life, and he had plenty to choose from. When we needed anything, we'd ring the hotel and they'd deliver gin, whisky, rum, chasers and whatever else we asked for. The maids were delightful, clothes were washed and ironed by the following evening, and Gladstone the gardener did a good job, including maintaining the pool. If we had company in the evening before returning to the Club, we'd entertain each other's visitors while the other showered. We worked long hours, and as we were committed to making CC a success, it was more like fun.

By now I was seriously getting stuck in to sorting out the mess the accounts were in and introducing financial controls. I organised a stock count, which revealed there was something like two dozen cases of Red Stripe and many bottles of spirits missing. Wanting reassurance, another count was carried out with a similar result, and I fined the bar staff, cashiers and storekeepers $5 each. A week later, same result, same fine. The third time, I had a riot on my hands. There were thirty very angry Jamaicans and me crammed into the MD's office—it had taken three attempts to get anywhere near what was being ripped off. It turned out that the back-yard manager, Mr Brown, a large Jamaican with a huge belly, feared by many, was operating two bars in the village with booze he was ordering and had dropped off by the draymen, which CC was paying for.

The hotel was desperately short of cash, and with none of the two hundred employees having bank accounts, there was a run to the bank every Thursday about midday. The staff knew there were difficulties, and in the afternoon they would congregate outside the window of the accounts office where the pay packets were handed out, the gardeners stroking their machetes. One week I panicked and called Bob Salm, RPS' father in England, and told him that we wouldn't be able to pay the wages the following day. A transfer was made and I received an angry phone call from the bank manager because I had gone to Bob Salm before I'd spoken to him.

It was when I was anxious about getting cash to pay wages that one of my fall outs happened, this time with Janice McNeil who ran reservations, a glamorous Indian/Jamaican lady with the longest painted nails. She was speaking to someone in the front lobby when I desperately needed her help; she could see my anxiety but continued to go on and on about things I thought were trivial. In the end I exploded with an expletive, and a torrent of abuse came back my way.

Another faux pas was when the police were making inquiries about a theft, and foolishly I allowed them to go into Salem village to speak to the housekeeping manager, a good lady who was doing an excellent job. She was extremely angry with me because neighbours seeing a police car outside her house automatically assumed that she was being accused of committing a crime; far from it.

One evening when I was on duty, a maid came to the front desk carrying a number of sheets which another member of staff had been stealing and whose boyfriend had been selling on. After a few weeks, the case was listed in Brownstown Court for a hearing before a judge. There were two women involved; one was young and pretty and the other a chunky mama. I was called as a witness, the only white face in the room, and after answering several questions, I was asked which lady had brought the sheets to me. I genuinely couldn't remember, the Judge put pressure on me to answer. I made the wrong choice—case dismissed!

Despite small altercations, I was feeling very much at home. I'd turn up to work in shorts and a tee shirt; I was building an excellent relationship with Harvey, my accountant, as well as the other accounts staff. Gradually, we were starting to sort out the mess. Peats/KPMG happened to be the accountants, and at a meeting with the senior partner, I was warned that RPS made everything as complicated as possible and had a habit of part paying suppliers' invoices, which made reconciliation to agree exactly what was owed a nightmare, especially when cheques were bouncing.

The atmosphere was relaxed, which I enjoyed, but it meant the hotel was much more difficult to run than a Marriott or similar, which had strict systems followed in every operation over the world rather than having to make many ad hoc decisions. There is a Jamaican expression, "soon come," which means mañana but without the urgency. This together with nothing much balancing, plenty of wrong postings and staff not taking responsibility was totally the opposite of what I was used to, working in one of the top accountancy practices in the world.

In January 1975, four cricket teams came out from the UK sponsored by Mackeson, all except for one was hammered each game; they even considered asking me to play as "my eyes should be accustomed to the light." They were looking for excuses. I witnessed one of the fastest sixty runs ever; in one over 6–4–6 (out of the ground) 6 (over a house) 6 and 0. The shots the Jamaican batsman played were a joy to watch. The following day, I was sitting at CC's bamboo bar in my shorts and tee shirt, working dress, flowcharting the systems, when one of the players approached me. He worked out of the KPMG Stoke Office, knew John Davies well and looked forward to reporting back what I was up to and conveying my good wishes.

In March I was assigned to meet Gerald Harper, who played Hadleigh in the TV series, at Kingston Airport and show him the town. Club Caribbean provided the accommodation and Air Jamaica the flights for the winners of a Capital Radio competition that Gerald hosted. There were several rounds, including dinner at Maxine's in Paris, and the final prize was Gerald Harper awarding the lucky winners a bottle of champagne at Dunns River Falls. We had a good time visiting various bars and places of interest, and the next day we hired a plane to fly to the North Coast. We buzzed the hotel, letting them know it was time to pick us up on the private runway in the cane fields. All went well; we transferred into the Club's Holden estate and waved goodbye. The pilot accelerated down the runway, filling the open-windowed car with dust and stones! Gerald took it in good spirits and on his radio programme invited Clare, from St John's days, to visit me in Jamaica, which her mother had forewarned her about, but she didn't take it up.

Gerald Harper

Sugar cane factory

Peaches, who was as lovely as her name suggests, had an important administrative role in the stores and was efficient and trustworthy. However, I was finding out how cunning Jamaicans were at foiling systems, and things were happening she couldn't be expected to pick up. We became suspicious that a certain storeman stayed late on one particular night every week, so we prepared an ambush. A truck arrived loaded with vegetables, and we stopped it half an hour later as it was leaving. When we looked under the remaining produce, we found a whole heap of lobsters—Club Caribbean was paying the farmer for vegetables, who then sold the stolen lobsters to another hotel.

Peaches

King

Ele

I loved the outdoor life. At the weekends, I played tennis with RPS, who also taught me to water ski. One of the commendable projects RPS started was a tennis school. Matthew and Dreamy were the professionals and were encouraged to find local youths who had potential and wanted to be taught the discipline of being ball boys; during slack times they learnt how to play tennis. Many young lives were improved in this way, with Giant and Fast Car making the Satellite Tour. I made friends in Water Sports, owned and run by King, whose right-hand man was Packet, assisted by Cap, Tony and Steve. They taught me to sail Sunfishes and scuba dive; no PADI or dive tables, just a quick fifteen minutes in the swimming pool to get used to the regulator and tanks, then down off into the sea. At the time there were no conservation ethics; I'd arrive at 6:30 and we'd go spear-fishing for parrot fish, mullet and gobies. It was only after I shot a five-foot barracuda with the boys that King told me that if I'd have winged it, the fish would have turned round with a frightening set of teeth and taken a chunk out of my leg. I'd go back to Encore, get ready for the day and call into Water Sports at lunchtime to enjoy the delicious food they cooked up. Sometimes we'd dive a hundred feet for black coral, which thankfully was soon banned. In return, I introduced Cap, Tony and Steve to rugby! There were several clubs on the island, the nearest being Montego Bay—not the best, but the Caribbean Championships were about to take place in Barbados later in the year and I wanted to make that trip. Bucky, who was a fantastic fast bowler and one of the strongest men I've come across, wanted to play as well. He once held up the front of a Mini to stop the driver leaving CC without paying. However, he had a bad temper, and one time when an umpire didn't give a batsman out, he stormed off the pitch and tore up the score book. The three others made the Montego Bay team; they were young, fit and natural athletes.

Cap

Tony and Cap

It was one of the most pleasurable sights watching Cap and Tony grinning from ear to ear as they travelled in an aeroplane for the first time to the Cayman Islands. Simon Marsh and RPS were also allowed to come, provided they played rugby. It was a 1945 DC-3 for twenty people totally filled with Montego Bay rugby players, and after fifteen minutes the hostess told us to help ourselves to liquor as she couldn't keep up with the demand. A few minutes later, a cry came from the pilot to sit down as, with so many at the back of the plane, he was having difficulty flying at a near to forty degree angle. The flight took one and half hours—it would have been twenty minutes in a regular jet— and Montego Bay Rugby Club and friends staggered off the plane about 6:00 in the evening to be met by immensely sober gentlemen dressed in white shirts and club ties.

Simon and I were very drunk by the time we landed in Cayman, and we were left at the shack which passed for a terminal while all the others were taken to the Cayman Arms by the hosts who were putting us up. Eventually, by some means or other, we joined them, and after a few more greenies were taken to a place to stay. It was terrifying awakening in the morning: wailing, banging and singing. We were next to a cemetery, and a burial was taking place.

Simon and I managed to find RPS for an appointment with the bank, and business was completed over a good lunch of mushrooms, bacon and, of course, a couple of bottles of wine.

We were well and truly beaten in the first match. A few drinks afterwards, then onto a party which lasted till 3:00 am. Time for the second match, and as agreed for being able to come on the trip, when wives of the Montego Bay players had flown out on a scheduled flight from Kingston as they were told there wasn't space on the DC-3, RPS and Simon were on the field warming up. RPS took a high ball, which broke his finger—he didn't make the first whistle. Simon played well, and we won easily, with yours truly scoring a try.

A swim in the sea instead of a shower, a good lunch of marinated conch and turtle steak, then onto the DC-3 for the return trip—not as drunken and boisterous as the way out, but fun nevertheless, with Richard holding his broken finger, Cap with a badly torn thigh muscle and Barney Eldemire with a twisted ankle and torn tendon! For a change, I had only a few bruises and scrapes. Cayman is fine for a couple of days, but I couldn't imagine living there. It's clean and tidy but devoid of Jamaica's interesting culture and heritage. In better circles, whites were not seen mixing with black women and men—we did something to bring them closer together. There is little doubt in my mind that apartheid in South Africa would have broken down sooner if sporting teams had continued to travel there, as they would have demanded non-white friends they had made be allowed into the celebrations. I also believe that racism laws promote racism by encouraging troublemakers on both sides to take improper advantage and promote distorted publicity; far better that laws should punish bad behaviour, whatever colour, creed or social standing.

Decades later, I was at Club Caribbean the same time as Tony, and it was wonderful to see my good friend who I'd shared so many experiences with after many years. He'd become a successful businessman in New York, owning two shops and a restaurant; however, he was overweight, stressed and had no family. I'm not sure if he'd have been happier living a simple life back in Jamaica, and I felt a tinge of responsibility for introducing him to travel.

Donkey

Two up

Pineapple Lady

The pineapple lady in Brownstown market became very angry when she saw me taking a picture, as she thought I was mocking her because of the sack shielding her head from the sun. I explained how beautiful she looked amongst her pineapples, and all was redeemed when a couple of weeks later I took her a hardcopy of the photo.

I was feeling part of Jamaica, and the fact I was born out of wedlock had no significance there whatsoever, as by far the majority of couples were not married and it wasn't uncommon for a woman to have several children by different fathers. With a mix of races from Europe, Africa and China, it was a true melting pot, although there was discrimination and some lighter-coloured Jamaicans would disparagingly call those with blacker skin Niggers. As Michael Holding related, education of white and black people is needed. Christ is portrayed as having pale skin, blue eyes and blond hair—how likely is it that someone from the Middle East of Jewish origin would have been so?—while Judas Iscariot is usually depicted as black. The world credits Thomas Edison with inventing the light bulb; what he created had a paper filament and was gone in seconds. A black man, Lewis Howard Latimer, made it into something useful, and who has heard of him? History is written by the conquerors, and those who have the power and ability to manipulate minds, it is a sad state when capitalism has been replaced by greed. In the age of social media, there is no excuse for heroes of every colour, creed and derivation not to be recognised and young children made aware of their own champions to look up to.

Unfortunately, prejudice extended to members of Montego Bay Rugby Club, who were predominantly white and for the most part from humble beginnings in the UK; because they had swimming pools, maids and gardeners they took on airs and graces. When I was off the island, Cap, Tony and Steve weren't looked after. Parties after rugby were held at one of the player's houses, often in lavish surroundings by the sea, and one time when I was chatting to my mates, the Water Sports guys, they asked why I wasn't with my big friends; I explained I'd prefer to be with them, real people. There was a similar reaction from Americans who were on the team. Russ Finsness owned companies in Jamaica and lived in a beautiful home in Tryall, a 2,200 acre estate with its own beach and luxurious facilities. I was invited to stay over for dinner and took Jennifer. At one point, she left the table and was in tears as it was pointed out that, because of her colour, she was not welcome there; I left, never to return again. However, the majority associated with Montego Bay Rugby Club were open and fair minded.

Generously, because I hadn't gone home for Christmas, RPS arranged for Oliver and Enid to come out for a month. I watched them as they came through immigration, producing their documents, and I was ready, waiting to take their luggage. What a joy it was that they felt able to make the arduous journey, as not only was I sure they would love Jamaica, but it allowed me to feel better about leaving Wales when Oliver wasn't in the best of health and some consolation for denying them my degree ceremony.

The drive from Montego Bay to Runaway Bay was delightful. We were soon leaving the airport past the manicured golf courses, the luxurious Half Moon Hotel, Rose Hall Great House—with the three coconut trees the White Witch was said to have buried the husbands she had murdered under—mountains to the south and the inviting blue Caribbean to the north. Through Falmouth, over the Martha Brae River, Duncans and Discovery Bay, where Columbus landed in 1494 after leaving Columbus Cove in Drax Hall. We soon passed through Runaway Bay then arrived in Club Caribbean, where my mum and dad were given Cottage 4, located right on the beach, two steps from the pool terrace and dining area. Most of the time, breakfast, lunch and dinner would be served outside unless the liquid sunshine fell. There was one near miss when a coconut fell from the tree directly above the table they were sitting at and narrowly missed Oliver's head, which could have been disastrous and taken him out if it had been a direct hit. There had been great excitement in Gresford when they learnt the Vicar was travelling to the Caribbean, which was still regarded as an expensive holiday destination in the days before charter flights. After a welcome rum punch, they settled into their cottage, which they enjoyed for the next four weeks.

Oliver was already up when I arrived at the hotel 6:30 the following morning, sitting on the wall outside his cottage in Winceyette pyjamas, talking to the man raking the beach—he had already made a friend—and soon afterwards the hatman made him a trilby from palm leaves. Oliver was as happy as a sand boy from day one and found the Jamaicans friendly, cheerful and captivating. Enid also felt at home, provided she was careful to stay out of the hot sun. I took them to Encore, which they loved, and when the maid heard that my dad suffered from hardening of the arteries, she made him ganja tea every time he was up there. Amazingly, Oliver wanted to go in the pool although he couldn't swim, and I'd walk round the edge of the pool dragging him on a rope; occasionally he would flip over and I'd jump in to right him.

We made several trips out, and Mum and Dad particularly enjoyed the journey up through the hills to Brownstown Market. There are beautiful views looking down on the Caribbean. The market was covered and the most colourful spectacle, with all kinds of vegetables, fruits, meats, and—what Oliver took a liking to—"donkey arse rope": lengths of twist tobacco which rolled up into a ball and were so named because the most flavoursome was the piece which wrapped under the donkey's tail. Another hit was punting down the Martha Brae on a bamboo raft. It was a long time since I'd seen my dad look so relaxed; he'd been on boats of all shapes and sizes but never one like that.

Brownstown Market

Martha Brae rafting

For several of the dinners, Jennifer would join us. My folks understood we were in a relationship and she received nothing but good vibes. It wasn't long afterwards that she handed in her notice at CC, being a Kingston girl at heart she was missing town life. No way could the relationship survive with Mount Diablo in between, and sadly it came to an end. Jennifer had done so much to make my initiation and integration into Jamaica a happy and stimulating event.

There was quality entertainment every night at CC, from native dancing to Keith Stewart, a renowned ballad singer. Another of my mistakes was to play Harry Belafonte before Keith came out to do his turn. One event that appealed to the guests, including Oliver and Enid, was crab racing. Helmet crabs were painted in different colours, and the main races were to see which was the first to make its way out of a circle. There was always a slow race, which would lead to arguments as to whether a dead crab could win. Bets were taken with a percentage going to the house; we found out that the crabman, Leroy, sold weed on the side but we didn't disturb his extra business. One of Oliver's favourites was Lord Laroo, who sang spiced up folk songs such as "Shame and Scandal in the Family", which always brought a smile to his face. The Jolly Boys, a small calypso band, played during the day, comprising Bongo Shorty the drummer, who I'd sail with in a good-sized boat, a lead singer and Luther, who played the banjo who became a particularly good friend of my dad. Even though most of them had limited academic education, they were articulate and knew the Bible well, which led to lots of interesting conversations with Oliver.

The four weeks flew by, and at the end there were many people at the front of the hotel to wave Oliver and Enid off. They'd had a wonderful time, made many friends, and my dad reckoned they were the most pleasant, happy people he'd ever met—and he'd done a fair amount of travelling, including on the Cunard cruise ships, when once a year he'd be chaplain. On the way to the airport, we called in at Half Moon, and Oliver chose a very smart wide-brimmed straw hat with a ribbon, not too dissimilar to the black ten-gallon hats he wore around the parish. It gave me the utmost pleasure to buy it for him, and he walked out of the boutique grinning from ear to ear.

Bongo Shorty was a huge character, a brilliant drummer but very small, and he had the largest Queen B partner. I would visit them on the fisherman's beach in Salem and enjoyed endless conversations and watched him carving, another of his skills. He knew the seas like the back of his hand and the location of many wrecks, and a dream of ours was that I'd return one day and we'd dive for sunken treasure—it didn't happen.

At night, a fair amount of ganja was smoked— not by me—through a chillum made of a coconut shell and a plastic pipe. The bowl in which the weed was placed was large, and there would be a thick cloud of smoke that the face of the partaker would be hidden behind. One of the enduring images, which I would love to have captured on film, was Cap's smiling face appearing as the cloud started to disperse whilst those around made Rasta chants and praises to Haile Selassie I, King of Kings, Lord of Lords, their divine heritage, who would take them out of slavery, oppression and racism.

One false rumour that spread was that locals threw stones at tourists' hire cars as they drove around the island. Nothing could be further from the truth; Jamaicans realised the monetary value holidaymakers brought to their lives. In fact, stones did hit cars, but that was because they were kicked up by their own tyres from the ramshackle roads. One stone was thrown at me in the depths of Spanish Town, but that was possibly deserved. I drove into what was a rough part of town as I was tired and hungry and wanted something to eat to help me with the two-hour drive back to the north coast. I found a hut selling bun and cheese, and when I reversed, I accidentally knocked a small motorbike over. I wound the window down to apologise and give the owner my insurance details, but he was extremely angry and in no mood for talking. Realising this, I hit the accelerator and rapidly drove away as a missile flew into the air and hit the back of the car.

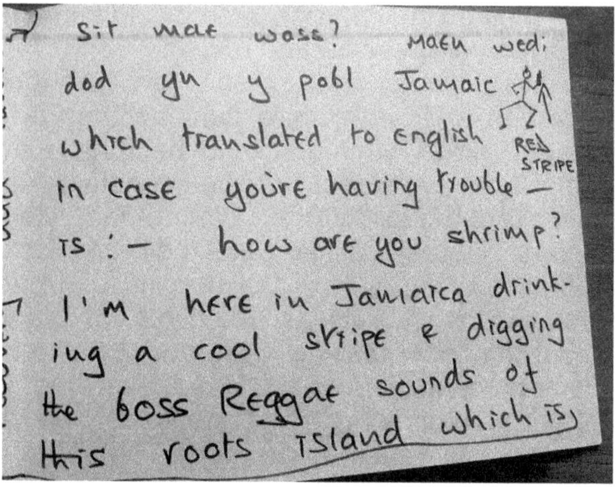

> Sit mae wose? Maeh wedi
> dod yn y pobl Jamaic
> which translated to english
> in case youre having trouble — RED STRIPE
> Is :— how are you shrimp?
> I'm here in Jamaica drink-
> ing a cool stripe & digging
> the boss Reggae sounds of
> his roots Island which is,

Shrimp was Oliver's term of endearment/insult for me. His request when I started on a journey was "bring me back a parrot".

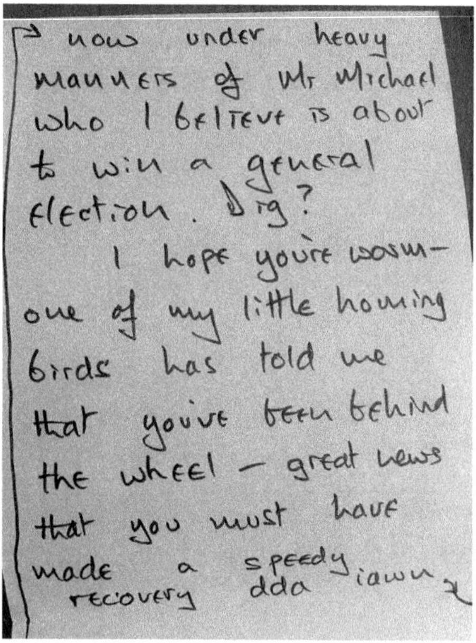

> now under heavy
> manners of Mr Michael
> who I believe is about
> to win a general
> election. Dig?
> I hope youre wosm-
> one of my little homing
> birds has told me
> that youve been behind
> the wheel — great news
> that you must have
> made a speedy recovery dda iawn

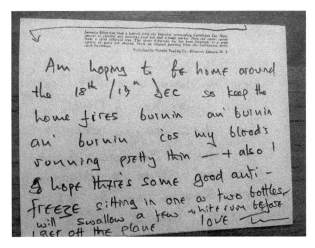

As managers, we took it in turns to do the evening duty, which involved handling any problems arising from guests or staff. I enjoyed going round each of the tables to make sure the holidaymakers were as happy as they could be. However, I never plucked up the courage to make announcements on stage over the microphone and introduce the entertainers. Running a hotel is one of the most difficult challenges; most businesses either have a large number of staff or many customers—hospitality has both, including all the safety and hygiene concerns. We learnt that if someone arrived at Club Caribbean expecting a Hilton experience, whatever we said or did they were not going to be satisfied, so we moved them on as quickly as possible. Others might have a leaking roof or an enormous crab might have found its way into their cottage, and those problems had to be sorted as quickly as possible or else you'd see guests gathering in groups and bad feeling could quickly spread. There was one precarious situation where it was deemed necessary to lay off a waiter who was popular with certain guests; it seemed he'd been supplying them with orders from the kitchen and making adjustments to the paperwork so they weren't fully charged. We only just avoided a riot, as that group of guests were acting as a union on the waiter's behalf.

Being in the country, staff were on the whole extremely friendly, and it always amazed me how they could leave their troubles behind and the bar staff became part of the entertainment, rocking to boss sounds or doubled up laughing at a funny comedian.

Although we had a good proportion of return guests, the cash flow was poor and we continued to lose money. How we managed to survive while making losses from the time Club Caribbean opened in 1968 until we became the first three-star all-inclusive hotel in Jamaica warrants a book in itself, and I learnt plenty of survival skills from RPS.

One day, out of the blue, a stumpy Jamaican turned up looking like Quasimodo. He sidled up to the front desk with his climbing gear and said he was going to cut the telephones off unless he walked away with a cheque—not just a regular one but a bank manager's cheque. By the time I got the message, he was halfway up the pole; the hotel was fairly full of Americans, and I managed to persuade him to come down before he cut us off and we paid him what was needed. Another important lesson I learnt was that largest savings could be made by attacking the biggest figures first.

The supplier of cooking gas wasn't so successful at collecting payment. In the end, the managing director, a good-looking Chinese lady, turned up and demanded that we paid a chunk of the tens of thousands US dollars they were owed. Because the debt had become so large, we were in a commanding position and we retired to Encore. She returned several times, but didn't once leave with a cheque.

One evening, there was an almighty fuss going on at the front desk. Concie, a well-known prostitute, was yelling at the top of her voice, "Where chef? Dat pussy tief, he tiefed me pussy!" The Pink House was a brothel in Ocho Rios, and the chef had turned up there, had his evil way, paid over the money then asked Concie for a loan, which was twice as much as he'd paid her, and he'd not done the honourable thing and returned to settle his debt; Concie soon had her money.

Aunt May had a small local shack restaurant in Runaway Bay where we'd regularly go for an evening away from the Club. Her food was excellent, and we'd order what she recommended from fish of all types, flyer chicken—which was a staple of the Jamaican diet and was cooked in many different ways, always delicious—Trenton, pig of one sort or another, curried goat and invariably rice and peas. My favourite drink at May's was carrot juice with condensed milk and stout blended in. The avocado pears were something to die for, as were mangoes, and another favourite of mine was Irish Moss, made of seaweed like a thick milkshake. With two hundred staff, there were plenty of mouths to feed each day, and we tried to persuade Aunt May to be the staff cook, which we thought would be pure luxury. However, there was no way the majority of the men would allow a woman to cook for them, although it must have happened in their homes.

Although I enjoyed the journey into Kingston, through the mountains, alongside the rivers and over Flat Bridge, I was never totally comfortable in the city. Partly because I didn't know my way around thoroughly, and one time I found myself lost in Trenchtown. The streets were crowded so I had to drive at walking pace through the ramshackle government yards. At night, the advice was to drive through traffic lights on red to avoid the chances of being held up. Once again, I found myself as the only white person and was very pleased to get back to New Kingston.

I used to call in at Stan's on the way back from Kingston, a Pimento farmer who kept a well-stocked bar on the road between Moneague and St Ann for his friends. He lived part of his life in Kingston, and there were always interesting people to chat to. He said he'd fix me up on a date with Roberta Flack who called in when she was in Jamaica, but that never happened!

RPS' wife Sam came out for the summer holidays with her two young children, Rebecca and Dominique. A fence was built around the swimming pool in Encore to stop them falling in, and I moved into Caribbean Village, a complex of sixteen houses adjoining Club Caribbean. That worked well; however, Richard had a girlfriend from England who was staying in one of the regular cottages, and he would be scampering round trying to keep all parties happy.

A group of university students from Atlanta, Georgia, checked into the cottage next door to mine. We soon found we had the Grateful Dead in common, and before long I was head over heels in love with Caroline. She was an excellent tennis player, and we took on all comers old and young, including the D'Allessandros and Taussigs.

A couple of weeks later, I travelled to Miami on business, then up to see Caroline, who studied at Emory University in Atlanta. I enjoyed the city— lovely houses and restaurants, particularly the Underground, a shopping and entertainment district in the old part of the city, and a jazz room called Down the Hatch. We flew in a small twin-engine plane to an airport outside Charleston, Carolina, where Caroline's brother picked us up. The family house could have been transported from St George's Hill, Weybridge in Surrey, with its smart drawing room and lovely paintings. There were outbuildings where the black servants lived. Her father was a lawyer and drew up the documents for Holiday Inn when they started out. He was offered either cash payment or shares; unfortunately, he took the cash. Charleston was a fascinating old city with quaint buildings, including the place where Gershwin's *Porgy and Bess* was set and a lovely waterfront. We visited an old slave plantation which had maintained many of the buildings and character of the days of slavery. The next day we drove back to Atlanta—a fun and interesting journey, stopping in a town to buy the Frye boots I'd been hankering after for my motorbike journey. We decided we would travel to Costa Rica together for two weeks.

Caroline came down to Jamaica and things went horribly wrong. I was up to my neck in preparing the accounts for the audit, and it soon became obvious the trip was going to be delayed. It wasn't the first time I'd been dumped, but never had it been as heart wrenching as this. I was sorely upset when Jude ditched me after a visit to the cinema in Chester, but I understood, went home, wrote a lovely poem and offered any help I could in the future. Harvey covered well for me, as my brain was total mush. Luckily, maybe, Rutherford Brown was staying in the out quarters of Encore. He was a well-educated, talented black Jamaican who had spent time in Europe, mainly Germany, and created the most intricate fine carvings out of black gold/coral. He also had a good supply of ganja, and we spent long periods of time chatting and getting stoned.

One of the hotel cars I was driving at the time was a Ford Capri, only a 1,600 engine but it went like a bat out of hell. The maids complained bitterly to RPS because the house was filled with chippings and dust from the driveway as each time I came down, instead of doing a five-point turn backwards and forwards, I would slam the handbrake on, flick the steering wheel and round she'd come. How I missed the house and garden wall I have no idea, but I put it down to the lessons I'd had from Chris Statham, accelerating from the Griffin at the end of Gresford Vicarage drive and getting enough speed up to do a handbrake turn in front of the house.

After Caroline left, I tried working at the hotel but I had no concentration, so one day I set off past Salem fisherman's beach and walked the five or six miles to Llandovery, striding through the sea when the beach ran out. I then waded a mile up Llandovery River, which looked as if there could be crocodiles amongst the reeds—which there were, of course, in Black River on the south coast. How I got back to Encore or when, I have no idea, just as I had no clue why I took that rejection so badly, but for months I couldn't stand to hear the Neil Diamond song *Sweet Caroline*, which was popular at the time and kept playing.

I had plenty of support, which helped me get back together and return a smile to my face.

Tourism was suffering from a lack of visitors to the island, so we made considerable efforts to attract local trade from Kingston. I was in Epiphany night club, chatting to a group of Jamaican girls who worked for a travel agency, and I put pressure on them as to why they weren't sending traffic our way. A few days later RPS got a letter from the owner, who was also a shareholder, complaining I was very drunk, slurring my words and being rude to his staff. Richard wrote back saying it couldn't possibly be so—I was in training to represent Jamaica in Barbados—and being from Wales people often thought I was drunk and found it hard to understand me because of my strange accent; all turned out well.

One attempt to get local publicity was to take photographs of Miss Turkey, who was staying in our hotel, and I managed to have an article with a picture in the local paper.

Miss Turkey

Dave Richards

By chance I was listening to the radio one afternoon, and I heard Dave Richards being interviewed having just won the Rothmans 747 Jamaican Rally; I couldn't believe my ears. I quickly discovered where that was happening and rang the hotel, who put Dave on the phone. The next day, he appeared in front of the Club driving his rally car, and soon crowds gathered. My kudos grew as I lowered myself into the passenger seat; a few roars on the accelerator and off to the cane fields. It was a blast and I showed him Papillon Beach, where *Papillon* was filmed. Jamaica was used as a location for many movies, often set up by Maxine, Ele's sister. There was plenty of tension on that film, as Dustin Hoffman would steal a major shot from Steve McQueen with a small gesture, which riled him no end.

One major source of revenue to the island, almost on a par with tourism and bauxite, was ganja. There were many private runways and up to sixty flights a day were leaving for Florida. A major problem arose because forged dollar bills had been used for payment, so guns were demanded instead as "hard currency". The ingenuity of Jamaicans was once more reflected by improvising, and new roads made perfect landing strips. The plane would buzz when it was approaching, the new road would be closed to vehicles and the old road temporarily opened up. Within fifteen minutes, the ganja was loaded and on its way back to Florida. The government gave orders for lengths of railway track to be erected every two hundred yards to prevent landing by threatening the wings. There was a gully carved out for the new road by Lilliput, where the civil engineers followed instructions to the letter and placed the railway track up against the rock face!

Another phenomenal experience took place on Sunday evenings every few weeks, when Bob Marley turned up at the lobby shop to collect money for his record sales. Afterwards he would come to the Purple Turtle, a private restaurant/club next to Club Caribbean and jam to ten/twelve of us. His family lived in Nine Mile up in the hills of St Ann's, and he'd call in on his way back to town.

I went to Miami for two weeks on a promotion trip trying to encourage the Floridians that Club Caribbean was the place to spend their time. It was hard work. I visited golf, country and businessmen's clubs, travel agents, backgammon haunts and swinging jet-set private clubs. It is difficult to say how successful it was. When I got into the swing of it, I really enjoyed the selling aspect and it was satisfying to win people over but depressing to have them pull out later after they had shown enthusiasm, also to be kept waiting and having appointments broken—I learnt an incredible amount about people and Miami. It was fun zooming about in big American cars, and the luxurious lifestyle was astonishing. Both cars I hired had air conditioning—essential in Miami, still a rarity in the UK. It was frustrating at first to have all kinds of buzzers and rings if seatbelts weren't fastened, a door left open or key left in the ignition, but sensible for safety reasons. One of the cars had a light on the front wing that lit up when you were using excess gas; it didn't go out for long periods. The wide six-lane highways were a challenge after Jamaican roads, but people drove much slower in the States.

I spent a couple of days checking out motorbikes for a trip round Mexico, Belize, Guatemala and San Salvador before I'd ship it back to Jamaica. I tried the 1000cc Honda Goldwing that had been tested by the Japanese cops round Tokyo for two years. It was out of this world, rode like a dream, just like travelling in an armchair, but the salesman following me was concerned when I took it up to 80 mph as the speed restriction of 60 mph was strictly adhered to. The other alternative was a 900cc BMW: comfortable, reliable and known by mechanics all over the world.

I met a lot of people in Miami, especially Jews, and by the end I felt I should kiss a mezuzah on every doorpost and decided I would try and persuade RPS that we should build a bagel factory in Runaway Bay. There was much wealth amongst the majority of my Jewish friends, who drove Cadillacs and Oldsmobiles. I ate in super restaurants, saw several films and visited the theatre to watch *Equus*, a gripping play. I went to Honey for the Bears, a swinging club in Coconut Grove, a couple of times and greatly enjoyed listening to Jo Donato, the sax jazz player. I flew with a friend to Freeport for $5 to gamble in the Grand Bahamas Casino one night and was pretty whacked when I boarded the plane back to Montego Bay.

On 6 September 1975, I was to have been best man at David Spalding's wedding to Joanna Marchant. I warned him I might have a problem fulfilling that most pleasant duty, and this is a copy of the telegram I sent:

HAIL JAH. Guidance and Praise to the Brethren and his Queen now one. Hail Roots Iree. If you want to survive you can't slip or slide. A Serious Thing. Love Natty Dread Locks, Tim.

He forgave me, and I was honoured to be godfather to Jessica, his firstborn, on 2 June 1979. One time, his mother told Enid she was pleased David and I were friends as I'd done a lot to make his life more exciting.

There was plenty to look forward to on my return, especially the Caribbean Championships in Barbados. I had been chosen for the rugby squad and was training hard, running round the golf course below Encore and dancing in the disco.

The big event before Barbados was the screening of the Muhammad Ali vs Jo Frazier fight on 30 September in the National Stadium, the Thrilla in Manilla, one of the best boxing matches ever, when Ali retained his world title. I travelled to Kingston with Harvey and Spence; the stadium was packed, the atmosphere electric, and though mine was the only white face I could see, I felt totally safe. It was an unforgettable night and strengthened even more my love for Jamaica.

The time arrived and we took off for Barbados; I was the only representative from Montego Bay RFC on the squad. Graham Boulter, another player, had lived in Barbados for a few years so knew the best haunts and had family there who owned the caves, a well-known tourist attraction. We hired a Mini Moke to get us round the island on our time off, an ideal vehicle for the narrow roads, just like an open-topped jeep. We stayed in a convenient hotel, and I shared a room with two other Welshmen. The atmosphere was friendly and inclusive from the beginning; we had come here to win but also to have fun.

The championships were a big deal for Barbados, and David F. Callaghan wrote in the programme "*It is during the championships that "rugby fever" grips the Islands. This year is no exception and when the teams meet in Barbados for ten days it will be an historic occasion as The Caribbean Rugby Football Union will be officially inaugurated and affiliated to the Rugby Football Union at Twickenham.*" Sandy Sanders, England's chairman of selectors for five years, was guest of honour. The matches took place at the Garrison Savannah, St Michael.

We played the first match against Guyana in heavy rain and mud, conditions we were used to back in Wales, not on the hard pitches of Jamaica. My left elbow and knee hardly healed as that was the side I naturally tackled with and it would only take a little scrape on a sheet for the wounds to open up again. I was number 8, Alan Jones from Crainant scrum half and Ifan Williams from Bangor, who had played soccer for British Universities, at fly. The ball didn't get any further down the back line the whole match. There were plenty of Gary Owens, and the poor guys from South America didn't know what had hit them as they had never come across such tactics; they were used to fast, open rugby, just like the rest of the Caribbean. I had moves round the base of the scrum with the wing forwards and Alan. Every game was televised live back in Jamaica—unbelievable, as rugby was such a minor sport there. Alan's wife, Pam, was glued to the screen with Sue, who was her good friend—Alan and I would have been within a couple of yards of each other for the whole of this game and close for the others.

We lost the second match against Trinidad, and there followed a hard game against Bahamas for the third, which we won. I received a kick in the head which required stitches in my eyebrow. I had become good friends with Hieve Alaloux who was playing for Martinique, a former first-division French player in the same position as me; he was a doctor and stitched me up, allowing me to play on and finish the match. I was delighted to be a Jaa Baa—Jamaican Barbarian— and proud to have shed blood for Jamaica.

We played five matches in eight days, and the crunch one was against Barbados, the home side, which we won. By this time I felt a physical wreck, having given my all, and the hot water being pumped into the sea where Graham took us to relieve our aching muscles wasn't enough. Three of us went to Sandy Lane's cave bar on their beach and had a few beers in the lap of luxury. We left via the hotel's pharmacy to pick up some pain relief, where there were three attractive black girls and I asked if any gave massages, to which one replied, "My sister does." She gave me the telephone number and I arranged to see her 7:00 that evening as her last appointment.

I dragged my body to the clinic, and she was a lovely roundish Barbadian with an open smiling face. She set to work on me with hot and cold compresses, oils, ultraviolet and vibrators and would leave me while the ion machines did their work. I left two hours later hardly able to move my limbs but with a wonderful warm feeling. Not only had she studied physiotherapy at a high level but she was also an expert in psychology and the relationship between the mind and body. She invited me to return an hour before the last match against Martinique the following afternoon. I apprehensively agreed and was there on time. She massaged the parts of my back to make me fearless, which the Greeks did to each other before battle, and my feet to get the adrenalin flowing. I left in a totally different state from the night before, as high as a kite, and ran round the pitch like a spring chicken; it took me three days to come down, which was great for the end of tournament parties. We played our last match against Martinique and won. If Barbados beat Trinidad the following day we'd be Caribbean Champions—they did, so we were. An unexpected bonus was that I came runner up for the most congenial and affable player on and off the field.

Barbados was much cleaner than Jamaica, and I was amazed how organised and friendly Bridgetown was. Considering it was a major port, I would have expected the bars and surrounding area to have been rougher.

The last day we went on the Jolly Roger, a fun boat which lavished us with rum punch, an excellent BBQ and snorkelling. We disembarked very happy. Alan Jones came with us; because of his car accident he was short of funds, and I subbed him through the trip when he thought he wasn't able to afford to accompany us.

Jolly Roger

Tie from Hieve

Dive

It was a lively flight back to Palisadoes, Norman Manley International Airport, and the TV cameras were there to welcome us home with the large trophy we had won.

I wrote from Jamaica to thank the therapist for the amazing work she did on my body. She sent back that she was delighted to receive my letter as it reminded her of the story of the ten lepers and that she'd massaged international tennis players and knighted people and I was the only one to convey thanks in writing.

RPS definitely thought I should leave the island for a while when he called a staff meeting. There were two hundred in all, and a large number attended, including all of the accounts office. Richard came to me first and asked whether I wanted to attend. I never liked meetings—I prefer action—so he inquired whether I wanted any messages conveying. The accounts office was being used as a café and there was a constant stream of people stopping to drink coffee and chat, both inside and outside. We still weren't on top of the work and there was plenty to be done to get the records straight and up to date, so I asked him to let the staff know that the accounts office wasn't to be used as a café and to give the staff space to get on with their work.

When the accounts team returned you could have cut the atmosphere with a knife; hatred filled the air. RPS had basically said to the general meeting that the accounts staff were no good, leave them alone and let them get on with their work. He had embarrassed my people and hurt their pride, which all but had me in tears.

CENTRAL AMERICA

It wasn't long before I started my travels in Central America. Ten months in Jamaica had been action-packed, full of colour and life experiences; and I'd made many mistakes, especially managing the forty staff I was responsible for, trying to impose the standards of a world-class accountancy firm on Jamaican culture, neglecting their "soon come" mentality.

I was flying out of Montego Bay airport, I checked in, and was passing through emigration when the officer looked in my small leather bag and saw my ratchet knife—ugh. I had to quickly find my baggage, which was about to be loaded on the plane and put it in my cardboard box! A true Jamaican way of travelling, as I thought I'd be putting all my gear into the saddlebags of my motorbike. I returned to customs, who emptied the light red rucksack I was taking on board, only to find Dad's Scandinavian knife—back to my cardboard box, back through customs, only to hear over the tannoy: "Would Mr Hill please check the Air Jamaica counter?" Back through customs to Air Jamaica only to find it was a false alarm, so back to customs and eventually onto the airplane and off to Miami, where I overnighted before continuing to Austin, Texas, to buy a BMW. I rode several 900cc bikes, chose the one I liked, arranged for different handlebars and panniers to be added, agreed a good price then tried to get "full insurance", only to be offered complete insurance without collision and theft! I couldn't risk riding through Central America with the chance of being knocked on the head and waking up to find no bike, or chaining it to a tree and discovering the tree had been sawn down and the bike driven off. I had been warned about atrocious driving in Mexico.

I spent an exciting few days in Austin thanks to various introductions from Roger Mill, who had stayed at Club Caribbean and I'd played tennis with a few times; he ran a head shop in the mall. When the purchase of the BMW fell through, he lent me his Honda 450 for a day, which I rode round the enormous Lake Travis; what a remarkably kind thing to have done. It was a sunny day with clear blue skies when I headed into the rolling hills, enjoying the scenic views and burning some rubber. I stopped for something to eat and a drink in a bar on a quiet road, which turned out to be full of rednecks. I was uneasy about the looks I received and could only reflect on Peter Fonda and Dennis Hopper being badly beaten up in *Easy Rider*. I was mightily relieved Roger's bike was still waiting for me in one piece when I stepped into the bright sunlight.

I left Austin, a great city, at 7:15 a.m., and I was in Brownsville by 10:30, having changed planes in Houston, a vast modern airport with its own internal rail system. I crossed the border in Brownsville and had only to wait forty-five minutes to catch a bus to Monterrey. In Matamoros, amongst the relative squalor and hundreds of Mexicans at the bus station, I wondered what the hell I was doing not flying direct and staying in comfort in good hotels around Mexico. I was tired, my Spanish unwound, and soon I was on the bus to Monterrey and managed to sleep for a good part of the four-hour journey. The bus was clean and travelled quickly along good roads—how fast I don't know, as the speedo was bust! In Monterrey I took a cab to the station where the night express for Mexico City was leaving in half an hour at 6:00 p.m., arriving at 9:00 a.m. the following morning. The $25 ticket included a private sleeping compartment, which was comfortable, all facilities appearing from the walls as you pressed various levers. There was also a restaurant and bar in the end coach that had a table with armchairs and windows providing all-round vision over the rugged countryside. The train was quick and relaxing, far cleaner than any British Rail train I've been on.

I woke as we were travelling at four thousand feet. It was cold and misty outside, and the temperature dropped as we approached Mexico City. The sun began to break through, and as I was wearing my Frye boots, at least my feet would keep warm!

The train arrived in Mexico City (DF) on time, no one robbed me, no one shot me—a good start. My first plan of action was to phone Helen Jones Perrot Mandri, the daughter of a neighbouring rector from long ago back in Wales—no ring, no ring—so I decided I should take a taxi. *Cincuenta* (fifty) pesos, the driver said. No, *cuarenta* (forty), I said, a miscalculation by me, so off we set at a rapid pace, missing cars, lorries, buses and pedestrians by millimetres with no apparent alarm—the judgement was excellent. The taxi driver didn't know "cerro de los numeros", the address, so we asked at the *correo* (Post Office) in the area. An old boy told us the direction and we set off again and saw hundreds of cerros, but not cerro. After half an hour, we were back at the correo, only to find it was not Numeros but Munecos. I had given the list of addresses to the secretary at Club Caribbean to type and failed to check the spelling. After another quarter hour, I had more than my money's worth by the time we arrived. Seeing me as a tourist, the taxi driver made out that his meter didn't work and agreed a separate price, for which he was sorry! However, there was no reply from the doorbell. I hammered again; no reply. Just before we left, the taxi driver nearly knocked the door down, and two maids came rushing. The electricity was off owing to a breakdown, so the telephone was out of order too. I decided to wait for Helen to return; the sun was shining and it was just like a beautiful spring day, as the weather continued to be. I lay back in a reclining chair in the garden and started reading about Aztecs and Mayans. Helen arrived quite soon after with an astonished look on her face, which broke into a welcome smile after we introduced ourselves. We had never met in Wales because of the difference in our ages, although I knew her parents well as our families lived in neighbouring Rectories. In fact, her mother and father had been visiting us at Shotton Vicarage when the devastating earthquake happened in Agadir, Morocco, where Helen was travelling with one of David Spalding's sisters.

Helen had seen my rucksack in the hall and my seven league boots but didn't know who had arrived, as my letter was to take six more days to get there. We had lunch and chatted about Wales, then took off as she was desperate to show me Mexico! I saw the fantastic university library, covered on each side in bright, colourful mosaics depicting the story of

Tenochtitlan and the rise of Mexico City. Then to a beautiful hacienda in the city, San Angel, a restaurant with lovely gardens, flowers and an open design based around courtyards and balconies, then to a convent/church. Very impressive, passing narrow cobbled streets and lovely little squares, mostly stone-walled with many fountains. The areas we passed through were clean and there were beautiful flowers everywhere—I have never seen so many flowers, growing, being sold on the side of the road, in bouquets and multitudinous flower markets; the scent could be picked up from a distance away. Afterwards, we went to collect her children—Alex, who was six, and Xavier, three, both full of life and abounding in character. Pepe, her husband was in Santo Domingo chairing a naval symposium.

Helen made it her project to show me more of Mexico City and its environs, although she had numerous other things to keep her busy, including college courses and her children, and not surprisingly, there was a close interest in my travelling with John Dickin in South America the previous year—I hoped they'd all come to Jamaica so I could repay their wonderful hospitality.

As soon as the sun went down, it became extremely cold and I piled on more clothes with marginal results. It was not much below sixty degrees, but it felt like minus sixty to me and my thin Jamaican blood.

That evening, Helen had been invited to a friend's for dinner and I was kindly asked along as well. It was a lively dinner party—eight or so people—and it was interesting to be in a Mexican home amongst natives! My Spanish ground slowly; however, several spoke some English and a good time was had by all.

Afterwards, inspired by the cold no doubt, we made off with friends from the party to Garibaldi Square, where life goes on all night in true Mexican style. We took a table in one of the bodegas and I was introduced to tequila in proper fashion. Each bodega had its own mariachi band, a group of six to twelve musicians dressed in black, loaded with silver buttons, who serenaded each table. There were vendors selling beautiful bunches of roses to buy for lady friends. With true Mexicans at our table contributing to the ambiance and joining in the songs with great gusto, we had a fantastic time and sampled some local Mexican dishes, including guacamole, which I love.

Afterwards we hit the square itself, which was swarming with all kinds of people and many bands of mariachis, skilful musicians whose instruments comprised large and small guitars, trumpets, horns and the small Mexican harp, which Helen was learning. They generated excellent music, and although I couldn't understand many of the lyrics, they were mainly either happy or sad love stories. They made songs up on the spur of the moment about the people present, and we had several of them serenade us. The atmosphere was vibrant, filled with music and people in various stages of sobriety, or rather inebriation. We heard the next day that one of the fellows we left there arrived home long after dawn.

For some reason, Helen asked me to drive; she couldn't have been more drunk than me. We were travelling on the Periferico when a police motorcyclist pulled us over. I stopped in the outside lane, which was just like stopping in the outside lane of the M25. He became aggressive, asked for my driver's licence, which I didn't have with me, and threatened to lock me up for seventy-two hours. All this was taking place in Spanish and I kept schtum, pretending I understood nothing of what was being said. However, because of my dark complexion and black curly hair, he believed I was Mexican and tall blonde Helen was the visitor. When he said "*carcel por tres dias*", I replied "*momento*" and he was sure I had been having him on. Ugh!

He took Helen's licence and the documents for the car and told us to follow him to the delegacion, a jail, and took off at tremendous speed, losing us, so we made our own way to the lockup, which stank and from which groans were emanating. We were told an officer had no right to stop us on that road so late to avoid people being robbed by bandits and he shouldn't have been riding at that time, and if he didn't turn up within half an hour we should make a protest to the British Embassy and file a suit of robbery against him. We hadn't expected this, and in our state of shock we didn't have his number. Not surprisingly, no one turned up, so after an hour in the police station, we left for home. I hadn't been in Mexico City twenty-four hours!

I woke up Saturday thinking that Mexico City was certainly a place of action. Later that day, we took off for Tepoztlan, a small town about an hour outside the city. A beautiful journey through the mountains, which were lined with trees and astonishingly green. By that time I was getting used to Mexican driving, which was on a close level with that in Jamaica except they were more aggressive. Along the flat, winding open roads I had some regrets I wasn't riding a motorbike. We soon arrived at Helen's friend's house, which was a beautiful country cottage sleeping twenty-plus people with an outside swimming pool! Stunningly laid out with rooms decorated with Mexican paintings, lovely heavy Mexican furniture and apposite blankets and cushions. The other family staying had lots of kids, so I lay in a hammock to have a little peace and quiet and read more about the Mayans. That evening, I went to the local town to a hop! People were dancing in the streets to Mexican rock bands. I met a fraulein and joined in the revelry. Later that night when driving home, I turned out of a country lane and was immediately confronted by a masked man on a huge horse. My heart fluttered as I saw two shining metal tubes on either side of his flank. Needless to say I hit the gas and was relieved not to have bullets zinging about me. I later realised the guy was an ordinary worker making his way very early in the dark, and the silver barrels turned out to be milk churns.

Later on Sunday, we set out for Taxco via Cuernavaca. Once again, an interesting journey, dodging in and out of the traffic screaming down to Acapulco. Towards Taxco the roads became narrow and winding, with countryside much like the Berwyns. The road surfaces were always good and I felt the distance between me and the edge was always far greater than it had been in the mountains of Peru. Taxco was a beautiful town set amongst the hills. I walked around the markets and spent time in the silver shops; I hadn't seen so much silver work in such a small place before. The streets were narrow and cobbled and the houses attractive. In Taxco we battled with another puncture, which was giving me good practice at changing tyres.

The cathedral was ultra-baroque, packed with different images and artwork. It would have been better if the adornments had been spread amongst ten or more churches.

On the way back to Mexico City, we were caught up in the Sunday night traffic from Acapulco and the south—incredible, all battling to gain three or four positions further up the grid. Thousands of cars were making their way home, and it was amazing we only saw one crash.

Monday, we tried to trace the car documents which had been stolen early Saturday morning on the Periferico. The Embassy was no use, so off to the Transito, the Traffic Police. They were surprisingly cooperative and didn't make us wait long to establish whether there was something important to be investigated, which was a huge relief. After seeing various people, we were told they couldn't trace the guy who had stopped us and recommended we go to the motorbike battalion to see if we could recognise his picture. Off we went, and as we drew near the castle gates, we were approached by unfriendly looking Mexicans in battle dress wielding machine guns; there were few military with guns on the streets in Mexico City, unlike La Paz, Lima and Bogota. We phoned the head of the division whose name we'd been given in the Transito to gain admission. Within minutes, a fully uniformed motorcyclist arrived on his 1200 Harley Davidson to escort our car to be parked then drove ahead of us at walking pace through the barracks. We felt very important, with many eyes gazing upon us wondering why we were there and, even more to the point, how on earth a tall blonde Welsh lady had been given a police escort together with me, wearing seven league boots with three-inch heels; I was a good foot taller than the average guy around. We were shown into the office of the head of the battalion, who was very understanding and let flow with his Latin charm upon the poor maiden in distress. He produced several huge bound ledgers with pictures of all the motorbike police in the city, which we steadily worked through to try and identify whether the man on the bike who robbed us was an off-duty policeman; no success. With no way of retrieving the car documents and Helen's driving licence, we stopped feeling important; however, Helen had made a good connection in case of further disasters with the police. I chatted to the boss about motorbikes and was impressed to discover he had been the world motorbike acrobatic champion and performed at the opening of the Olympic Games. Helen had to set about the costly and time-consuming task of obtaining duplicate papers.

We went to the Ciudadela, a market of artists, which was disappointing as much was modern and more like Woolworths than the market we were expecting. We passed another beautiful flower market on our way to San Juan Market. The quality was much better, but there was still a lot of trash and it was so different from the old Peruvian markets I'd visited. It was located in a modern building and appeared far too clean and devoid of character, but there were beautiful ponchos, quality leather work and lots of rings, which I tried but came to the conclusion that my hands were not designed to bear finery.

That evening we returned the key of the house we had visited in Tepoztlan to Bob and Nina who had the most beautiful home in the city. The living room could well have been taken from a Norman castle; it was huge, with a high ceiling and wonderful artefacts. They were both well versed in Mexican art, archaeology and anthropology; it was a wonderful evening. Bob was a photographer and had worked on the Cancun project on the Caribbean coast of Mexico and gave me names of people involved in the venture I could meet. The hotel/tourist project was on a grand scale with a tremendous amount of planning and forward ideas. Richard Salm and David Rickham had carried out a survey there as consultants to see whether their client should open a hotel, so I could be returning to Jamaica with new ideas abounding. I visited the Museum of Anthropology—wonderfully interesting with excellent replica models of various Mayan sites, many images and carvings, but most impressive were the stone carvings, especially the intricate Mayan Calendar, which was more accurate than our twelve-month calendar. They were advanced in astronomy and astrology, which governed their lives. However, they didn't seem to be as advanced in surgery, brain operations in particular, as the Incas.

I tried to get back to the house in the south but there were no taxis and I spent ages trying to find out how to get there; when they were around, VW Beetles with the front passenger seat removed were often used as taxis. I had to resort to the Metro system, which I found hugely complicated, to cross the city, but it was well worth it in the end. That evening Pepe returned, without the contract, only to learn about Helen's tales of woe; the telephone being cut off with the electricity, the car headlights stolen and the car documents being taken. When Pepe was away, there was always a long series of tragedies. Pepe was a great guy, highly intelligent, with a deep knowledge of the Mayans and other tribes and was genned up on the new discoveries continually taking place that were turning upside down the existing opinions about the dates and importance of ruling tribes. He was a naval architect and designed the raft that followed the *Ra II* across the Atlantic, which Genoves captained. We had the most amazing discussions about the various religions and philosophers of all ages.

I went to the Guatemalan Embassy to get a visa, and luckily there was no military trouble despite the Belize situation. I was told I wouldn't have a problem crossing the border from Belize into Guatemala to visit the ruins at Tikal. I decided to phone the British Embassy before leaving to make sure I wouldn't be passing through a war zone. I visited the Zocolo, the main square containing the cathedral and palaces; spacious and beautiful. The cathedral was under repair inside so I didn't see much of it, but I went into one of the palaces. Impressive stone buildings, high arches and murals with Latin American art in strikingly bright colours. Stone was used widely for all buildings, houses and walls with stunning effect. While I was in the square, there were hundreds of school children with brightly striped umbrellas doing formation dances in readiness for the 20 November Revolution commemoration. The music was modern and they created wonderful designs with the spinning, swinging umbrellas. Then onto the Casa de Azulejos, a wonderful tiled house with outside walls covered in blue, lightly patterned tiles, fairly old, and inside were shops and a restaurant, again with high arches, beautiful paintings and murals. Next through a park to Palacio de Bellas Artes, a large exhibition building showing modern paintings and a British design exhibition, not very impressive.

I returned that night with Lucia, a Chilean girlfriend of Helen's, to watch the Ballet Folklorico, a splendid show incorporating pre-Columbian dances and music. The colour, sound, rhythm and music were fantastic, a variety of instruments being used for different dances, including guitars, drums, tambourines, brass and wind instruments, beautiful flutes and reeds, also marimbas, large wooden xylophones. There were post-Columbian dances displaying colourful costumes and bright music. Twenty-five hundred years before Columbus set foot in what Europe ironically calls the New World, five hundred years before the birth of Greece's Golden Age, Mesoamerica's first great civilisation was flourishing on the coast of the Gulf of Mexico. It was a splendid show, and I hadn't ever enjoyed watching dancing so much. The Deer Dance made an impression that would stay with me for decades.

Afterwards we went to a Pena "El Condor Paso", which was a type of pub where they played folk music. When we arrived there was a group with two guitars, drums and a flute playing Latin American songs; the music in general was far happier than the melancholy music in the Peruvian Andes. The flute produced a beautiful sound, which made me think I should learn how to play. The second group included the Veracruz Mexican harp, guitar and drums; again beautiful music. The third was a funny chap accompanied by a guitarist; much of the humour went over my head but the audience was often in uproar—possibly the Mexican equivalent of naughty rugby songs.

My days were full of interest and excitement.

I went with all the family Mandri to the great pyramids of the sun and moon at Teotihuacan in the north of the city. Temples have been excavated displaying beautiful murals and wall paintings in the most vivid colours. There are many still standing built of magnificent stone, although the stonework is nowhere near the quality of that around Cusco and the buildings are a different style, probably from a much later period though not declared as such by the archaeologists. The temples were beautiful with spacious courtyards. We went down the "Walk of the Dead", so called because any plebeian who walked that way was about to be sacrificed to the gods, not "pour encourager les autres" but to encourage rain to fall and the crops to grow.

I climbed the pyramid of the sun, a most impressive structure in an excellent state of repair and the steep steps in good condition. From the top there was a brilliant view of the vast area the city covered, many square miles. After descending, we walked back along the Walk of the Dead towards the pyramid of the moon. The passageway was wide with temples along each side, and the pyramid appeared most impressive at the end of the causeway, a beautiful sight. An intricate design with various sections framing the pyramid in wonderful symmetry most pleasing to the eye, especially when looked at with the great area/square below it. I have never seen any structure/complex of buildings so grand and with such an air of spaciousness; a wondrous spectacle built by man for the gods.

We had a delightful Mexican lunch in a cave nearby and continued to the temple of Quetzalcoatl, a fantastically spacious complex with the main temple in the centre and various others around the edge of the massive square. Compared to its awe-inspiring grandeur and splendour, Rome was ten miles behind. The main temple was still being excavated, or rather the older temples which had been constructed every fifty-two years, the time span of the short calendar they used; each temple was rebuilt over the existing one. The discovery of new temples completely shattered many of the prevailing theories about the history of these amazing peoples. I returned enriched from our day at the pyramids, my first taste of what I hoped to see, or rather what I thought I would not see at Palenque, Chichenitza, Uxmal and Tikal. These Mayan "settlements" I was sure would be impressive, but not compare to the style at Teotihuacan.

We visited Chapultapec Park together, parts of which were the public estate of Montezuma, a vast area of beautiful trees, lakes, flowers and yet more fountains. Coincidentally, this was on the day the newspapers reported General Franco of Spain's death, 20 November 1975.

San Angel Sabado market was full of all kinds of crafts and the most beautiful works of art in silver, leather, gold, wood and calico. I could have spent a fortune but settled for a couple of dollars as my carrying space was limited and I was likely to be clambering on and off buses in the next couple of weeks.

I went with Pepe to the Bellas Artes for a concert, Orquesta Sinfonica Del Estado De Mexico, with Director Enrique Batiz playing Bartok; a Japanese lady, Yuriko Kuronuma, was the soloist. The concert was outstanding and was the first I'd attended for two years. I also saw a very poor first division football match at the fantastic Aztec Stadium, capacity 100,000; Wrexham could have beaten either of these less-than-mediocre first division sides watched by a crowd of five hundred at the most. It wasn't difficult to imagine how remarkable the atmosphere would have been with a packed stadium for the Football World Cup or recent Panama Games.

In the afternoon I went with the Mandris to Xochimilco—what an amazing place—the last remnants of a vast water transport system built by the Aztecs. There were all sizes of colourful, gondola-like boats, highly decorated. Families of twenty-plus would take a boat and be punted down the river. Although there were a fair number of minor bumps, it was amazing, it didn't look like the Suez Canal after it had been bombarded a few years ago. As well as the passenger boats, there was a large market going on, with food cooked by a big fat Mama in a small narrow canoe. There were beautiful displays of flowers and wonderful bouquets which were bought by the men enticed by offering them to the lady; needless to say, some of the more wicked younger punters would occasionally try to pincer these Mamas and try to cause them distress. Clothes of all kinds were being sold, but perhaps most charming were the boatloads of musicians who would be punted around until a song was requested, then they would latch themselves broadside and let rip with trumpets, drums, harp, violins, bass and all sorts, dressed in their beautiful black Mariachi uniforms and, of course, grand sombreros. There were boats with marimba, and we had a tremendously enjoyable couple of hours.

That evening, Helen held a dinner party with Barbara, who had been at Tepoztlan, and her husband Ricardo; Nina and Bob, who owned the house; and a guy from New York who that day had a full-page colour article in a Mexico City periodical about him and his native masks; apparently he designed the Mexico Metro system. We had great fun.

Every day, Helen and Pepe provided different kinds of the most fantastic food: spicy, very tasty, but not as hot as Indian food can be. They used a lot of mild chilies; there are hundreds of different varieties, many of which appear in mole, an exceptional Mexican dish prepared by one of the maids as a treat for a special visitor. It looked black, had the consistency of thick porridge and tasted absolutely delightful. It contained chicken, banana, avocado, rice and about twenty other different ingredients, including bread, and took more than a day to prepare. The final flavour was a most beautiful fusion with no recognisable individual flavour. That was a huge dish, and we had it with various barbeques and breakfast for three days.

The next day, I ordered a beautiful leather waistcoat which was too good a deal to miss, and Helen was hoping to carry it home to Gresford as they needed more than twenty-four hours to make it. After a quick glance round a couple of markets and another lovely lunch, I said goodbye to Helen and the kids, then Pepe and I went to visit a church and museum of colonial art outside the city, forgetting it was Monday when all museums were closed. The church, one of the best examples of Baroque in the West, now part of the museum, was also closed. However, the setting in the hills was beautiful and we saw part of the rehearsal for one of the Christmas plays, humorous with singing; they are performed all over Mexico and usually depict Angel Gabriel and company fighting the bad angels—a nice tradition. Then to the station to catch the 8:00 p.m. train to Palenque. I had my little sleeper fully fitted out again but unfortunately this time no observation carriage. After a cold beer, I tried to sleep. It was difficult as we left Mexico City because we must have been descending steep mountains; the sleeper was the last carriage and I seemed to be leaving my mattress three feet below me on occasions.

The hospitality given to me by Helen and Pepe, the warmest, kindest and most interesting of people, was overwhelming, and they couldn't have done anything else to make my time in Mexico City any more enjoyable.

In the morning I awoke to sunshine and wild countryside, open and dry, not quite a jungle but prolific. As there was no observation car, I took up a position as rear gunner on the platform at the back of the last carriage, overlooking the railway tracks. We arrived in Palenque a mere one hour late, which was not bad for a twenty-four hour journey and the possible delays I was expecting. En route, I met interesting people— Margaret Atwood and Graeme Gibson, two Canadian writers—so the journey flew by. At the front of the train in regular carriages, food was being sold as well as on the platforms of the stations by people walking up and down the train; it wasn't as "local" as the train from Cusco to Machu Picchu.

In Palenque, I stayed at La Canada, a group of huts and restaurants—not up to the standard of Club Caribbean but ideal none the less. Most fortunately, they turned out to be built and owned by the person Helen and Pepe had advised me to get in touch with; unfortunately, he was out of town. I got up early next morning and took off to the ruins. Once more, magnificent buildings. I roamed around the "palace", admired some of the stuccos, beautiful figures, some with Mongolian features, and Moroccan arches. They used arches extensively, and much of the "palacio" was made up of doubled cloisters surrounded by grass quadrangles. It's likely that the walls were completely coloured red and blue; they were in good condition. There was a central tower, almost certainly for the thinkers and astronomers. I climbed the most impressive temple, the Pyramid of the Inscriptions, then walked down to the sarcophagus of the Jade King/Priest, which had only been discovered within the last thirty years. An amazing tomb and pyramid to house Pakal, the first leader of the Acropolis of Palenque. There was a massive stone over the tomb with beautiful inscriptions and carvings, and there were many stuccos around the edge of the sarcophagus. The stone is one Eric Van Daniken claims resembles an astronaut, which is clearly recognisable. The buildings in Palenque had tremendous warmth and feeling and were friendly compared to the severity of Teotihuacan. The setting added incredible atmosphere, being on the edge and partly contained in a rainforest with thick green vegetation and set on the side of a hill overlooking miles of open plains, a little like Marford overlooking Cheshire.

It was when I was climbing the hundreds of steps to the top of the Temple of the Inscriptions and chatting to one of the site guards that he spotted Moises Morales, Mr Palenque, who knew more about those ruins than anyone else in the world and had lived there for the last twelve years, having given up government work. He had been with the governor of the state and had flown back especially to take a group of Americans around. I ran all the way back down then up the palace steps and introduced myself. He invited me to accompany him as he acted as a guide to the Americans. He pointed out that what had been written about Palenque up to then was ninety per cent false. His narrative was fascinating and gave an insight into the people through the buildings and surroundings, including the clothing the priests and rulers would have worn. I spent the rest of the day wandering around the temples and ruins, a peaceful place, and thanks to Mr Palenque's guidance, imagining what the Mayans who lived there were like, visualising the ceremonies they performed; maybe no human sacrifice, considering the calm ambiance.

I spent the evening listening to Moises Morales with Maria, a psychiatrist from San Antonio, a good friend of his. Then came my second encounter with Mexican police. The captain of the police force in the area joined us as his uncle was staying there. By this time, Moises had left, and I learnt this man was a pig of the first order and hideously brutal. Before he joined us, he had been playing with his machine gun outside, not firing but quite drunk, and after a few more drinks, he started to take offence at our presence, thinking that every time we laughed we were mocking him; this wasn't quite true. He called his bodyguard to the edge of the bar, and after a while I realised—later than the others, poor simple me—that the situation was hot. Graeme had had a gun pointed at the end of his nose in Oaxaca some years previously. We made an opportune exit through the door and away—could have been nasty.

Margaret Atwood

Moises Morales

The next morning Maria, Peggy Atwood, Graeme and I set off early to the ruins with Moises. Some way in front, he paced up and down the hedge and beckoned us to follow through a thick mass of jungle, which soon opened up. Inside, the rainforest was clear as little light could penetrate through the massive vegetation and other foliage at the roof of the jungle. He led us on a two-to-three-hour hike and pointed out many pyramids and tombs which were as yet uncovered, and this was part of his theory that Palenque was not just a few temples but a massive acropolis with huge burial grounds. He related a myriad of stories, funny and real, which showed him to be a charming person with much feeling; I was delighted and honoured that I was able spend so much time with him.

One of his tales was about Jacqueline Kennedy, the former president's wife, and leading her through the woods a few months earlier. He thought she had very human qualities and was most pleasant during the days he was with her and Gil; Moises was taking us to the same streams and waterfalls. We were able to see a different aspect of the people and temples of Palenque through Moises' eyes, rather than just looking at the buildings and stones, which were in themselves beautifully designed. Grey stone and Dutch barn-shaped roofs, often with a lot of decorative weight on top to assist the centre of gravity, and the thin walls supporting heavy false arches. The structures had withstood centuries of the destroying hand of time.

Palenque was the most beautiful place I'd visited so far. What amazed me, but in fact was obvious when pointed out, was that the astronomers only needed narrow slits a couple of feet deep to trace the stars through the heavens, as once they knew the trajectory they would pick them up later, descending the other side.

I was very fortunate to be travelling in November/December and not July/August when the temperatures and humidity would have been ghastly hot and lots of Americans would have been on their school break—there were few tourists anywhere.

It was in the Mayan ruins of Palenque that I received the inspiration that would make so much of my life in business rewarding and enjoyable, remembering the main reason for this trip was that I had screwed up badly regarding the attitude I had taken with staff. I had no previous experience managing numbers of people, only a few trainee accountants, and most neglectfully I hadn't spent time contemplating what made the happy, sensitive, fun-loving Jamaicans tick. I remembered the wise words of Francis Glyn Jones when we were talking about the offer of a partnership I received from a Wrexham firm of chartered accountants before I went travelling, when he said, "You are fortunate if you can make your mistakes abroad." I decided that instead of expecting everything to be right and on time and getting upset when it invariably wasn't, I would expect that things would be wrong and work with staff to ensure things were right going forwards.

From Palenque I took the train to Merida. I walked down to the end of the train and clambered up to the restaurant car from the track as there were no steps at the sleeper end. After a while I found the chief in charge of sleeping cars and was led to a cabinet I had travelled in before; however, I had almost no cash, only travellers cheques, and these he would only change at a very low rate against the US dollar. We then went back to the other carriages and argued about changing money. Finally I gave him all the money I had, 140 pesos, and he made up the difference of five pesos. Big deal, as I'm sure the 140 went straight into his pocket. The bunk wasn't too bad as the upper one was a large steel panel, and amidst the occasional snore I soon got to sleep and woke up with just two hours of the journey remaining. Hungry and with not one peso, I went back to the restaurant car and the porter from the night before. By this time he must have been feeling sorry for me, as I managed to coax a small breakfast out of him. I couldn't borrow any money from the companions I'd met at the station as they were in first class, i.e. were going to try and sleep sitting in regular chairs. On the run into Merida I met a young English couple who kindly said they'd post a letter to my folks in Gresford when they got back to Miami, which thankfully they did.

After finding what turned out to be a seedy hotel, I went to the bus station to arrange my trip to Uxmal and further journey on to Chichen Itza, and I met a forlorn girl who had been working in the British Virgin Isles for the last eighteen months and had also landed in Merida that day, which was very different from the Caribbean Islands. She came from Pontypool and was in St Mary's College the same time as I was in Bangor Uni, so we travelled together to Uxmal on an amazingly funky bus, which I don't think Tommy Morris of Llanfyllin would have been proud to own. An hour late and carrying a mechanic on board, we set off on the one-hour trip! The driver had great difficulty finding a gear and after forty minutes could find none at all. The mechanic got out and between them they eventually engineered a couple of gears and we arrived at the site at 7:45, two hours late. Luckily there was a special showing of the Luz y Sonidos for a number of Mexican school kids. The show was most impressive, set in the central quadrangle of the ruins, and incorporated the surrounding pyramids. The commentary was in Spanish and told of the Mayan city of Uxmal, their daily lives, praying to the gods, harvesting, teaching by the great Chacmool and, most importantly, sacrifices to Chaac, the god of rain. There was no maize, no crops, and that's possibly one of the reasons why the ruins in that area had been deserted. The lighting effects were colourful and impressive, highlighting different temples and characters/gods at different times. They portrayed the great snake of knowledge, Quetzalcoatl, and played voices, music and singing as the processions crossed the temples—it was excellent. Although I didn't see many of the fine sculptures, I was happy to leave Uxmal as a fantasy world with my own interpretations of the Mayans.

Earlier that day, I had my rucksack fixed, the loops on one side had pulled away, and I also bought a hammock. The next day, I took it easy and wandered round the cathedral, the mediocre anthropological museum, an interesting national monument, then spent time in the pleasant Zocola. Merida was clean with narrow streets; however, it was modernish and not that interesting compared to what I had been seeing.

I spent the afternoon with Mr Dutton, the consul, and his wife in their home; not formal, with white pillars and servants thronging around, rather like a vicarage kitchen with many books and the consul's electronic equipment everywhere—very homely. A most interesting afternoon; he was from South Wales and had lived in Mexico for many years. His wife did much of the talking!

He was knowledgeable about Mayan ruins and was able to give me several interpretations and theories about the local sites and their societies. We got into religion, and they were keen advocates of the Inner White Temple. They advised me that the problems in Belize could blow up; however, the other day when Mr Dutton was there, it had been peaceful. I decided I would go to Tikal via Cancun and cross the border from Belize rather than flying to Guatemala City first.

On the Sunday I caught the bus to Chichen Itza, noble Mayan and Toltec ruins and pyramids. There were many shrines to the gods, different from the impressive but "lived in" buildings in Palenque. The ball court was fascinating, where games were apparently played to determine military or government action, rather like interpreting chicken's entrails, but with the losers most likely losing their lives and the belongings going to the winners and their supporters. All around Chichen there were remarkable effects from echoing stones placed in various parts of the buildings and pyramids, most likely to make the voices of the leaders sound more powerful when speaking publicly and help raise morale. Though magnificent in many ways and more splendid than ruins in Peru, these had less of the mysticism and feeling of Machu Picchu and felt less divinely inspired. Once again, they used false arches and headstones in Chichen.

That afternoon I proceeded to Puerto Juarez, and as a boat was about to leave, I couldn't resist taking the trip to Isla Mujeres—a beautiful crossing in the setting sun, to a small island with a couple of lovely beaches, reefs and clear water. I spent the night in my hammock, which turned out to be extremely comfortable, strung up from beams and pole sections amongst several others in a series of sheds: incredible value for $1 a night, and a great place to stay on an otherwise very expensive island.

The next day I tried to contact Jorge Gibson and Sergio Ortiz, executives of Fornatur, a Mexican Government development corporation for Cancun and another project in Puerto Vallarta, which would eventually turn Cancun into another Miami Beach; they were friends of Bob, the photographer from Mexico City. No success as there was difficulty with phones, so I left the islands.

After a brief chat, I set out on a Honda 50cc to inspect the Cancun properties, pining for my BMW on the good roads and comfortable heat. The project was about a third complete and there were one or two very nice hotels of the fifteen that were finished, and workmen were constructing others next door. The guests I spoke to complained that the food wasn't good and there was a lack of things to do. The sea there wasn't the best for diving, unlike the beautiful Cozumel waters.

That evening I caught the bus to Chetumal, a four-hour trip at night, and I managed to sleep part of the way. Another seedy hotel in Chetumal, and I was very glad I had my sleeping bag to keep me away from the sheets. I survived the night—in fact, for a seemingly filthy city it had a pleasant waterfront—and I left at 10:00 a.m. that morning for Belize.

Mexico was a most enjoyable experience: fascinating ruins, dramatically changing topography and peoples for the most part extremely pleasant and helpful, not living in the poverty I'd expected, but nevertheless they didn't appear happy and were possibly oppressed by the government, local officials and police! Their history was turbulent and very much in the shadow of the United States. The country is still developing and possibly confusing for a lot of the Indians/peasants who are used to a simple agricultural life. There are constant rumours about the rise of communism and shipments of arms into the country, which no doubt is not pleasing the big eye of the CIA. It wasn't a country where I'd like to have lived. The free spirit of the Latin Americans combined with their boisterousness meant Mexico City had a fantastic amount to offer in the way of culture, interest and people, and the kindliness and hospitality of Helen, Pepe and their friends was exceptional.

Only one hour to the border, easily out of Mexico but very stubbornly into Belize, and with only $50 on me they turned their noses up in front of everyone to show they were the most important people at the Customs Post. All rucksacks had to be emptied, not for inspection but for what appeared to be only inconvenience. The four and a half hour bus journey to Belize City was fascinating: through heavy vegetation, woods, rice and sugar fields, tidy little villages with houses on stilts beautifully constructed with walls cut from planks of wood. The road was good for the most part, and we frequently passed rivers and water. Halfway, a black guy who claimed to have gained an English degree in months and was about to qualify as a doctor joined me. He was interesting company and let fly with his political views and anti-American feelings. Much exaggerated, but maybe the greenback was getting settled in here as the politics in Belize was to the left.

Belize City was lovely: neat, tidy, wooden colonial buildings, many balconies, canals and rivers running through, with plenty of fish and a safe distance above the water line and crystal clear waters compared to Venice! The people, mainly black, were friendly with a desire to be helpful, intermingled with a few who wanted to rip you off. There was a calm, easy and orderly feeling in the city, possibly like Kingston one hundred years before. I wandered around the fruit, vegetable and fish market and into the bars to sample the local food and rum. My two-day-old cold was clearing. Good music was emanating from several haunts although there weren't many people around. I met interesting people, including George Gapp, a sculptor, and Joseph Fitzroy, a Commonwealth boxer. There was the possibility of a football match followed by a piano concert that night, then hopefully across the border to Guatemala the next day, *Si Dios lo quiere*. Warm, light rain was falling, and there was a feeling of Christmas approaching.

In the afternoon, I wandered over to George Gapp's, and he was sleeping in his hammock in a corner of his small workshop. His apprentices showed me his amazing work; his sculptures were beautiful, crafted out of a wood peculiar to Belize—Zerricote, black with creamy streaks flowing through. They also showed me pictures of his exhibitions, including one of a child holding the cross he'd made in commemoration of the Aberfan Disaster in 1966 when a coal tip slid down the rain-saturated mountainside and killed 144 people including 116 school children. George was a wonderfully kind, gentle and humble person, and when he woke we chatted for a couple of hours about many things, including the US, for which we both saw as hopeful and an example to the rest of the world. What!!!!!

We went for a drink in a local bar where we'd met the night before. He'd turned down many opportunities to travel and earn vast sums of money in favour of staying amongst his own people. It was touching to see him with the locals, who gave him their utmost respect.

That night I went to a concert by Francisco Peneau, who played Chopin and works by several other composers. It was good, and fascinating as a study of local sociology. I met the local vicar, Gareth Thomas from Wales, who George Gapp knew well. We sat and chatted outside as the Belize Auditorium, even smaller than the one in Llanfyllin, filled. All the local gentry, black and very much colonial white, attended in their finery, followed finally by the Governor General who arrived in his Land Rover. A great evening, which was preceded by a very good meal in a Chinese restaurant, which are all over Central America.

Thursday I set off on the local bus for Guatemala. It was a good journey with changing topography, beautiful rolling hills and heavy vegetation.

It took about three and a half hours to reach the city of Cayo, the road deteriorating rapidly towards the end of the journey. Time passed quickly as ever, having made good company with two girls from Canada, Heather and Brigette (who was also a Swiss national). At Cayo, we took a taxi to the border Melchar de Mencos, through the Belize customs and on to the Guatemalan, where I was anxious about my British passport. However, they were the most friendly customs officials I have ever come across, laughing and joking, and they didn't even want to look in my luggage. There was a short walk to the local village where we waited half an hour for another local bus to take us to Flores.

We found a hotel by the side of the lake, had a meal which inevitably included frijoles, beans, and a bottle of wine, then the three of us with a French couple set off in a taxi boat across the lake singing "Alouette" and various sea shanties, much to the bewilderment of the driver. He was even more amazed when we asked him to take us straight back as soon as we arrived at the other side. It was a beautiful night with a star-filled sky. The next day we took a transit bus to Tikal, two hours along a rough road, which was well worth any amount of pain getting there.

We stayed in the Jungle Inn owned by the Artiz family. I'd been given the address from a girl who'd stayed at Club Caribbean. We took a tour in the afternoon, led by a rather pompous Indian, but nevertheless an amusing and interesting guide. The ruins were a magnificent experience, set in the jungle amidst the sound of monkeys and many kinds of beautiful birds. It was wonderful to experience Tikal with only a handful of other people, but I thought that might change following the recent *National Geographic* article. The ruins were vaguely similar to those at Palenque, much more lived in than those of Chichen and Uxmal, and resplendent, made of magnificent stone, and the architecture was always beautifully balanced. We wandered through the jungle and ruins for a couple of days and spent time in the museum, which was most enlightening with carvings in stone, pottery and jade. There were carvings in the wooden lintels of the temple doorways.

Three days later, we boarded a very old DC-3 for the flight to Guatemala—I didn't feel up for twenty-four hours on and off buses. The flight was smooth over the hills, rivers and forested mountains, landing through cloud in Guatemala City. That night, I paid $1.50 for three meals and a hotel! Not very clean, but I was too tired to schlep my increasingly heavy luggage through the streets looking for something better. I slept through a Sean Connery/Candice Bergman film about Arabs in North Africa and managed to survive the night. The following morning, a move was made to the Ritz, a lovely little hotel with a pleasant garden where I left my rucksack while I travelled to Atitlan. When we arrived on Sunday, they were celebrating the burning of the devil. At first, I thought my dad was there, because at six o'clock there were of piles of rubbish and litter burning in the streets; Oliver would get rid of rubbish people had appallingly abandoned that way, and I'm sure it was a festival he'd like to have participated in. I'm not quite sure of the significance, but it was quite a spectacle, with lots of noise and *cohetes*, firecrackers, which weren't allowed in Mexico City. We travelled round the markets, much like those in Peru, bought good artefacts, and saw the cathedral and palace. The city was clean and modern, abounding with motorbikes! I sat on a bench in San Salvador and listened to soft music and admired the Christmas decorations.

There was another large celebration on Tuesday, the Conception of Virgin Mary. Amidst clouds of incense, the procession of images trailed out of the cathedral, many small and one large, carried by forty women struggling heavily. The parade went on for several hours, and men carried the large figure back to the cathedral.

We spent a most interesting evening with Joya Hairs, a girl from Jamaica, who was a celebrated archaeologist and photographer who threw a party attended by equally celebrated people including a tea planter. I was able to glean more information about Guatemala and plan the rest of my stay.

Wednesday we went to Antigua, the old capital which had been badly damaged by earthquakes but was still very fine with many colonial buildings, churches and cloisters, a traditional municipality with a small market. We went by bus to San Antonio Aguas Calientes, a small Indian village where you could see the ladies making *tejidos*, textiles—beautiful people—and I left my heart with a five-year-old girl.

We enjoyed a three-course lunch including a bottle of wine and a bottle of champagne for $6.50! The following morning, I bade my amigas a sad farewell as they returned to Canada and I set off for the Thursday market at Chichicastenango. It was a pleasant two and a half hour bus journey through the appropriately named Country of the Eternal Springtime. Rugged mountains, rolling hills, much vegetation and farm crops of wheat and maize... Vaguely like the Alps, Scotland and Wales rolled together, changing continually and with glorious sunshine all day.

The first view of Atitlan was delightful, looking magnificent through the mountain peaks. A change of buses in Los Encuentros, and off down the Pan-American Highway along a very twisty steep road, up and down to Chiche. Beautifully located and the most well-known of all the markets, abounding with tourists, and the Indians quite rightly very much on the make and continually looking for sales. I resisted many temptations and bought little. The materials here were exquisite, the blankets made out of heavy wool; however, the bright designs of reindeer and other animals weren't for me.

The wooden carvings were crude, and I'm sure the original ceremonial masks were beautiful, but these, alas, were cheap replicas. The market was a lot of fun with a jolly atmosphere, and there was an Indian section selling all sorts of vegetables, pots, ropes, and string bags of all sizes. The native dress of the Indians was attractive with different designs for each village. The Mayan Inn was quite something. A colonial building with beautiful gardens, cloisters, elegantly dressed waiters in native costumes and one old guy playing the marimbas in the middle of the lawn: quaint sounds from an original marimba made from gourds. Later that afternoon I saw the player carrying his instrument through the streets. They'd put a sling over their foreheads to carry heavy weights while balancing the extending rope round the middle of the bundle— bags of vegetables, clothes, even fifteen foot planks of wood were carried down the main street by one person who would turn sideways when cars approached; old men and young girls used this method to transport their goods.

Most remarkable was the church, which was a combination of pagan witchcraft ceremonies mingled with those of the Roman Catholic Church: masses of incense, many candles and a vibrant atmosphere.

That afternoon, I went via Los Encuentros and Solola to Panajachel on the side of Lake Atitlan. The short journey from Solola down to the lakeside was fantastic: completely surrounded by volcanoes rising from the blue waters and clear blue sky. That evening, there was the most glorious sunset, but I didn't have my camera with me—ugh! The falling sun went through several enthrallingly beautiful phases, with the mountains and clouds changing colours before disappearing behind a volcano. I was thrown into a room for three with two air hostesses, which may or may not be good luck—no action, sorry Dad! The next day, I went to the market at Solola, which had more Indians and far fewer tourists than Chiche. Lots of colour and *alegria*, and I bought my beautiful boasty white woollen jacket with black finery. The textiles were lovely reds and bold, deep colours.

In the afternoon, I took a boat trip across Lake Atitlan to San Perla. Three boats, which together should have housed one hundred at the most, arrived to carry what appeared to be two hundred people.

We all managed to fit on board, including chickens. I had a place on the rear deck with just enough room to sit over the side. In my boat they were all Indians speaking their native language but pleasantly conversing with me in Spanish from time to time. The trip was amazing and took an hour, around a very large lake which seemed relatively small amongst the volcanoes. We dropped the remaining people at a small village opposite San Perla then continued back with a crew of three and two passengers. The sunset from the boat was delightful; however, not as good as the previous evening. I'd had an excellent dinner with wine for $2—what value! To bed, up at 6 a.m. to take the boat ride to Las Lucas on Saturday, my day of rest. The journey took an hour and was a beautiful ride, getting hotter all the time; the last part of the return trip on the lake the previous night had been very cold after the sun had disappeared. I ate breakfast in the small village of San Lucas then returned to Panajachel, where I wandered around and met some glamorous Parisian girls who looked as if they'd walked straight off the Champs Elysées. Early to bed, suffering slightly from flatulence, after the whole trip had been almost completely free of stomach upsets.

The next morning, I caught the 7:00 bus to Pazun. It was interesting to see the colourful market being set up while waiting for the bus in Panajachel: beautiful, richly embroidered materials—lots of red—plenty of fruit and vegetables and much *alegria*. Heavy weights were being slung from people's heads—possibly that's why they are so small and I appeared such a giant! There weren't many tourists, and altogether it was a massively pleasant experience. I left my luggage in one of the shops with much confidence, as although they bargained hard, they were lovely people. Mass was being broadcast from the church.

I caught the bus and enjoyed a two-hour ride to Guatemala through beautiful countryside, fields full of crops and many volcanoes. I returned to the Ritz to find my luggage in one piece, took a last flip round the market, picked up a letter from Joya Hairs for her parents, ate a Chinese meal then bed. I didn't sleep much, thinking about the fantastic holiday I was so lucky to have experienced! I was sorry it was coming to an end, but in the five weeks I'd seen and experienced masses, met amazing people and was wrapped in thoughts about what was awaiting me in Jamaica, especially the hard work ahead.

I arrived back at Club Caribbean at 6:00 p.m. to a warm welcome from Maisie Lyn on the front desk, RPS and David Rickham—otherwise the hotel was deserted, as it was the night of the staff Christmas party. I was made incredibly happy by so many of the staff coming and welcoming me back with hugs and kisses; it was touching and humbling. I'd been apprehensive about the reception I might receive as I'd left under a cloud, thinking there was plenty of animosity towards me, especially from Harvey, but our relationship was stronger than ever. They were surprised to see me return, as many had thought I'd gone to pastures new; goodness knows the financial comptroller, who I replaced after he was fired, must have been a really bad act. There were many extraordinary benefits to living in Jamaica, particularly Club Caribbean, but the biggest by far was the people.

JAMAICA ABRIDGED PART 2

Life in Jamaica had been amazing and I couldn't have dreamt it could improve, but it did. After my revelation in Palenque that inspired the new way I'd relate to staff, the day job got better and better. I spent as much time as was necessary each morning with those in accounts, reception and on the front desk to ensure they knew what was expected of them that day, and the next morning I'd review what they'd achieved and what they'd struggled with. This was time-consuming initially but the rewards came quickly. We were still pushed for cash, so we let our suppliers know that calls for payment would only be taken in the afternoon, which diminished disruption and allowed us more time to get on top of the work.

It was a relief to find that my few belongings—tape machine, radio and clothes—were intact, as Encore had been open for the five weeks I was away, which included two weeks when RPS was in London. January was a busy month, with Renate visiting from Germany, Heather from British Columbia and Wendy the White Witch from California on her way to South America. Clifton, a young boy from the fishing village, helped take care of visitors during the day in his boat. Wendy and I had a memorable meal in Sans Souci. The atmosphere was enchanting, enhanced by a small spliff, grand piano and quartet, ceiling fans, excellent service, delicious escargots and lobster. Wendy discovered that the pastry chef, Presser Foot, so-called because of his gammy extremity, had a sideline to supplement his income, which was having guests buy cake mixtures from the local supermarket, charging them for adding ganja and baking the brownies—we didn't interrupt his trade.

I greatly enjoyed water sports and was on the verge of conquering mono-skiing, made much easier behind RPS' stunning Riva boat with a 200 hp Chrysler engine. The staff took much delight watching my frequent mishaps, like hitting the water about twenty feet after dropping the left ski whilst transferring that foot to the right ski.

I was becoming an accomplished Sunfish sailor and able to handle it reasonably competently in fairly high winds, single handed. Controlling the wind against the sail and finding the best direction to drive the boat the fastest at daring angles to the water was a superb sensation and something I'd never have achieved in the UK's deadly cold waters. Sailing was also a good way to get a tan, though I wasn't looking particularly brown at the time. I was feeling healthy though, despite my body falling apart with all sorts of dreaded fungi, which had delayed my mastering of the art of scuba diving and spear fishing. I visited a consultant in Kingston who analysed the whys and wherefores and prescribed medicine to clear up the fungi in my ear, and I was able to dive again fairly soon. I had never worn more than a tee shirt to dive and couldn't imagine how confining it would feel in a wetsuit.

I became good friends with the D'Allessandros and Taussigs, two great families who owned cottages and came back to the Club year after year. Vinny D'Allessandro was a paediatrician from Rhode Island, with Carol his wife and Dana their twelve-year-old daughter, whose infatuation with me became a source of amusement. John and Ann Taussig had four older children. Vinny and John were amazingly generous, and their restaurant and bar bill after two weeks, which they shared equally, amounted to thousands of dollars, which David was happy to settle in Jamaican dollars receiving US dollars in return, which were scarce for the general public; they also tipped the staff handsomely. My tennis improved thanks to RPS and playing with John and Vinny almost every night of their two-week stay. John was an ex American football line backer, a big man who would start his service game with four tennis balls in one hand and continue rallies holding the remaining three. By the time they left, my service was flying and I was even playing some reasonable ground strokes. I had a great time with the families during their visits and was always sad to see them go. When Emily, Sam and Kate were young, we had a wonderful reunion with the Taussigs at their "cottage" on the edge of Lake Winnipesaukee, New Hampshire.

One evening I was called off the tennis court to deal with what turned out to be a serious incident. I was the manager on duty and was taken to the back yard, which was the access point for the laundry, wet and dry stores, maintenance, linen and kitchens. Quite a sizeable crowd had gathered and had become excited. A young lad, one of the kitchen cleaners, appeared with a long gash across his face, from which blood was flowing. There had been an argument with a fellow worker who had chopped him with the metal part of a large squeezy mop. I doubt whether he had meant to do so much damage, but he had taken refuge in the changing rooms, refusing to come out. I opened the door, and he looked menacing with an angry scowl on his face. I persuaded him to accompany me and we headed towards the offices—what to do then, I hadn't a clue. Just as we left the yard, he pushed me away and took off down the drive. I set off in hot pursuit and rugby tackled him to the ground; soon the noisy throng caught up and a guard escorted him away. The cry went up: "Big Bird can't half fly"—my nickname from *Sesame Street*.

I even managed to fit in a game of squash at the Liguanea Club when I was in Kingston and tried to hit some golf balls.

Life was good, and I got an immediate high when I looked at the Caribbean—the mountains, flowers, birds, animals and rich vegetation. I felt thoroughly spoilt and didn't know how England was going to hit me in July. It would be almost impossible to work for the likes of KPMG or take a position as a management accountant having experienced the luxury of working conditions in the tropics and advising the board about the direction the Club should be taking. I needed to expose myself further, stand on my own two feet, collate my education, background and experience to create a lifestyle and standard of living I'd enjoy. This was why RPS' offer to extend my contract for a further year was so attractive and gave me the chance to prove myself and build confidence to go it alone. If all went well, I could spend a couple of months a year in Europe and time with my folks, which is what I'd missed over the last eighteen months; Oliver and Enid were constantly on my mind. I wrote home: *I am so happy to think I am what I am because of you and I am proud of it, which you know but I hope not to excess, and I am so thankful for my appreciation of life and nature which you have given me. I don't think I would be satisfied to live an entirely basic life of sea, country and sunshine which Jamaica could offer. I think you will be pleased that I have spent time visiting the local hospital not because people are ill but I appreciate now the amount of happiness and recharge of spirit your visits to Chester and Liverpool gave your flock, I visit the infirm of Club Caribbean.*

The other boost we had was from Ketchum McLeod, one of the top marketing/PR companies in New York, who looked after Japanese Airlines and the Jamaican Tourist Board. We couldn't afford their rates but were able to barter rooms for expertise. Jim Foley was the president and the family of his wife Priscilla had an interest in Jamaica Inn. We were offered some head office expertise, and Linda Gianforte was allocated to work with us to create a strap line and a new brochure. It was invaluable experience and resulted in "Lazy but Lively", which perfectly described Club Caribbean, and we put together an enticing brochure utilising words like *luxuriate*. Our internal slogan was "Built on Guilt", epitomising the reason for any work being done—tongue in cheek, of course!

Rugby created a tight community, and I'd often bump into Alan Jones, my pal in Barbados, and we'd reminisce about the fantastic time we'd had winning the Caribbean Championship. The main pitch was outside Kingston in Caymanas Park amongst the cane fields, and it was the home ground for Kingston, Privateers, Arawaks, and the Jamaican Defence Force. Mandeville RFC was in the hills in the centre of the island and Montego Bay on the North Coast. Close by was Caymanas Racetrack and Golf Course. There was an active bar whenever a rugby match was taking place, and one Saturday evening Alan and I were the last to leave. Alan was still without transport, so I offered to give him a lift to his home in Kingston, where I met his wife, Pam, and her friend Sue: a very attractive, lively, bright-eyed young blonde who was teaching in Catherine's High School, Spanish Town. Ever wanting to please, I was more than happy to drive them to the party that evening, and I arranged to come back the following weekend for a date. It was 10 April, my mum's birthday, and Sue took me to Devon House, a Georgian-style building set in beautiful grounds that was erected on a property once known as Devon Penn. George Stiebel, the owner of the house, significantly was the child of a German Jew and a Jamaican housekeeper. He was a carpenter, shipper and gun-runner.

I maintain Sue got me very happy on Devon Duppies and the rest wasn't quite history. As Sue and Pam watched every rugby match in Barbados live, and Alan and I were at each other's shoulders, working together every game, I've always insisted it was what she saw on television over those ten days that really attracted her to me.

My heart pounded after spending a wonderful evening with Sue. We laughed a lot, the time sped by, and I felt I had found a soulmate in our love for Jamaica. Happy as a sand boy the next morning, I visited King, who ran Water Sports in Club Caribbean and was spending time in Richmond prison. A really nice guy, who unfortunately was caught after driving a Public Works Department garbage truck laden with ganja down from Alexandria. He had fled from the coast where the boat was to have been packed but was picked up the next morning in Port Maria and his lawyers didn't manage to get him off; Packet, King's Water Sports manager, got away. I knew King enjoyed my visits, but I would have been fooling myself if I denied the good feeling it gave me to see him happy when I turned up, and we both enjoyed our long philosophical discussions—Jamaicans know a lot about life. King had a good brain; although not an academic he provided plenty of food for thought and offered me insights into life and human nature I had previously overlooked. The prison was open air, fairly relaxed and clean, not like the cess pits in Spanish Town and Kingston. He got on well with the officers, so life for him wasn't too bad, but captivity of any sort must be heartbreaking. His spirit was strong and his sentence had been cut from three to one and a half years; yet again life showed itself to be tough but sweet.

I drove back to Runaway Bay via Constant Spring Road and the "Junction". It was raining heavily; several of the roads through the mountains had turned into rivers and there were minor landslides—one bridge was flooded and we had to cross in single file. The torrents below reminded me of Lake Vyrnwy after the cloudburst when the water level rose so high that trees swept down from the hills were caught in the tops of the bridge arches.

At the end of April, Neath RFC toured Jamaica and the Caymans. Montego Bay did amazingly well against them, only losing 22-3, helped by several of their players suffering from sunburn and others playing out of position. The following week, I represented Jamaica as a Jaa Baa in Caymanas and was startled by the aggression of Steve Williams, a crazy player for Neath. I was up against Glyn Shaw, who propped loose head for Wales, and halfway through the match he brought his knee up and cracked a couple of my ribs; I left the field in agony. There was an incident at the afterparty when Glyn was getting on well with ex-Miss Jamaica and someone tried to queer his patch; he immediately dispatched them down the stairs. I have a Neath RFC tie which I still wear with pride.

Sue hadn't been in touch for a few weeks, and I thought all was lost. What I didn't know until I tracked her down in school was that she had phoned, but when the switchboard operator contacted me at my desk, I'd misheard what she'd said, thinking it was someone chasing money and told her to relay the clear message that I didn't want to speak to them; the operator had left the line open and Sue heard every word of my animated dismissal.

George Dixon played a notable part in the development of my romance with Sue. He was the Club's driver, and with his pointed eyebrows, additional little fingers, wicked laugh and luring smile he could be mistaken for the devil. An ex-policeman who liked his liquor and told me it would take him three days to drive me round the island for him to introduce me to all his pikni. He had a heart of gold, but not as large as that of Miss Lou, his partner who worked in the kitchens, and her son Fitzroy; both remained long-time friends.

I would look forward to Friday evenings more and more as time went on and I was falling deeply in love with Sue. George would regularly take care of hotel business in Kingston on Fridays and pick Sue up in Spanish Town on his way back to the north coast. Exasperatingly, the time she'd arrive at Encore was a movable feast as George would make stops on the way for a drink and disappear to keep his liaisons happy. I only hoped Sue was looking forward to spending time together as much as me.

Weekends were wonderful; I had the run of the hotel and excellent food—lobster in a hollowed out "pineapple boat" was one of our lunchtime favourites, together with chef's salads, delicious fresh fish, steaks and fruit. This was pure joy for Sue as the economy was tightening and supermarket shelves in Spanish Town were getting emptier the whole time; even rice was kept under the counter for regular customers. We both loved swimming and spent a lot of time in the sea, which we discovered was a good place to eat succulent mangoes. Our love grew as our laughter increased, and I felt so lucky our love for Jamaica was bringing us closer together. We enjoyed meals in great restaurants, including Moxons towards Port Maria, and Aunt May's of course, invariably eating outside surrounded by wonderful night sounds, especially friendly chirping tree-frogs and the sweet smell of midnight jasmine. We'd lie in the hammock at Encore pleasantly stoned, watching shooting stars rocket across the sky.

After a few weeks Sue wanted to demonstrate her culinary skills and decided to cook a romantic meal for us at Encore. We had drinks on the terrace overlooking the golf course, watched the sun set over the Caribbean, breathed in the sweet scent of jasmine and listened to the night sounds warming up. Sue looked beautiful and brought out a delicious-looking meal of steak and colourful vegetables. We drank more wine and the warm, glowing feeling continued to grow. Sue had taken a good time procuring and, even more, planning the banquet. After a couple of attempts to cut the steak—it was tougher than I'd expected—I threw it over the wall for the dogs. It was many years before she told me how upset she had been at my unfeeling behaviour, and her friends were horrified that she ever cooked anything for me again.

One time we decided we'd make brownies. They smelt delicious when they came out of the oven; however, we never got to taste them as the dog gobbled the lot, having stolen them from where they'd been left to cool. Maybe he regarded them as a belated dessert following the steak he'd been tossed a few weeks earlier.

There was only one stumbling block in our relationship, and that was Sue's smoking habit as for years I'd not been able to abide cigarettes. I nearly got into serious trouble in a cinema back in Liverpool watching *Papillon*. The person next to me was a smoker, and every time he took a draw I would cough, each time a little louder; luckily no fist came my way, and even luckier, Sue chose to give up cigarettes rather than me.

There was a system of robots throughout the island where minibuses travelled the roads, got flagged down and filled up to way over capacity; it was a cheap and convenient way to travel but not very comfortable. On Monday mornings at 5:30 I'd drive Sue down to the main road from Montego Bay to Ocho Rios and wait while she hailed a robot and waved goodbye. It took between thirty and forty-five minutes to reach the main roundabout in Ochi, which was a staging point for journeys to Port Maria, Montego Bay and over Mount Diablo to Kingston.

Sue quickly became a celebrity, not only because she was the one white girl on board but the only person doing a three-hour commute to school; she would be greeted with "Hi, Teach," and regular travellers looked forward to seeing her on Monday mornings.

Sue regularly travelled into Kingston from Spanish Town to Rex Nettleford's dance classes in New Kingston. One time, a lady handed Sue her baby while she got off the bus as it was very crowded and difficult to make her way through the aisle with her little one. The bus took off but was immediately stopped by people banging on the side and yelling "White girl got de baby," who was readily passed to the worried mother through the window.

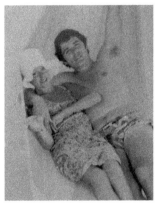

I was delighted when Chris Statham announced he was coming out and enquired whether there was anything I needed. No one comes out from the UK empty-handed, and much to his surprise, I asked if he could bring some cricket kit, followed with, a couple of days before he left, "By the way, could you bring a front cross member for a Ford Capri?" Courtesy of those scallys at Skellys Ford Liverpool, Chris acquired one.

The weight of the cross member was too great to be checked into the hold, so he bound it with tape and took it as hand luggage on good old Air Jamaica. Check-in were a bit surprised by the size and the sharp jagged edges, together with all his hand luggage, which included cricket pads and bats as they wouldn't fit in his suitcase! But they didn't seem to mind enough to make him leave anything behind.

I had warned him that import duty would have to be paid on all the stuff he brought in, but it was better that way than having to wait months for the local dealer to get the parts. Once on the ground in MoBay, Chris made his way through immigration, then there to face him was the customs official. He, of course, wanted to know what all the stuff was, as it was rather difficult to conceal a front cross member, which must have measured three foot across and the suspension towers at either end nearly one and a half feet! Heaven knows what it weighed!

He then demanded to know what he was doing in Jamaica, and Chris said he had come to play cricket; he had strategically placed a bat across his luggage, although it hardly concealed the cross member.

At the time, the West Indies were touring England and had got off to a particularly poor start in the second test, despite their strength with Viv Richards, Michael Holding, Andy Roberts, Gordon Greenidge and others—no doubt as a result of partying till the early hours and Captain Clive Lloyd having difficulty getting his team to bed. England were well on top with Amiss, Underwood, Bob Willis, and others, and looked likely winners. The customs official was clearly a huge cricket fan (who wasn't, out there?) and was very depressed and upset that the Windies were going to lose. Somehow, Chris convinced him that England's success up to that point had been entirely due to the weather and pitch conditions and that things would soon turn around in their favour and there was no doubt the Windies would win the series. At that point, he said, "Do you really think so?" Chris told him he was certain and that it was inevitable with their quality line up. A huge smile appeared on the official's face, and he just waved him through without any further questions about the luggage or import duties! As an extra bonus, Chris brought me a cassette of The Doors album *Riders on the Storm* and the track "Patricia, the Best Stripper in Town".

We had a ball while he was out. I introduced him to the pleasures of living in Jamaica and some suffering. A Welsh regiment of the British Army were out on the bi-annual Calypso Hop, and a rugby match was arranged against Montego Bay in the bushed-out cane fields in Llandovery, which Chris questionably agreed to play in. He said he enjoyed the game despite the bloody scrapes down his legs.

We were invited to a bash in the Sergeant Major's Mess that weekend. Sue came up from Kingston with Pam and Alan. I lent Alan the yellow Beetle, and Sue, Chris and I took one of the other Club vehicles. It was quite a rowdy affair; Sue and Pam went to let tents down then, when Sue was in an ad hoc loo, there was a knock on the door and a young kid of about twelve with a bottle of white rum under his arm propositioned her. Chris later placated Sue while I was dancing with an attractive Jamaican girl, bettering local relations, and assured her that I had spent the last few days extolling her virtues and telling him how much I loved her.

We left very merry and we heard the next morning that Alan had decided he wanted a swim and drove the VW down the steps of Dunns River to the beach. He couldn't reverse it back up and Pam had to push, but somehow they'd extricated themselves from a precarious situation.

One evening, Chris and I went to the Playboy Club in Oracabessa, the other side of Ochi—a beautiful excursion towards Port Maria. Chris drove the Capri back at speed and was going particularly fast through the tight bends before Dunns River, hanging the back end out while the tyres screeched on the hot tarmac and could be heard way ahead. We were broadside, laughing away, as we came round the corner just in time to see three pairs of feet disappear over the bridge; they must have feared for their lives, not knowing what was about to happen. Our laughter only subsided by the time we got back to Club Caribbean.

Chris later recollected feeling guilty about the Capri as it was fixed whilst he was out, and as we drove back to Encore one night, he put it into exactly the same pothole he thought had broken it in the first place. I'm fairly sure it was hammering around cane fields that had done the damage.

A couple of weeks later, I was invited to the officers' party in Moneague, which was altogether a smarter affair than the sergeant major's, with full dress uniform and elegantly attired soldiers waiting on. We had been there a good while enjoying the company of the crew of an army sailing boat that had competed in a transatlantic yacht race to Bermuda, when Sue asked me to take her home. She was agitated and most insistent; I had seen her disappear backwards over a small wall without spilling her gin and tonic. She had been worried about attending the event in case I was side-tracked in a similar way as at the sergeant major's party, and as there was no Chris to look after her, she had quickly downed several gins. She had shown amazing balance as a gymnast, as it was apparently the third time she had reappeared after tripping over backwards.

One weekend we gave free passes into Club Caribbean to members of the paratrooper regiment who were part of the Calypso Hop. They looked to be about sixteen years old and the scrawniest bunch of teenagers; far from it, they were battle hardened and really wished they were with their mates, who were involved in the Troubles in Northern Ireland. You wouldn't have wanted to face any one of them individually, let alone as a team. They had a great day in and out of the swimming pool carrying out daring escapades and sank a few barrels of Red Stripe.

One of our favourite pleasures was snorkelling in a "secret" place in Discovery Bay where the sea is enclosed by volcanic rock. By crushing sea urchins, beautiful little fish of various shapes, forms and kaleidoscope colours appeared to feed on the meat. There were heaps of squid swimming backwards, forwards, sideways—amazing-looking creatures.

There is so much beauty in Jamaica whichever direction you travel. The journey to Port Maria was breathtaking and we walked around Goldeneye, where Ian Fleming wrote his James Bond books, then down to Dr No Beach whence Ursula Andress appeared from the sea. The view from Firefly, 1,200 feet above, which Noel Coward moved up to, must be one of the most stunning anywhere in the world, with the remains of Captain Morgan's stone cottage in the garden. The house had been left as a museum exactly as it was when Noel Coward died, other than someone having painted bathing costumes on his picture of boys swimming in the sea—maybe his butler, who'd found his body and who showed us round. His mausoleum had a two hundred and seventy degree view of the craggy coast line of the blue Caribbean, with the mystical Blue Mountains floating up to the sky in the other direction.

Summer of 1976, we planned to return to the UK. I travelled via Canada as I had work to do with Treasure Tours, owned and run by Stuart Lunan a good friend of Club Caribbean who'd sent many guests from Canada in tough times. Mind you, the cheapest deals were out of Montreal, and those were the people who made the most complaints and caused us the biggest problems.

Max Lyn and I flew to Toronto from Montego Bay and straightaway went to visit Max's Jamaican Chinese friends, who were intensely embroiled in a game of mahjong. They hardly gave him a sideways glance until their game had finished, then he received the warmest of greetings. Arthur Wint came round later, the first Jamaican Olympic gold medallist, who won the 400 metres at the 1948 Summer Olympics in London. He was extremely tall, with the largest hands I'd ever shaken and was the most placid, kind gentleman who at the time was High Commissioner to Britain.

I completed the work at Treasure Tours, and Stuart Lunan offered me tickets to two football matches in the new Olympic Stadium, which I gratefully accepted, and off Max Lyn and I went to Montreal, where we stayed with a friend I'd made when a Canadian rugby team toured Jamaica. There was a festive atmosphere in Montreal and great excitement with the whole city focused on the Olympic Games. There was special signage wherever you travelled from the underground to the streets which became more intense as you approached the various venues. We had seats in the gods and saw Brazil draw against East Germany. The design of the stadium was so good that we felt as if we were sitting right on top of the pitch. There was meant to be a roof which opened and retracted like an umbrella, but because of union disputes it was never finished.

As well as there being the special atmosphere that accompanies the Olympic Games, when the nations of the world gather to support their greatest athletes, Montreal also maintained its wonderful French flavour, especially in the old part of the city with its beautiful stone buildings, quaint streets, garlands of flowers and sumptuous restaurants. As ever, it was terrific to be shown round by somebody who knew the city. We watched the Soviet Union beat Canada, then Max returned to Jamaica. By this time I'd made contact with David Broude, a good Jewish friend from KPMG in Liverpool, and he'd sourced several tickets for me, including two track and field events, one of which was the penultimate day, which we attended together with seats thirty yards from the finishing line and twenty rows back.

It was amazing to have witnessed the Cuban Juantorena opening his legs and leaving the rest of the field behind, winning the 400m gold medal, having already won the 800m two days earlier. I saw Brendan Foster in the 5000m final when he was calling fellow Brit Ian Stewart to come through to give him a chance to take a breather. Stewart didn't come, and cries of "Brendan, Brendan" echoed with him as he raced round and round the track, reaching a crescendo as he crossed the finishing line; he came fifth. I watched two Asian teams competing in the lady's volleyball, and the shrieking from the supporters was almost deafening.

MONTREAL OLYMPICS

I flew out of Montreal to Paris at the same time as the East German Ladies Team. We were in W H Smiths together, and I gawked in awe at those beautiful blonde women in ideal proportion but a good twenty-five per cent bigger than my six-foot-one and two hundred pounds.

I had time in Charles de Gaulle airport to buy a Hermès silk scarf for Sue, which she still treasures, flew to Heathrow and hired a zippy Ford Capri and drove to Conway Crescent in Melksham, where Sue was staying with her parents. It was the longest we had been apart since meeting on 10 April earlier that year, and I hoped she was as pleased to see me as I her. Next morning, her dad chuckled as I struggled to start the car, which I eventually worked out needed choke—what, in summer?! Then home to Oliver and Enid in Gresford, and I was so pleased they had settled into the School House and a system of electric storage heaters had been installed to keep them warm. They had a steady stream of visitors to make sure their needs were being catered for, including Eddie Wilkinson, who performed faith healing on Oliver.

Sue came up for a week with Robert, her three-year-old brother, and I was able to show them round my favourite places, including The Boat Inn, Erbistock, the waterfalls at Pystyll Rhaedr, Lake Vyrnwy and Chester. We visited many of the cousins, and to this day some believe that Rob is Sue's son and not her brother!

The weather was glorious, and I enjoyed a week at home with my mum and dad and spending time with friends. One delightful lunchtime was with Richard Llewellyn and Les Bonenfant, a Border Breweries brewer, in the gardens of the Nag's Head, Ridley Wood. The sun beat down, the steaks were excellent and the beer equally as good. Richard recalls me telling them that I had experienced so many adventures, met wonderful people and had enjoyed such immense pleasure that if I was called in and my life was to finish at that point, I couldn't complain. Topping the list was Sue, who I was driving down to meet at Jo and Geoff Pitt's in Winchester while she hitchhiked from Wiltshire. Jo and Geoff had been close friends with Oliver and Enid since the 1940s and had given me some great experiences when I went to their house on exeats from St John's. Jo, in her wisdom, warned that two years was the maximum time I could take out playing in the Caribbean if I wanted to make it in mainstream corporate life. The next day, we took them to see *Chorus Line* off Leicester Square, which we all enjoyed, though it must have been a long time since they'd watched a show from the gods, then out for a meal as a token gesture for the indulgences they'd afforded me over the years.

We stayed with Jill Dinnage in Margaretta Terrace off Fulham Road, a great mate of Sue's who she'd lived with in Richmond while on teaching practice and ran villa parties in Greece for Colin Murison Small. We had a fun time and I witnessed some great reminiscences. We met several more friends of Sue's and went out with Yolanda, another Muiri Bird, to a Greek Restaurant in Fulham Road. We had delicious food, and three bottles of Retsina between the three of us, and laughed the whole way through the evening. I carried Sue on my shoulders down the middle of Fulham Road to find Yo's Mini and off we drove to Bruce, her boyfriend's, flat. While Yo was fetching Bruce to continue the night's celebrations, I turned round and reached over to Sue, who was in the back of the car, and asked her to marry me. There was no doubt in my mind that she was the one I wanted to spend the rest of my life with. Admittedly it wasn't the most romantic proposal; she said "no". To which I replied, "Okay, if you change your mind, let me know where and when you want to get married, and I'll be there." Her explanation for her refusal some time later was that she was worried we'd wake up in the morning, and she'd be bubbling and excited in her own inimitable way and declare how thrilled she was to be engaged, only for me to deny any knowledge of what she was talking about.

We were eventually married on 9 June 1979 without ever having being formally engaged. Our fortieth wedding anniversary fell on the day after Elen Moore married James in the most wonderful wedding ceremony in Kefalonia overlooking Antisamos beach. Our anniversary coincided with a tremendous pool party the happy couple had arranged. We felt privileged to be amongst so many young talented people, delightful friends of Elen's who held various positions in TV, film, theatre and Welsh opera and accepted us oldies as one of them. Late in the evening, after we had been celebrating hard throughout the day, Charlotte Church asked me how on earth can you achieve forty years of marriage, to which I responded with trite and serious comments, including that any major argument needs to be settled before going to sleep, preferably by making love, and concluded by telling her I had not committed adultery since I proposed to Sue in Fulham Road.

Antisamos

Charlotte Church

Elen Moore

The holiday was coming to a close, and I returned to London on the train from Chester and couldn't believe how scorched and brown the fields were. I joined RPS for some business meetings and excellent lunches in Lloyds of London and the RAC Club, then went to swap cars with John Cleese, who owned two cottages in Club Caribbean—not his Bentley. Richard had borrowed an estate car as he was having dining room furniture made. We arrived at the Mews, unloaded a chair, knocked on the door, and out came John Cleese and pleasantries were exchanged. The chair was on the pavement, and all John did was sit on it and I wanted to roll about with laughter—an amazingly natural funny man. He entertained guests when he was in Jamaica by performing his Ministry of Silly Walks on the beach, as well as other skits.

Sue and I crossed the Atlantic separately, not because I'd failed to persuade her to jack in her teaching and come live with me on the north coast; she had a two-year contract and nothing was going to stop her finishing it. I didn't make the flight to Paris, so flew straight to Jamaica, arriving back at Club Caribbean to the friendliest welcome anyone could dream of, several of the staff wanting news of Oliver and Enid. The hotel was still short of money, and by means of much ducking and diving, we struggled through.

Life continued to be exciting, full of ups and downs, with the election campaigning under way. There was a strike in the hotel, so for a couple of days I waited on tables and enjoyed the experience.

The saga of me rushing round the ministries and banks continued to no avail; it was disheartening to have hopes built up then dashed. Rising at 5:00 a.m., zooming into Kingston for 9:00, watching an official reading his newspaper with his feet on the desk through a crack in the door while I waited outside, back to the club to produce figures, having phoned Harvey to let him know what I needed so he could start to prepare, and returning to Kingston before the offices closed the same day. I had a lucky escape going through the hills, driving the Capri on empty roads at seventy mph around Moneague first thing in the morning. I didn't clock the dampness on the road coming out of a bend, and the back end came round 180 degrees. Luckily I managed to hold it and drove backwards for a hundred or so yards until I was able to stop, turn and continue in the right direction. There was nothing coming the other way, and it was fairly wide at that point. Coming back one evening in the Mach 1 Mustang, I was even luckier, as the road was narrow with stone walls either side. I had just overtaken a lorry and touched the accelerator too hard coming out of a bend. She flipped round 180 degrees, and not wanting to have to overtake the lorry again, I reversed as quickly as I could until I found a gateway, then turned and headed the right way. Though tired, I was able to enjoy the rest of the drive looking at the beautiful views across rolling hills then over the sea, but it could have been so different. A third lucky escape I had was when I was driving steadily on wet roads in the relatively new HiAce van to rugby practice in MoBay. I touched the brakes going round a corner and slid to the other side of the road, and an open truck coming the other way carrying fifty chairs took evasive action and drove into the ditch. I immediately got out to assess any damage, and three burly Jamaicans approached me in a threatening manner, totally unnerving me. I persuaded them they were covered by my insurance, and things calmed down. While this was happening, one of them had gone to the driver's window and taken the van keys: a smart move. The vehicles had only just touched, there was no real harm and we went our separate ways; well, I turned round and followed them back to Salem as by then it was too late for the practice. A few weeks later, a claim came from their insurance company asking for a stupid amount of repairs to the beaten-up truck. We contested the claim and landed up paying nothing, but I would have been happier to have paid what was fair.

One time I was lucky to get an audience with Scree Bertram, the local MP for St Ann's and a senator, in the prime minister's office in Kingston to put our case for a government loan. As I didn't hear back, I decided to track him down in Brownstown, and he assured me he'd speak to Michael Manley, the prime minister. I played what I thought was an ace by turning up with King's two-year-old boy on my shoulders at a PNP political meeting in Runaway Bay. I stood in front of the stage, the only white person amongst a small gathering of eight hundred, on the road opposite Rose Bros awaiting the arrival of Michael Manley. Scree Bertram was on the platform with other senior members of the PNP, and every few minutes they would crank up the tension by looking down the road for Michael then reporting, "Joshua soon come." The expectations were built up, then there were huge cheers as he turned up with his rod of correction given to him by Haile Selassie. Jamaica is very religious in its own peculiar way, and the campaign around Manley was built with biblical connotations, including his nickname Joshua, after the prophet.

The mayor of St Ann's spoke at Runaway Bay, and at a much bigger meeting in Brownstown; he was quite amusing and an amazing character to look at with his woollen cap and bobble. I could have taken my camera, but I wanted to show my true interest and not just that I had come for the spectacle. The scene was as you'd envisage in the Po Valley, with Giovannino

Guareschi's Don Camillo being introduced as comrade! They had the "insight" to have a gospel preacher call for God's love and guidance upon their people and party in no uncertain terms. There were hymns and party songs, but nothing to compare with Brownstown. The whole of the market area was swarming with between five and six thousand people; again, mine was the only face that wasn't black—except for Michael Manley's, that is. There were more speakers here, such as Carlyle Dunkley, head of the NWU, who I had met previously; he was not as impressive as Scree Bertram, who was convincing and fair. They hammered the JLP on various scores and Bertram called for conversion of the JLP to PNP and spoke heavily against violence. His main focus in Brownstown were the eight landowners who owned 25,000 acres of the best land. Bertram was astute and an excellent speaker—maybe one of the three closest people to Manley. It's not difficult to point to the wrongs of capitalism when there is so much wealth shared amongst the few and poverty for many. In the speeches, especially by Michael Manley, there was a heavy slant towards the Bible, entwined with glory to socialism, with the clenched fist raised and much rhetoric. It was a tremendous experience to be part of the crowd, which he so readily controlled with his exceptional oration—I felt safe at all times.

The speech by Michael Manley in Runaway Bay was a shortened version of that in Montego Bay on the Sunday, which I didn't attend but listened to on the radio, and the one in Brownstown was almost exactly the same. "Heavy Manners, rod of correction, Haile Selassie, lie lie lie of the JLP, high up crow, hail socialism, Jamal can read letters from foreign and bible, wicked capitalist—master servant, January burnings, oil on road, malicious press, tidal wave, pacific ocean, accusation of communism, democratic socialism, violence of JLP, up park camp, do not mind the businessmen in the supermarkets, and the capitalists that don't exploit cheap labour are still welcome!" Brownstown was a great experience; beforehand I was apprehensive about my safety, but everything was cool, and if Michael was told of my presence by Scree Bertram, it might have improved our chances of financial support.

There was a catchy song as part of Michael Manley's campaign about Joshua leading his people with his rod of correction:

"Joshua a lion
Don't trouble lion
Cos lion will devour you
Joshua a lion
Bertram a lion…"
Just like the Welsh rugby chant:
"At full back we've got JPR Williams
At scrum half we've got Gareth Edwards

At fly half we've got Barry John…
We've got the best team in the land."

Over the previous month I had hardly done any work other than preparation and rehashing of figures to obtain a loan. I'd enjoyed the challenge but would have been bitterly disappointed if we'd had to close.

Before I flew to NYC for a business trip, I was running around the government ministries in Kingston trying to borrow money to keep the Club afloat. The inefficiencies, lack of knowledge and consideration were amazing, and there appeared to be total breakdown in communication between the various departments. I was being bounced between the Ministry of Industry Tourism and Foreign Trade, the Ministry of Finance (or no finance!), the Jamaican Development Bank (which was meant to lend money on behalf of the government) and the National Workers Union. We had approached the Union as a last resort because we were making no headway and needed dollars in a hurry—the Union could exert influence on the government, especially coming up to election time. Each person employed in Jamaica was reckoned to have up to ten dependents—maybe one thousand mouths were dependent on CC's two hundred employees. If it closed, they would have a hard time getting fed and the village of Salem would be in a sorry plight. By then I was on good terms with the Union leaders and had been preaching the cry of the South Wales miners to encourage them to get us help from the government, which they kindly—or rather sensibly—did. Clive Dobson, who was the Union leader on the north coast spoke to the Parliamentary Secretary for Industry, Tourism and Foreign Trade, who said, "Okay, take some dollars." However, no one seemed to know where the dollars were to come from, and each ministry denied knowledge of the funds and then demanded reams and reams of information about the Club. The undersecretary looked in a drawer but couldn't find three million! It took nearly a week of sweet talking to secure an advance. The saga of the initial loan from the government had a happy ending; the company seal and directors' signatures were quickly obtained and the deal done.

While I was presenting the business case, my love for Jamaica came across, and I'd make suggestions as to how the tourist trade in general could be improved and costs cut. I was invited to write a detailed report for the Ministry of Industry, Tourism and Foreign Trade. This included:

Advertising and Promotion – Duplication of costs by the Jamaican Tourist Board (JTB) and Air Jamaica, who were using different PR companies, Doyle Dane and Ketchum MacLeod. I suggested bringing JTB into NYC and sharing frontage with Air Jamaica.

Road Transportation – Rude hustling by cab drivers and atrocious driving on bad road surfaces caused many tourists to have a bad impression of Jamaica from their first day.

Donald Sangster Airport – There was often severe congestion at the airport between 2:30 and 4:30. I suggested, where possible, to re-schedule arrivals.

The location and design of the Tourist Board Information was poor.

Hotels – There should be personnel continuously moving around the hotels who could perform the role of inspectors and public relation officers. I was in favour of close liaison between hotels and local villages so that visitors could experience Jamaican culture, local dance and theatre groups, local fishing trips, and a day release programme whereby all hotel employees could regularly attend courses in hotel skills and guest relations.

Security Law and Order – It was essential that visitors to Jamaica feel safe without feeling imprisoned.

A system of light immediate fines on visitors in possession of ganja would serve the dual role of being an added attraction for Jamaica as a destination for tourists and a fundraiser for internal revenue.

Two Tier Dollar Exchange Rate – To increase the flow of foreign exchange to Jamaica by enabling the price of holidays to be more competitive and increasing per capita spend by tourists on vacation without the burden on the nation of a total devaluation against the US dollar. (Within twelve months the government introduced a two tier exchange system which was a total disaster!)

Having a close view of politicians and their behaviour opened my eyes beyond the study I'd done for A-Level politics and British constitution. Scree Bertram, two years previously, had been a schoolteacher; after coaching Michael Manley at tennis, he was jettisoned into the cabinet. I realised things weren't so different in the UK, except relationships and promotions happened in private clubs over gin and tonic.

With the election, gun crime was on the increase and the Gun Court had been opened in Kingston to counter crime, enabling criminals to be incarcerated following an in camera trial with no jury. There was an attempt on Bob Marley's life in early December 1976, and he performed at the "Smile Jamaica" concert a couple of days later in an effort to bring peace amongst the warring factions.

Bongo Shorty

Mount Diablo

After succeeding in obtaining the government loan, I flew straight to New York from Kingston, touching down in Montego Bay on the way but only after three attempts to land. It was the worst flight I'd ever made; there was torrential rain and lightning, and the pilot at each attempt was unable to see the runway because the deluge was falling so heavily. Eventually we approached from the opposite direction, which made me feel more comfortable because if we overshot the runway, landing in the Caribbean would be relatively warm.

Richard was at JFK to meet me and drive into Manhattan. We managed to accomplish quite a lot of work and enjoy some good meals (one with Gilbert Barker), and saw a couple of good movies: *The Front* with Woody Allen, which is all about the '40s and '50s and leftist tendencies—it was at the same time most amusing and a serious criticism of the stupidity of bureaucracy; and *The Harder They Come*, made by our Jamaican friend Perry Henshall and a cult showing. I thoroughly enjoyed it and thought it an excellent reflection of the harsh and cruel life in Jamaica: ganja, police corruption, and the ripping off of a singer by an ugly record producer who had a monopoly of the market.

We visited Prisclla and Jim Foley at their lovely home in beautiful Richfield, Connecticut. Sun was shining and autumn had started, with leaves in glorious shades of yellows and browns and some red; there needed to be more frost before the colours caught fire.

Shortly after returning to Jamaica, a few of us had an impromptu party mid-week in Encore, which was located in Cardiff Hall, a smart residential area. We were well lubricated with alcohol and high when the lounge doors were simultaneously kicked in from the driveway and patio and men in black pointed handguns at us. A sobering experience, and for a while we expected to be beaten up or worse because we didn't have cash or valuables to give the robbers. Then a Jamaican voice asked, "Tim, are you alright?" It was members of the local police station who were patrolling the area and had seen cars in the driveway they didn't recognise—what fantastic protection. If things had become really rough, I'd have relocated into the middle of Salem where I'd have felt safe amongst the locals. I was also concerned for Sue's safety in Spanish Town and travelling into Kingston at this time, but no way was she going to stop her dance classes.

Sue was head of the PE department in St Christopher's School in Spanish Town, which housed many of the villains who had been chased out of Kingston, and her job involved running the annual sports day. Everything was going fine when suddenly there were shouts and screams and a crowd started running away from the field towards the school. There had been a row between two youths at the cinema the night before over a girl, and the street boy involved had turned up to the event, which was attended by the public, bookmakers and stall holders. The pupil saw the culprit, drew a knife and killed him. To prevent the schoolboy getting lynched, the headmistress bundled him into the boot of her car and took him to the police station.

There was a strong belief on the island that the CIA were responsible for a lot of the trouble, as they were concerned that Michael Manley was too close to Fidel Castro with a growing Cuban influence and investments and the strong communist leanings of some members of the cabinet. The world press exaggerated the violence, reporting women being raped on the beaches and soldiers patrolling the streets. This had an adverse effect on tourism—half the hotels closed—and bauxite shipments were curtailed, having a severely detrimental effect on the two major sources of national income. The economy was being brought to its knees, and Jamaica has suffered the consequences for decades since. No doubt Eddie Seaga, leader of JLP, had sold his soul to the USA for the promise of millions when he was elected. I recognised Seaga one time in Miami airport and introduced myself— I'll always remember his cold, limp handshake.

We had a high proportion of return guests at CC as the quality and variety of food was good and facilities excellent, provided you didn't want luxury. The Rondavel Cottages offered plenty of space inside and out; no way could a three-star hotel be built to run economically today with so great an area per guest. Land had been bought in Portugal, a country which the Founding Fathers loved, and a ski club in the Alps was high on the wish list. However, RPS had constructed the ownership in such a complicated way the whole operation couldn't be bundled together to sell at any time in the future. Shareholders owned the freehold of the original sixty individual cottages, with the paths, grassed areas and main buildings owned by a separate company. In phases two and three, the cottages were leasehold with different voting rights, so it would be impossible for a couple of hundred people with so many differing interests to reach agreement, especially as a good number would never want to sell.

Miko Blanco had put a troupe together to perform in the hotels. He was an apparition: six foot tall, skinny, and ponced around like an exotic Indian prince. He was extremely athletic and could limbo under a pole a mere foot off the ground with his *mawga* chest—a great character and talent. He had a number of beautiful girls, scantily dressed, and men in similar attire who performed rhythmic exotic dances.

Another character was Count Frank, who wandered round the hotel during the day with a tall pyramid straw hat playing calypso songs.

The weekly beach party was always popular and there were various games, some involving drink, and one of the funniest was "round the bottle", where the participants had to run as fast as they could in a circle with their finger on a bottle then in a straight line for ten yards—most staggered aimlessly then fell in a heap. From time to time there was goat racing along the sand, where the runners would start with their goats on a tether then race to the finishing line.

The most exciting show was Ross Kananga, who we booked without knowing exactly what his show comprised and without arranging extra insurance. He had a crocodile farm in Trelawney, where he had stood in for James Bond in *Live and Let Die* and ran across a bridge formed by the backs of his crocodiles; he also wrestled the crocodile for Steve McQueen in the mud swamp in *Papillon*. He had scars across his body from taking out a lion just in time in mid-air as she pounced on him. The reason he went back to fighting crocodiles was the tax authorities wouldn't allow him to claim a new fence to keep the crocs in against profits, and he was left with a large tax bill; we didn't pay him much more than $100 for an evening's star entertainment!

He asked for a wooden tank twenty foot by ten foot and three foot deep. We ordered this to be built in Salem way in advance. I went to check on the tank the morning of the first show, which I should have done a few days sooner as it was not finished. Following frantic activity at four in the afternoon, I accompanied the ten men carrying it across the road on their shoulders like a turtle with long legs, and it was neatly placed in between the bandstand and the swimming pool. Next challenge was to fill the tank with water. It didn't leak, but when it was halfway full, the sides began to bulge, so we made an emergency call to the ship's carpenters who shored up the sides. Eventually the tank was full and appeared to be stable. In plenty of time, Ross Kananga arrived in his Land Rover with a twelve foot croc strapped up in the back with a sack over its head. He and his helper carried it through the lobby, removed the covering, slid it into the water and placed the wooden boards on top.

An hour later, the guests started turning up for dinner and took their places in the open air around the swimming pool—still all well. The show started with his young native Indian girl taking a baby croc around the tables for guests to touch. Lights went up, and Ross Kananga took to the stage. The boards were removed, and the diners saw for the first time the croc lazily resting in the tank. Our hero steps into the tank, does a head catch and the tail thrashed around. By this time, some foolhardy audience had started to gather close. Next he hauled the croc onto the stage and fought it for a while as if it was a bull, with the jaws crashing so quickly you could hardly see them but you could certainly hear them. Then came our first big lesson. The concrete floor was dry; the croc had traction and slid off the stage past the tank into the swimming pool and made for the deep end. Amazingly, this didn't faze Ross Kananga—and all he'd had for sustenance was a couple of swigs of white rum. Somehow, he coaxed the croc to the shallow end, where he once more dragged it onto the stage. He demonstrated how, if you're in trouble, just roll the creature onto its back and it will red out. Also, provided you clasp your hands round the tip of its nose and keep its mouth shut, there is little power to open its jaws, but once open they have pneumatic power and will crush almost anything. Lastly he rolled the croc onto its front, climbed astride its back, lifted the head with the tip of the nose under his chin and shot his arms horizontally in the shape of a cross. End of the show—other than collecting loose teeth from the stage.

It was rumoured that to supplement his income to pay the taxman, Ross Kananga performed similar shows in Canada—however, the crocodiles would have cocaine safely packed in their mouths as they went through customs. Sadly, Ross Kananga died in 1978 of a heart attack while fishing off the coast of Florida.

I arranged to take Sue to Disney World for half term, and Max Lyn warned me not to give her too much all at once, which I don't think was my reason for hiring a Ford Pinto, one of the worst cars ever built. It was a long drive to Orlando on straight roads, and I was pulled over by the cops for doing seventy miles an hour and given a ticket; I was warned that if I didn't pay it I'd be arrested next time I entered the States. I even went to the trouble of completing a cheque stub before tearing up the cheque. To help time pass, we played backgammon for the remainder of the journey—more dangerous than exceeding the speed limit.

I'd booked into the Contemporary Hotel, which hadn't been open long. It was a beautiful A-framed building with a station, and the monorail went through the middle to take us into the heart of the Magic Kingdom. The room was massive, with four doors off the bathroom to the various facilities and a giant bed. The television was controlled by a button on the light standard, which confused Sue, who thought she'd broken the TV when it kept switching channels. Disney World was a mirror image of Disneyland in Anaheim but with acres more space and Epcot yet to be started. We had a fun time over the three days going on all the rides, and especially enjoyed Pirates of the Caribbean, Mark Twain Riverboat and the Haunted Mansion.

There was an annual hotel cricket competition which was a high standard; Club Caribbean took this seriously, and being a star cricketer could be key to gaining employment. Sparrow was one of our quick bowlers and had trials for Jamaica, and the only reason he didn't claim a regular spot was that his best bowling happened when he was stoned. Precious was another excellent player who played at the top level. The matches were played at quality grounds and attracted good crowds. There were other interesting fields such as Beverley, the home of Charles and

Bucky, where the pitch was at an angle, not from end to end but across.

Michael Holding

Kaiser Bauxite

No such handicap at the Kaiser ground in Discovery Bay, where I saw "Whispering Death" glide elegantly and release the ball with venom at the end of his blisteringly fast run up. He said he could bowl as quickly off a short run up but that took much more out of him.

There would be plenty of beer drunk round the ground and invariably a number of domino games where the closing bricks were slammed down from a great height.

Montego Bay rugby team played a match on the Kaiser grounds at the same time as a cricket match was taking place. When there was a break, a fair number of spectators came over to watch us "whities" knock lumps out of each other, much to the amusement of the local Jamaicans, who were doubled up in laughter.

There was a medical clinic near the ground, which Kaiser made available to the local community, and it was where I went to get my hand x-rayed after a rugby match, only to find out the metacarpal of my right index finger was fractured. I was on the way to St Ann's Bay Hospital, having been warned that my fingers to my elbow would be in plaster for several weeks. On the way, I called in to see my friends at the marine lab that was part of the University of West Indies. They advised me to go to Miami and have a fibreglass cast fitted as a wrongly fitted plaster could cause all sorts of infections in the heat and humidity. I tried to make contact, but without success. RPS decided to send me to the doctor in Harley Street, back in London, who had fixed the finger he had broken in position so that he could hold his ski pole when he competed in downhill in the Winter Olympics in Innsbruck 1964. I turned up with the x-ray; the doctor took a look at it, called his secretary, asked her to bring some Sellotape, and he attached the first two fingers together the second acting as a splint and charged me £10! Sue sitting on my hand on the way to the airport hadn't caused any more damage.

It was an opportunity for me to visit my mum and dad. I also called to see Chris and Gary Talbot, friends in Chester. Gary was an ex-professional footballer who had scored the fastest hat trick in the league before becoming an excellent photographer, and he asked me if I wanted any publicity. He replaced the clear tape with black so that it would show up on the picture, sent it to Reg Herbert, a journalist friend, who got it on the front page of the *Wrexham Leader* and inside pages of the *Express* and *Mail* with the caption "Boss thinks so much of his Financial Comptroller that to get him back at work quickly he flies him to Harley Street for seven inches of tape at £100 an inch."

When I originally arrived at Club Caribbean, RPS spoke about his intention to put a two or four man bob into the Winter Olympics; there being no snow in Jamaica we could go to Bariloche in Chile, where the

Founding Fathers had been before buying the land from which CC grew. Unfortunately, because we were losing money, there was no spare cash to fulfil this dream.

In those days, flying Air Jamaica was a fun experience. The attractive hostesses offered all passengers rum punch, which set the tone. When they finished serving the main meal and drinks, they would all partake in a glamorous fashion show gliding up and down the aisles. That no longer happens, and they even banned the carrying of overproof white rum, at 151% proof, as it was regarded as potentially dangerous.

An opportunity arose to open a recording studio in the Purple Turtle, right on the sea. It was an ideal structure with a bar downstairs, where Bob Marley jammed, and a large room upstairs, windows on three sides with amazing views, and the building itself needed little structural alteration. There were sixty other studios on the island but none in the Runaway Bay area, and we could offer Club Caribbean for basic accommodation, Cardiff Hall for serviced villas and the incredible Unity for total luxury. It was an original stone building owned by Tim Andre's family, over two hundred years old, where the Queen Mother was reputed to have stayed; more recently Jefferson Airplane, who RPS had met on the plane from the States and persuaded them to play at Club Caribbean in return for accommodation. When the driver went to pick them up, he was bowled over by the sight of a huge open suitcase overflowing with ganja in the middle of a polished dining table with silver candlesticks that seated twenty-four. The lounge was furnished with several settees, and the garden led down to a secluded beach. Success wasn't assured, but we saw we could put together a tantalising offer that included a sound engineer from a New York studio who'd recorded Elton John, James Taylor and Carly Simon. Many rock bands liked to record in Jamaica, which was where the Rolling Stones recorded *Goats Head Soup*.

I attended the initial meeting in Negril to discuss the project, and as it had legs, a follow up was held a week later over dinner in a villa where the New York studio owner was staying above Ocho Rios and the White River towards Upton Golf Club. Sue was with me, and we turned up in the Mach 1 Mustang. There was a jovial atmosphere, enhanced by "Fuck Up"—a Rasta who was an excellent chef but, as his nickname implied, had a track history. As well as cooking several delicious courses, starting with magic mushrooms, conch and lobster, he rolled spliffs, and when the dinner party didn't need one, he'd smoke them himself. We made excellent progress, and there was agreement that the recording studio should go ahead. We couldn't understand why the girlfriend was disappearing to the bathroom at regular intervals and was paying attention to her nose; it was only several days later Sue suggested she might have been topping up with cocaine. As a parting gift late into the night, we were given a bottle of ganja honey that had been produced by hives placed in the middle of fields of herb. I wasn't in the best condition to drive, and we went cautiously and eventually joined the main road. Barely a chain later, we were pulled over at a police roadblock where half a dozen soldiers and armed officers were searching for drugs, and especially for guns. I lowered the window of the left-hand drive car, tried to understand what they were saying to me and with even more difficulty stuttered a reply. Whether they realised I was in no condition to be running guns or if they recognised me, I don't know, but luckily we were sent on our way and fortunately didn't land up interred in St Ann's gaol, where the consequences could have been dire.

Sue had planned to visit Mexico with Avril and Denea, her housemates, together with Pam and Alan but we decided to return to the UK for Christmas. We were flying out of Montego Bay the day before the elections, and because there was talk of roadblocks and potential violence, we stayed in Half Moon hotel the night before in the lap of luxury. We arrived in Heathrow, having joined the mile high club courtesy of Air Jamaica, with no problem other than freezing temperatures. Sue had to delay her trip to Gresford from her parents' home in Wiltshire as the trains had stopped running because of the snow.

She eventually came up, and David Mayers took us to the Horseshoe Pass above Llangollen, where people were skiing and sledging. We spent a few days in London in Simon Marsh's flat behind Baker Street, and I attended meetings with the Founding Fathers in Box Cottage where Robert Salm lived in a small gated community behind Harrods. Nobby was a fount of knowledge on everything from the City to journalism and anything to do with sport and was a positive stabilising influence on RPS. He would also remind me whenever we met that one is never too old to start skiing. We went out for a boisterous meal and a surfeit of wine which resulted in a taxi driver kicking RPS, Sue and I out for nothing other than being a little rowdy. I accompanied Sue to Victoria Bus Station the next morning, where she caught a coach to Heathrow somewhat the worse for wear. It was a most uncomfortable flight back to Jamaica, where she turned up to school two and a half weeks late, luckily with no adverse consequences.

Her housemates delayed their Christmas celebration lunch for a week so that I could be with them. As Alan and I were considered to be getting in the way while they prepared the dinner, we were ordered out of the house and went to the beach, swam, had a few beers and paid a visit to a rough rum bar on the way home. Only the gate stopped me driving into the side of the house! Everything was going well until I fell asleep with my head on my plate of painstakingly prepared food. Sue was livid, quite rightly so, but because I was so inebriated it had little effect and I went to bed. Pam told her that it was a waste of time giving a man a row when he was drunk; it had a much better effect if you waited till the following morning.

The hotel continued to struggle financially, and RPS, who had a most creative brain, came up with the fundamentals of Passkey. We knew we'd lose money in the summer months, as in the mid-seventies it was outside the high season when the best rates were achieved, and heavy discussions took place to decide whether or not we should close for those months. The main difficulties with that course of action was that we'd lose the best staff, the hotel would dilapidate and require refurbishment, and continuity with the travel agents would be lost, necessitating a large marketing spend so the decision was to stay open and grapple through. What we realised was the marginal cost of having additional guests once the hotel remained open was a few bars of soap and washing powder, and the fuller the hotel the better the atmosphere and the greater the spend. This problem was the same for all hotels in the off season, and our research showed that golfers were happy to travel outside peak season to play courses around the world. We contracted hotel space with thirty-six of the top golfing hotels, Half Moon in Montego Bay being the first to sign up, then The Rose Garden in Thailand, El Paraiso in Spain, British Transport hotels in Scotland and Sandy Lane in Barbados, and we were selling twelve weeks of vacation which could be taken at any time over a twelve-year period at any combination of the hotels at up to 50% discount at current prices. There was a watertight contract between the hotel, Passkey and traveller, and monies could only be transferred from escrow when the vacation was taken. We started to put the programme together in February 1977, and by the time we launched at the Open in Turnberry in July there was an excellent brochure with sheets for each of the resorts, including a picture and description of the golf course holes. It was decided that I should relocate to Miami in time for the August launch in the USA.

Part of our research took place in New York, where we presented to Don Fugazi, who owned Fugazi Travel and had the contract for providing limousines to the United Nations and was the first to sell vacations door to door. Bob Hope only lent his name to Exxon and Fugazi, and there were pictures of Frank Sinatra and Dean Martin, who he considered friends, on his office wall. We were invited to sit in on the weekly management meeting with managers, according to race, from the main areas of New York including Brooklyn, The Bronx and Queens. Don Fugazi accepted our offer to take him to dinner afterwards, and unknown to him, RPS had selected Raos in Harlem. I was driving a Capri which had a dodgy shock absorber, and we bounced around the potholed streets. It was dark and there were plenty of unsavoury characters hanging about as we looked for the restaurant; there were a few blocks of the Italian Quarter in Harlem, which are easily recognised by the flags flying. We went down the steps and saw punters playing the numbers game. Immediately, Fugazi was greeted like a long-lost friend by the doormen, bartenders, waiters. The owner appeared as soon as he heard who had arrived, and from then on we were onlookers. We had a fantastic evening, with Fugazi and the owner choosing the food and wine between them. When we left several hours later, Fugazi told me it was foolish to have parked the car on the other side of the street because of the potential dangers that could happen in the time it took to cross over.

There was a meeting of the Founding Fathers, and because I had played such a big part in preventing Club Caribbean from going under, including getting a government loan, they decided to give me a directorship. RPS approached me in the front lobby and made me the offer. I still had a lot to learn; instead of saying how delighted and privileged I was and could he please give me twenty-four hours to think about it, I told him *no thank you* before the words hardly left his lips, which displeased him for years afterwards. It was the right answer, as I knew what measures had been taken to keep the hotel afloat and they were not all kosher. As a servant of the company being told what to do by the directors, I was not comfortable but was content to go along in order to survive. It would be a different matter to be sitting on the board as a chartered accountant, and no way was I prepared to put my head in that noose.

Sue and I continued to have fun, not forgetting the wise words of Valda, one of my dear maids: "Count your blessings every day, every single one of them."

Harvey and Wong arranged a surprise birthday party for me in Encore with over a hundred people, which I was delightfully shocked by and thoroughly enjoyed—I had come a long way in two years.

Every month I was travelling away from Jamaica, mainly for business reasons, and as large as Jamaica was, it helped avoid island fever. In March I went to Toronto to visit Treasure Tours. Foolishly, I left the warmth of Jamaica and didn't take any winter clothes and we landed in a temperature of seven degrees Fahrenheit, or minus fourteen Centigrade. Once I'd bought appropriate clothing, it was a comfortable dry heat and I hardly felt cold.

Sue enjoyed crewing in a Sailfish, and we'd head north out of the reef, tack to the east and come back inside the reef, then a broad reach back to Water Sports. The circuit would take about half an hour if you didn't continue further out to sea.

One day, there was good stiff breeze blowing, and I asked Sue to hold the rope to the single sail as we sped with the wind so that I could unscrew the bung that would empty the cockpit of water. Next minute we did a somersault when the bow ploughed under water as she'd let go of the line. We were both in the water; Sue was upset as blood was flowing from my arm and she thought she'd wrecked the boat. She asked what she could do. "Swim!" I shouted, as I pointed north to Cuba. All was well, and we were soon back at the bar having a celebratory drink.

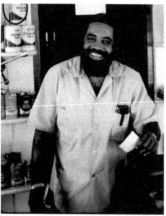

Friends of Sue, Jill Dinnage and Jane Bibbings came out to visit, and we showed them round the island. A wonderful trip through Port Maria to Rio Grande, a beautiful wide river which flowed into Port Antonio. There we took two bamboo rafts and floated peacefully down the river with luscious vegetation either side and looking up at the mountains and the blue sky. There were stops for Red Stripes and local food. The trip lasted about two hours, and we were having fun, embellished by a mild spliff. We went to the side of the river, as Sue needed a wild pee behind a large white rock. All of a sudden there was a loud shriek as the rock turned out to be a cow that got to its feet and walked away.

We took Jill and Jane to Harmony Hall outside Ochi, a gallery run by Annabella Ogden that had beautiful Jamaican artefacts and paintings, and later included an excellent Italian restaurant which Mick Jagger regards as one of his favourites, as do I. We drove them around Cockpit Country through hamlets including Wait a Bit and Quick Step and watched cascading waters.

I moved out of Encore down the hill to After All, which I shared with David Scales, the new general manager. There was an equally beautiful view overlooking the golf course and the Caribbean. The swimming pool was being repaired, so we celebrated Sue's birthday with a disco in the empty pool, which was a weird experience. There was a BBQ, and Robert Salm, Richard's father, cooked the steaks.

Robert Salm's behaviour didn't help the working capital of the hotel. RPS would ask his father for money to cover losses, which he'd eventually provide, but instead of it being used to help the cash flow he'd come out from the UK and embark on a project such as building a large two-storey building overlooking the ocean, saying that as he'd put the money in he could spend it as he wanted. This had several bad consequences. Firstly, we remained strapped for cash. Secondly, compound interest was charged. Thirdly, the building in question required retrospective planning permission from the local authority, which was not forthcoming without a bribe as it had been built too close to the sea.

A couple of weekends later, I took Sue to Negril, or rather she drove the yellow Beetle, which in hindsight was fairly risky as she didn't have a driving licence and I was teaching her to drive. We stayed in Negril Beach Village, a brand new hotel that had opened the previous December and had been full ever since. It operated like Club Med, with sharks teeth to pay for drinks and any purchases from the shops; meals were included as well as Rosemont wine, which wasn't the best. There was a great atmosphere and one bar had a side open to the swimming pool, which was fun.

I arranged to go scuba diving, and a few of us set off in a boat as Sue waved goodbye; she didn't have a good feeling. The dive leader asked what weights I wanted, and I said I didn't need any as I'd never worn them back at CC or at Sunset Divers in Cayman. No comment was made, and we flipped backwards into the water. Very soon we entered a cave and I realised something peculiar was happening as I arrived at neutral buoyancy; when I breathed in, I would rise towards the roof of the cave and when I breathed out I'd sink. The others had gone ahead and I was soon touching the roof of the cave on the in breath. Without panicking, I breathed out, searched the floor and found a couple of conch shells which provided enough mass for me to make my way out. I had a suspicious feeling that the guide had done this on purpose to teach me a lesson that could have been fatal; I had always dived with steel tanks and this was the first time I'd encountered aluminium ones. I was asked if I wanted to go down again with weights, but I politely declined. It was as frightening as seeing a moray eel leering out of its little hollow on the drop off from Club Caribbean; if one got hold of you it would expand so that it couldn't be budged, and there would be no way of escape.

We enjoyed walking along the seven-mile beach and swimming in the coves, which at that time were unspoilt. The other big attraction was Rick's Café, where we drank cocktails and played backgammon until the sun began to set and provided the most spectacular views. Sue drove all the way back to Runaway Bay without incident.

The diving in Cayman was amazing. They had been eco-friendly for years and had wrecks with many incredible fish of sizes not seen in Jamaica, such as grouper, snapper and jewfish, and wonderful coloured fish of all shapes and ranges; it would go dark as massive rays glided overhead. Visiting the Turtle Centre was also fascinating.

David Scales' decree nisi divorce papers came through and we decided to celebrate by going through all the cocktails on the board one by one, starting at about

11:00 in the morning. Sue went shopping in Ochi with Diane Lucy and when they returned three hours later we were still playing backgammon and drinking cocktails. We finished well into the afternoon, and I "walked" with Sue down the beach, escorting Diane to her cottage, and for a reason I can't remember, I threw my Yellow Bird down the front of her white dress before heading back to After All. Sue and I came down for dinner; I was much the worse for wear and spent a good while explaining to Bill Bailey, the head bartender, that I was in the "goathouse. Not the doghouse, the goathouse." A disaster was somehow avoided when for some reason I decided to go into the kitchens and tried to go through the exit door, only to be met by a waiter carrying a tray laden with dinners coming the other way. The more serious accident was averted when Claudia found David Scales in the swimming pool about to go under for the third time and rescued him from drowning.

I continued to visit NYC, and one time I travelled on the train from Grand Central Station to the Foleys through heavy rains. There had been storms and tornados all over the States, and with delays on the railway tracks and power and telephone lines down, it was almost like Jamaica. The winds and rains had subsided by the time I was leaving NYC, and for fun I took a helicopter ride from the Pan Am building to JFK, and to make it more of a journey—much to the surprise of the check-in clerk—I went via La Guardia. It was a thrilling experience flying over the Manhattan skyscrapers, and it cost little more than a cab.

It was an amazing day when I picked Shirley, King's partner, up from their family yard in Runaway Bay early in the morning and set off for Richmond gaol to collect King. It had been a long eighteen months and the day couldn't arrive fast enough for them both. We left the prison with no ceremony, carrying the artefacts King had created. He had turned some beautiful bowls, jars and candlestick holders in mahogany mahoe, and lignum vitae; they had graceful lines, and one gift for me was an frame inlaid with a story of African kings. King was interested to hear that

Oliver had made furniture and woodcarvings, including toys for children after the end of the Second World War, and I told him about Puffin Billy, the engine he'd made for me as a small child. As well as sending his regards, he suggested coconut water and a little lime as a medicine for Oliver's hardening arteries.

The major question was where King would like to go and what he'd like to do. Without a second thought it was Blue Hole, Port Antonio, which was an idyllic bit of sea surrounded by the most beautiful scenery, protected from the inshore sea breezes. He chatted to a friend who operated the water sports, and within minutes we were in a ski boat, the tow rope taking up the slack for the most amazing reverse start; as King came out of the water, he snorted what appeared to be gallons of water through his nostrils, just like a massive beast of burden, as he blew away the horrors of the last eighteen months; for me, it was his cry of freedom.

We had lunch and headed for Spanish Town to pick up Sue, then back to the north coast. It was dark by the time we arrived in Runaway Bay, and we still had over an hour's drive into the hills above Alexandria, the heart of the ganja country.

Baa, a serious drug dealer, had seen me visit King in the open gaol a couple of times while he was working in the fields and made it known that he wanted to buy the Mach 1 Mustang, which fortunately RPS was wanting to sell, and we'd agreed a price. The four of us drove up through Brownstown and continued a further half an hour as the roads became narrower and narrower, eventually arriving in a hamlet in the pitch dark with no street lights. King called out and two forms appeared through the darkness and a whispered conversation took place. Although I had no doubt I was in safe hands, I was in totally new territory, and Sue, who I was deeply in love with and felt a great responsibility for, was in the back of the car with Shirley. All was well, and we dropped King and Shirley at their home and, totally drained following an exciting, emotional and very long day, grabbed some dinner and much needed drinks at Club Caribbean and headed back to After All.

Time was fast approaching for me to move to Miami to launch Passkey in the United States. It was au revoir rather than goodbye, as I would be returning monthly to oversee the financial systems and whenever needed to run the hotel if RPS and the general manager were off the island. The biggest joy was that Sue and I would be starting to share our lives together, and nothing could have made me happier. During the week, I would be able to read poetry to my beautiful little whale in bed from *Verse and Worse* and *I Touch the Earth and the Earth Touches Me* by Hugh Prather, wonderful pieces of love and wisdom.

Jamaica had certainly changed my life. With the associated travelling, it was no surprise my passport, issued in Liverpool in 1974, had run out of space and had to be renewed in 1978 as there was no room for any more visas and stamps. I had met phenomenal people from all walks of life—Fred Perry, the brilliant Wimbledon

Champion amongst them, who was director of Runaway Bay Golf Club. I made wonderful friendships, and the work experience was exceptional. It was a pleasure reading Morris Cargill, who wrote a daily article in the *Gleaner*— he was one man who didn't pull his punches. He was erudite, tearing government ministers and bishops apart for wrongdoings and faux pas while being quick to praise accomplishments.

Jamaicans are survivors, extremely resourceful, with the ability to remain happy in the face of adversity. I learnt a lot from them and was eternally grateful to Jamaica for helping me rediscover the happiness I knew as a child growing up in rural Wales, and I was proud to have shed blood for my second country. I was incredibly lucky that I was allowed to make mistakes, maybe too many, and have the chance to learn from them. RPS, in his Chairman's Statement, wrote that it was unusual for a financial comptroller to be as popular as Tim and yet maintain control.

I loved the Jamaicans' sense of freedom, warmth and sensitivity and built a rapport with many, some as a consequence of the sympathy I had with their suffering over the centuries. I explained that the Welsh had more similarities with Jamaicans than the English, compounded by my inherent feelings of rejection. We were a conquered nation; castles were built to keep us down and efforts made to destroy our language. My mother experienced the Welsh Knot, where school children were humiliated if they were found speaking Welsh in the playground by having a slate with *WK* written on it hung around their necks. I'd point out that slaves had hospitals provided for them and their welfare considered, not forgetting they endured being branded and whipped. In a similar way, those who worked in coal mines had their freedom taken away. They'd go down into the black in cages early in the morning, and the sky would be dark when they surfaced. Their lives were locked into company shops when they were unable to pay their debts and credit had run out. *How Green Was My Valley* by Richard Llewellyn and *Rape of the Fair Country* by Alexander Cordell describe the sensitivity of the mining communities and the hardships they faced.

One of the achievements I'm most pleased about was coaching Harvey to take over from me as Financial Comptroller; twice before he had failed when given the opportunity.

Another of my prodigies was Carol Spencer, who had talent but lacked self-belief. She was a quick learner who I eventually encouraged to gain qualifications. In May 2020, she sent me a message the morning of my third chemo treatment in Clatterbridge that brought a tear to my eyes:

Tim, may God go with you today and I am happy you are feeling really good. You were good to Jamaica as much as it was good to you.

LUCKY BASTARD

4 February 1949 was a traumatic day for Beryl. Her parents had kicked her out of the house when they found out she was pregnant, and she went to stay with an aunt in Liverpool. In later years, her mother blamed her father and her father blamed her mother. They lived on a social housing estate in Manchester; her father drank a surfeit of alcohol and made a living by travelling to Ireland to buy donkeys and selling them back in England.

This I found out in 1990 after tracing my birth mother. Throughout my life, I felt I never fitted in, especially in St John's, where it was very much stiff-upper-lip and showing any emotion was regarded as a sign of weakness. Boys would gather like wolves, as in *Lord of the Flies*, to take advantage and do their best to make a wounded soul's life even more hell. The word "bastard" resounded round my brain whenever I heard it called—which was often, amongst teenagers in a boys' school—even though ninety-nine percent of the time it was not aimed at me. From the age of eight, I knew I was born out of wedlock, as when I was sitting on the tumbling down wall of the Rectory grounds adjoining the local council estate, chatting to my friends the Wright brothers, they asked whether I'd been born or adopted. Of course I didn't have a clue what that meant, so I asked Oliver. He replied saying that I was their chosen child and that was good enough for me.

I had bountiful love from the amazing people who adopted me at seven months, and my dad, the Rev. O. J. Hill, was one of the most enlightened people who ever walked this earth. He understood me and was always forgiving despite the atrocious way I carried on at times, particularly in Shotton, which was a rough town, and with me going to a "posh" public school in the South of England I felt I had to prove I was one of them through even worse language and behaviour. Enid exuded calmness and love. Oliver tried to encourage me to read during my teens, particularly books I might enjoy, such as James Bond, which is why I felt able to relate the story about sharing a three-bed hotel room in Lake Atitlan with two air hostesses. I remember going excitedly to him at the age of nineteen having been enthralled by Victor Hugo's *Les Miserables* and being astounded that he knew so much about the characters in a book I had just put down that he hadn't read for thirty years. Enid enjoyed him reading all sorts of literature to her in bed. At about the same time, I asked him what classical records I'd enjoy for my new sound system, and he reeled off a few. I went out and bought and massively enjoyed them. Where did that knowledge come from, as I don't remember him listening to classical music on the radio or going to classical concerts?

It was a good friend, Gordon Taylor, who, in around 2010, helped me understand a part of my emotional state of mind which I had carried throughout my life. He'd been watching a series of programmes on television and one of the conclusions was that anybody who had been adopted had a feeling of rejection. This had never occurred to me, as throughout my years I have always received so much love.

I knew I was different, and for years I'd wanted to discover my roots, as a fluent Welsh speaker at the age of eight and having the emotions associated with Welsh blood flowing through my veins. In my teens I was asked whether I was from America because of the way I spoke and my looks, and people would ask if I originated from places from Argentina to South Africa. One cousin even questioned if I had a touch of the tar brush in me. Mari, my late father's sister, said she was pleased I now had my own family because I was never really a Hill. At my Aunt Gwyneth's funeral, my cousin

Meredudd asked that I sit with Sue in a different pew from the rest of the immediate family. When I was asked directly where I came from in my teens, I replied saying I didn't know but whoever my birth parents were, they must have been fucking good looking and clever. I had long before determined I would attempt to trace them, but not while Oliver and Enid were alive, out of respect for everything they had done and the abundant love they had heaped on me.

I shed tears of joy when I recently came across this letter. There are things I regret saying and doing, in particular not asking my mum and dad if it was okay for me to go to America in 1970 as it would mean missing my graduation ceremony. This meant nothing to me, and I selfishly took the opportunity without thinking of the pleasure it would have given them after all the sacrifices they had made to see me receive my certificate in cap and gown. It was not a proud moment when I realised years later I had taken that moment away from them.

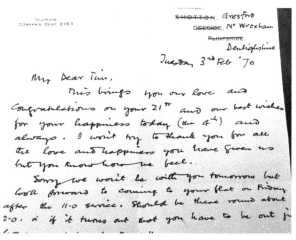

One of the many influences Oliver had on me was to be frugal. I had printed the letterhead above on the Adana printing press with Gill Sans type face whilst we were living in Shotton. There must have been sheets left over, so to avoid waste Oliver struck a line through with his fountain pen and substituted Gresford for Shotton. He would straighten drawing pins for reuse and buy white sticky labels to cover addresses on the letters he received so that envelopes could be reused. I still continue to reuse envelopes, often those provided by HMRC to send PAYE returns; I've not paid myself for over five years, so there are still plenty spare.

My birth certificate was smaller than most and read *Paul Edwin Hatton, Smithdown Road, Sefton Park, Liverpool.* I didn't want to go through Social Services to find my birth family, although there are many good people who work there. I wanted to be in control of the situation and there was a chance I would be handled by someone with whom I had little empathy. My plan was to view the situation from afar and decide how to make the connection. Without Sue knowing, I went through various government records and eventually came across an address in Longsight, Manchester. I couldn't find a telephone number, so I made a couple of trips to find the address with no success. I used to regularly work in Lincolnshire for Badley Ashton and Associates, so one dark, wet, windy night on my return I made another attempt to find the address. I walked around the streets and was just returning to my car when two elderly ladies appeared. I asked if they knew where Beryl Hatton lived, although it was forty years since she had been ejected, and to my great surprise and relief they directed me to the house, which wasn't far away. I knocked on the adjacent door, which an old man answered and pointed out my mistake. The right door was answered by a lady who was Beryl's mother. I was smartly dressed in a pin-striped suit and overcoat. We spoke for a while and she told me Beryl would be visiting at the weekend and gave me her telephone number. My blood grandmother suspected I was something to do with Beryl's son but not that she was speaking to her actual grandson. I called Beryl at the weekend, and we arranged to meet at her house in Abergele.

It took me a long time to find her cottage. I drove up and down the road to Llanrwst, and just as I was about to give up, I found it off Compton Road. I knocked on the door, which was answered by a smartly dressed lady of small height and slight stature. We hugged, and very quickly she asked me, "Why did it take you so long?"

We went to the Kinmel Hotel and I ordered two gin and tonics, and as I stood at the bar, holding the glass, she told me I looked just like Harry, my father. Her main concern was that I'd had a happy childhood. Oliver had written to her for the first three years then stopped for whatever reason. I told her I'd had an amazing life, not a great time in St John's, but plenty of good experiences. She said it was good for me that I'd been adopted. I discovered many years later while she was heavily sedated with morphine in hospital that she'd had post-traumatic stress disorder after giving birth and was placed in a home for unmarried mothers. Beryl told Emily that there was not a day that she hadn't thought of me and been very sad. Since we met in 1990, it had always been too painful for Beryl to speak about those early months. As our family increased, the love she received grew.

I learnt Harry was an Orthodox Jew, which immediately explained my looks, and although he'd wanted to create a life together with Beryl, she'd realised that couldn't happen because he would be disowned by his family, who would tear at their hair and rip their clothes—bloody religion. As a teenager, Beryl used to spend time in the Quaker Friends Meeting House and was later drawn towards Buddhism and meditation, and for two years she was president of the Theosophical Society. She was also involved in the Peace Movement with Fr Owen Hardwicke and the Cohens.

She married one of three brothers who had a building company together but never had another child. All three turned out to be alcoholics, and the two other sisters-in-law divorced their respective husbands, but Beryl lived separately in the same house. When he died, she was left with enormous debt; did Harry help her get back on her feet? Her close friend, Val Knowles, I think is the only one ever to have known about my existence until Beryl went into hospital and I was recorded as next of kin. Val drove her to Rosebank, where we had lunch and spent the afternoon together with my family; Beryl never learnt to drive. Our relationship built, and Beryl spent most Easters and Christmases with us, as well as other weekends, and we had lunch or dinner together monthly, somewhere around Abergele or Llandudno, until her health failed and she was housebound. Sue and our children couldn't have been more welcoming, and Beryl became an integral part of our family. A couple of years ago, Beryl asked whether I'd like to have her three cottages left to me in her will. I thought carefully, and replied that her grandchildren and great-grandchildren would be delighted. Her face lit up. The will, dated 1 December 2017, confirmed this.

I was now desperate to meet my birth father to understand more about my roots. Beryl had told me his name was Harold Hoffman and he lived in Blackpool. At the time, I was working a couple of days a week in Karp's Greek Street, Liverpool, and had struck up a life-long friendship with Harvey Abramson, one of the directors. As his name suggests, he was Jewish, and there was no better person to carry out investigative work. A couple of weeks later, through his synagogue connections, he gave me an address in Blackpool. A few days later, well dressed, I travelled to Blackpool unannounced and knocked on the door of 440 Queen's Promenade. A lovely lady answered, mezuzahs on each of the doors, and I asked whether Harold Hoffman was at home; how different the next thirty years might have been if he had been. She said he was in Blackpool Casino if I wanted to speak to him. Feeling apprehensive, I walked into the casino early evening. There were few people, and I asked a waiter for Harold Hoffman. He went over to a table where four people were playing cards and returned to say Harry would be over soon. He came, tall and dapper, and I introduced myself. I wish I had a recording of the conversation, because it must have been the best talking I have ever done. I asked if he remembered Beryl—oh, yes, he had a friend in the army called Beryl. No, someone he'd had a relationship with—and I was the result. It's hard to imagine what was running through his head, suddenly being confronted by his offspring. *Is this guy after money? Does he want to ruin my reputation as a founder of the Reform Synagogue and a leading light in the Blackpool Sportsman's Aid Society as well as President of the Parachute Regimental Association, or is he just looking for vengeance?* Luckily after, a few long moments, he acknowledged the situation and said he would return when the card game was finished—no doubt he wanted time to collect his thoughts.

My confidence wasn't at its highest as I was still recovering from my totally unjust firing as financial director of Zeta and was in the process of suing them in the High Court. Nevertheless, we had the most enlightening two to three hours together. We had similar stature—huge barrel chests, long legs and long slender fingers. He regaled me with his wartime experiences in the SAS and North Africa; he didn't have a favourable opinion of Field Marshal Montgomery, and it was even lower after the Market Garden slaughter. He told me how he'd helped two Americans escape from German captivity in Sicily, and after rescuing them from a burning boat returned for the log book, for which he was awarded the Purple Heart, a phenomenal honour for a Brit. He was captured three times by the Germans and escaped three times. Many were captured and, for various reasons, that's where they'd remain for the rest of the war. When asked how come he'd kept escaping, he replied because he didn't like the food. His nickname was Tony the Italian because of his dark curly hair. The first thing he had to do after burying his parachute was hide his dog tags, which would identify what burial he should have, therefore his Jewish religion. It is amazing that I'm here today, considering his exploits as a war hero and his ability to escape from the Germans who annihilated so many Jews. He wrestled and boxed for the army, swam and played water polo for Lancashire and was a member of the Caterpillar Club. I'm sure he was proud of me, especially my sporting abilities, with my long-standing swimming records, ten international rugby caps and captaining Florida to victory over the all Southern States.

He told me he had two children, a daughter and a son who was a chartered accountant with severe mental health difficulties. I didn't want that meeting to end.

I was high as a kite all the way back to Wrexham. I had discovered my roots and been accepted by my father, who not only was an amazing athlete and war hero to boot, but one of the few Brits to receive the American Purple Heart for bravery. I couldn't wait to tell Sue. During the next week, I'd attack her from various hiding places around the house and pretend to slit her throat, just as Cato Fong attacked Peter Sellars in the *Pink Panther* films.

I made attempts to find his son and daughter with no success. I had recently started T H Consulting Group, a limited company to help small-to-medium companies increase productivity by better use of IT and sound business strategy through Professional Quality, Personal Encouragement and Emotional Support.

I formed the company as EuroTOH, and thankfully a friend in PR produced a smart A4 binder for me which I sent to Big H asking for his opinion, but really I was trying to start a relationship. I didn't hear back, which wasn't surprising as he'd said when we met that it was too late for this to happen.

I wasn't slow to let my family and friends know that I had a father who was one of the most enlightened men ever to have walked this earth and another who was in the SAS, a war hero.

Nothing much happened on the genealogy front until 15 October 2005 when a surprise 60th birthday for Harvey was held in the Crowne Plaza next to John Lennon Airport, where Neil, his youngest son, was one of the head chefs. Harvey was expecting a dozen immediate family to celebrate with a meal, whereas there were well over a hundred guests. When everyone was seated with drinks and canapes, the "This is Your Life" show started. There were six of us behind closed curtains, and we came out in turn to relate something hilarious about our good friend. I was the fifth to speak and Rabbi Norman Zalud was the last; he was a long-time family friend of the Abramsons, and Harvey used to blow the shofar in his Liverpool synagogue. In the few minutes we had together, having just met for the first time, we found out that he buried my father on 18 November 1997.

Harvey and I were in touch regularly, and out of the blue he let me know the following posting was made on 7 September 2017 in the Jewish Small Communities Network Blackpool United Hebrew Congregation:

Hello I wonder if you could help me. I am related to Harry Hoffman who died in 1997. He was a WW2 war hero with two Purple Hearts. In an obituary it states he was the president of Blackpool Parachute Club – not sure if they still exist or whether there are still members around. He volunteered for the Sportsman's Aid Charity. I am trying to find anyone who knew him or his family. Hope you can help. David Firth

Do coincidences happen? For Harvey to have looked at this site at the time of the post!

I got in touch with David Firth, who asked me to describe myself and whether I had any athletic ability. He soon realised I was telling the truth—I was Harry's son and had met him. It was several months before David was able to find his daughter Debra's contact details, and a further six months before he got round to phoning her. He started by making sure she was sitting down, then asked if she was aware she had a brother other than Paul, who had died of cancer of the oesophagus in 2006. She was astounded, and as they spoke, Sarra, her daughter, googled me, and there were close family resemblances to the photos she found, including the one with Mark Carney, governor of the Bank of England.

I looked like her father, but Paul had taken after his mother, short and stocky with size 7 shoes. Patricia, Debra's mother, was very short even though she was a Tiller Girl.

Debra phoned me straight away on Tuesday 26 June 2018, and we arranged to meet in Chester Grosvenor at 2:00 p.m. the following Monday. As well as being wonderful for me, it was something Debra had dreamt of, having watched programmes about this happening to other people, but never did she once imagine she had "unknown" family. She cried for a week, spoke to her aunt in Laguna Beach, Los Angeles, who said if I had hammerhead toes then there was no doubt—"But how can I ask him to take his shoes and socks off in Chester's smartest hotel?"

Tim Portugal and Harry Sudan, note the vast rib cages

The days couldn't pass quickly enough, and eventually the hour of the meeting arrived. We made our way into the hotel, and I anxiously looked around and saw a woman who obviously must have been Debra. Sue relates how I went straight up and we gave each other the most enormous hug of friendship and love—hard for an onlooker to believe this was our first meeting. There was no need for Debra to ask me to take my shoes and socks off, as it was a beautiful sunny day and I was dressed in shorts and open sandals. Sarra, her daughter, the same age as Emily, accompanied her and her partner of thirty years, Brendan Ward, an ex Blackpool golf professional.

Debra had married at eighteen and a daughter was born. Harry wanted Debra to call her Sarah after his mother, but Debra didn't want that name. Harry offered to buy her a brand new car if she did, and a compromise was reached whereby she was called Sarra and Debra received her car. The marriage didn't last long, and Sarra spent much of her time living with Harry and Patricia. Sarra attended Rossall School in Fleetwood, and she disliked the experience of independent schools as much as me; the junior school was on the same circuit as Lawrence House.

There was the most wonderful feeling of joy and exultation as we related stories about our lives and any doubt about mis-identity disappeared. Debra said it was just as if her father had walked into the room with a huge smile and more of Harry's idiosyncrasies. I was bowled over when she produced Big H's beret, cap badge and a war medal as gifts. A further coincidence was that the staff in Club Caribbean had nicknamed me Big Bird from *Sesame Street*; they didn't know my dad was called Big H.

Much to Sue's surprise as she "hadn't tidied up and there was no food in the house," I invited everyone back to Rosebank. The joy of this was that Sam could join us and join in the celebrations.

The atmosphere was thrilling. We found out that there was little in the house that Debra and Sarra would eat, as Debra's staple diet was chip butties and Sarra ate little more, so we adjourned to the Pant, the love flowed and we parted at 8:30.

Stories about Harry were told. How his family was very poor in Manchester, and when he signed up for the army, they each contributed towards buying him a washbag and brush, which was stolen on the first night; from then on, he determined anything that moved was potentially his. He was bullied in the army because he was Jewish and was nicknamed Tony the Italian because of his long curly hair; most others had short cuts. One of the things he was most proud of was the defence of the Pegasus Bridge, which helped the Normandy landings become a success. Towards the end of the war, he climbed the outside structure to the top of the Eiffel Tower, intending to parachute down, which in the end he deemed too dangerous. At the end of the war, he thought he would become a stunt man and auditioned in Pinewood Studios. After being thrown down a flight of stairs for the sixth time, he decided there were less painful ways to make a living. He had a successful career in the Rank Organisation, also Pearl and Dean with offices in Mayfair. While some were earning £100 a week, Harry would be making £3,000. He had a large flat in Dolphin Square and would fly to Hong Kong for two days at a whim. He always wanted large cars, not to show off but because of his size. He was seriously into horse racing; Patricia never knew how much he lost or won but would receive gifts worth thousands from time to time. As Patricia refused to fly, they would travel to her family in California on the *QEII* to New York then cross the United States by rail; amazingly, I was on the second voyage of the *QEII* and Debra might have been there at the same time. Once, Cunard set sail early and they had to put Debra and her mother up in one of the best hotels in New York for a month. They regularly holidayed in luxury in the South of France. A few years ago, I went with Gordon Taylor to "An Evening with Peter Alliss" in Northwich—Debra and Brendan were there that night!

Family: message on back of family picture: *Thought you would like the photo frame as we are family now "Thank God" With much Love Debra & Sarra XXXXX*

Harry had been courting Patricia and, because he wasn't interested in marrying her, she left to join her family in Canada. No doubt Harry could see he was going to lose another goyim he loved. After two months, he went out and persuaded her to return to the UK. When the boat docked, Patricia asked to arrange the date they were going to get married, which Harry laughed off; she made straight for the bursar's office to buy a ticket back to Canada, and Harry sensibly decided that they would definitely marry. Patricia converted to Judaism and they tied the knot in Blackpool, 1953.

It was a mystery to Debra why Harry didn't invite me back to his home after meeting in Blackpool Casino. Debra remembers the THC folder arriving in the post and Sarra recalls it being in the middle drawer of the chest in the hall where he kept his treasures, including war medals, a gold fox with ruby eyes from Burlington arcade which he wore on special occasions and SAS books. Harry was a generous and kind man who helped lots of people including in later life, many at Christmas organising food parcels. Debra had no doubt her mother would have accepted me with open arms, as one of her relatives rescued a little boy from an orphanage who they found cleaning steps—he had been abandoned by another relation in a marriage dispute. It could well have been because Harry's son was going through serious depression at the time, and the arrival of another son the spitting image of his war-hero dad might have done him untold damage. The reason Harry hadn't replied to my letter was that he had suffered a series of heart attacks, dying several times on the operating table, and strokes; Patricia had had to help him shower, while Debra drove him where he needed to go, so they would have discovered the unburied secret. Another important reason is that it would take some explaining that my birth name had been registered as Paul, and his son by Patricia was Paul. No doubt he would have been quizzed as to who I was and what I wanted when I knocked on the door of Queens Promenade, looking very much like Harry when he was forty.

Another mystery for Debra is why they'd gone on holiday several times to Llandudno, close to Abergele, when Blackpool was on the sea with many more attractions and was a fashionable place at the time—could it be that he'd been visiting Beryl on the side, as she had told me he lived in Blackpool? They must have been communicating. Not long after Beryl moved from Manchester to stay with a friend in Abergele, Harry had turned up and tried to persuade her to make a life together.

Big H was captured during the Market Garden operation: Fangmanweg Street.

Debra's Grampa, who was in the First World War at the Battle of the Somme, and Harry were very close and they shared wartime experiences. Ernest Green volunteered at the age of fifteen by exaggerating his age. Debra has a picture of his platoon with thirty-five people, and the next day, everyone else was dead. A truck with the bodies was being wheeled to a mass grave when the brigadier who he served recognised him amongst the dead and had him removed and taken to hospital, and amazingly he survived. Another miracle that Debra and I were given life.

That's lovely ☺ what a wonderful photo I am so happy 😀 you are having a lovely time My uncle went to the cenotaph in London yesterday for my grandpa who was at the Somme and wore his ⚕ 🎖 🎖 medals and marched for him. We cannot tell you how thrilled we are to have you in our life so fabulous hope you all have a wonderful day in London for Kate's Birthday 🎂 (12 November 2018)

Love 💝 Debra and Sarra 💝😊🎂💝💖

My heart was bursting with pride as Sue filmed me walking the exact same street with my hands behind my head as my dad had done seventy-five years earlier, but he'd been surrounded by Germans carrying machine guns.

Re-enactment and Tim rode with Matthew Hallett in his Kobler in the Race to John Frost Bridge for the 75th Commemoration September 2019. Right hand picture wearing the jacket Harry would have worn for parachuting and was captured in.

Email:

On Monday, July 2, 2018, 10:23 p.m.:

Dear Tim, Sue & Sam,

We have just arrived home safely. Thank you so very much for one of the most amazing days of our lives. It was such a pleasure to meet you and your beautiful family.

Our Dad would have been so proud to see us together and I'm so thrilled to have such a wonderful gentleman as my Brother (& Uncle). Thank you for inviting us all to your lovely home and for a lovely meal.

Several cards arrived:

Dearest Tim, It was an absolute thrill to meet you and your lovely family on Monday. An Amazing Day I will never forget. I love having a very special Handsome "chosen Brother" With much Love Debra X

Dear Tim

Monday was such an amazing day! One I will never forget. I hope we can have many more like that, very soon. Lots of love Sarra XXX

Dear Tim

It was so great to meet you, Sue and Sam at long last. Can't wait to meet everyone! Lots of Love Sarra XXX

To which I replied:

Just opened your cards, and eyes full of joyful tears

Yes one of the most memorable happiest days of my life. As I keep telling anyone who'll listen and emails coming back full of wonderful congratulations

Monday was amazing (seems an age ago) and gave me a special sense of belonging and completed the circle of my life
Much love
Your chosen brother (and uncle)
😄🐙😆❤️😊😊😊
Didn't want to wait to put these feelings in a card!!

In my diary to myself:
Last week was one of the best of my life, rather this week! It has given me a sense of belonging and completed a circle bringing another shed load of happiness. Jamaica had brought back to me the happiness I knew as a child growing up in rural Wales for which I will always be indebted. Being accepted and receiving so much love from my own flesh and blood wiped away the hang ups I carried with me about not fitting in and any notion of rejection. Whatever happens from now on that feeling of exultation can never be taken away.

It all happened so quickly after Sarra emailed, and Emily burst into tears when she heard. We went to her's in Liverpool the following Wednesday, and Kate couldn't wait to meet them either.

Everyone got on incredibly well at Em's, and not long afterwards, Sue and I went to Debra's lovely house in Pickmere Lane, Cheshire. There was a wonderful spread from M&S, including a beautifully decorated cake which Debra and I cut together as a token of unification and love. Gold cutlery was brought out and used for the first time since her mother had died in Stratford-upon-Avon in 2000—it was one of the rewards Harry had won for exceptional performance; he was the go-to marketing person in the UK at the time, Cunard being one of his clients, as was the launch of Concord. We met Debra's dog, called "Harry", and saw the portrait of our dad overlooking the staircase, which Debra waves a finger at each night as she goes to bed, saying "naughty boy".

There is no doubt that I am Lucky Lucky Lucky.

Sanskrit proverb by Kalidasa, Indian poet and playwright, fifth century A.D.:

Look to this day, For it is life, The very life of life

In its brief course lie all the realities and verities of existence

The bliss of growth, The splendour of action, The glory of power

For yesterday is but a dream, And tomorrow is only a vision

But today, well lived, makes every yesterday a dream of happiness

And every tomorrow a vision of hope

APPENDIX:
KPMG ALUMNI ARTICLE 2015

Tell me about your time at KPMG?

Initially it was challenging. In 1970 I graduated with a degree in economics which was for the most part understanding theoretical concepts and suddenly my working life was dealing with minute detail – the discipline did me a lot of good! As I progressed I gained more business knowledge and these years have been an excellent foundation and invaluable guide throughout my assorted career.

What are your fondest memories of the firm?

The people I met, camaraderie, celebrations, staying away on assignments (memorably The Blue Bell, Heversham) and building friendships several of which have lasted over 40 years, amongst them Chris Statham who was my best man. I was in turn best man to John Davies; both Chris and John visited me in Jamaica. It was a privilege and enlightening experience to serve articles under the inspirational Alan Pownall.

Clients were varied such as Hawker Siddeley, Lostock where they developed the Blue Streak missile, Lines Brothers at the time of the selling on of Meccano, and the audit of Border Breweries Wrexham was always fun. John Holt, which was part of the Tiny Rowland empire was an interesting experience with different bands of gold circled tea cups depending on seniority, prints of the slave trade from West Africa on the walls and excuses for non-compliance such as 'documents have been eaten by ants'. I learned the foundations of business and I have been able to apply these across the hundreds of organisations I have been involved with since.

Is there one thing you learned at the firm that has served you well in your career?
Always keep an open mind as things are often not as they first appear.

Since leaving KPMG, you have had an interesting and varied career. Can you tell us more about your life after KPMG?
After leaving KPMG I spent a few months travelling around South America before returning to Jamaica as Financial Comptroller of Club Caribbean. I was straightaway managing 40 people and demanding accuracy and precision from those in accounts in particular, and trying to impose tight deadlines soon led me into trouble. After nine months the MD sent me off the island and I travelled round Central America. It was in the Mayan ruins of Palenque that I received the inspiration that made my life in business rewarding and enjoyable. Instead of expecting everything to be right and on time I decided to accept that things would be wrong and I would work with staff to ensure things were correct going forwards. The welcome I received from the staff when I returned to Jamaica was overwhelming, they thought I had moved on and expressed their emotions openly. At Club Caribbean I continued to introduce new systems as many of theirs were seriously lacking, and successfully trained Harvey to take my place as FC after he had not succeeded in the post on two previous attempts prior to my arrival. In Jamaica I rediscovered the happiness I knew as a child growing up in Montgomeryshire, Mid Wales, before going away to boarding school. My time in Jamaica was a wonderful lesson in life. There was a free spirit and despite the tough conditions many staff lived in there was no hesitation in cracking up to a joke from a comedian or rocking to a reggae band; the bar staff were part of the entertainment.

The economic climate was grim in Jamaica following the 1976 elections when it was believed in certain quarters Michael Manley was courting Fidel Castro too closely.

I relocated to Miami to help put together Passkey, a forerunner to timeshare, as well as returning to Jamaica each month for financial duties. From our experience running Club Caribbean and being faced each year with a decision as to whether to close the hotel for the summer to reduce losses it was obvious that the marginal cost of an additional room night was minimal once the decision had been taken to keep the hotel open. We contracted hotel space with 36 of the top golfing hotels throughout the world from The Rose Garden in Thailand to Sandy Lane Barbados on the basis that golfers want to play different courses and are happy that this is out of season. We were selling 12 weeks of vacation which could be taken at any time over a 12-year period at any combination of hotels at up to 50% discount of current prices. I was also involved in opening Bacchanalia, Coconut Grove, the first wine bar in Florida before returning to the UK in 1979 for family reasons.

Soon after arriving back in North Wales, Michael, who also worked for KPMG during my articles, asked me to join him and I became a 40% equity partner in M D Coxey which he had already established. I looked after the larger clients including Ifor Williams Trailers, Gerrards Bakery, Cable Services and Badley Ashton and Associates Ltd, preferred suppliers of high quality geoscience consultancy to the oil and gas industry worldwide. The eight years were exciting as we grew the practice and amazingly there was never a single argument about expenses or cars bearing in mind that while I was in between transport Michael lent me either his Porsche 911 Turbo, Range Rover or Renault 5TS!

It was a sad day when I left Coxeys to join a client who designed and manufactured data communications equipment as FD with the intention of taking it to the Aim stock market – it didn't happen and in August 1990 I started T H Consulting to provide business and financial advice, focusing on increasing profitability through better use of IT and sound strategy, to small and medium sized organisations. The directors of Club Caribbean soon heard that I was working for myself and invited me back to Jamaica to help solve some of their challenges. I was back four times a year for the next twenty years during which time my children came to love Jamaica and my grandchildren are now building up an appetite for the beauty and culture.

Some of my best experiences over the last 25 years with T H Consulting were with David Clapham, an old friend from Chester in the 60s who qualified as a chartered accountant about the same time as me. While I was in the Caribbean he became a Parisian and over ten years we carried out Intellectual Property Verification for Hollywood Majors together throughout Europe. I am godfather to Chris, one of his twin sons and looking forward to attending the other twin Jonny's wedding this September.

Mark Carney   *Dungeon Electronic Arts*

Recently I have taught Finance and Risk Management on the higher degree MBA course at the local university and because of the success in this I was asked to teach finance to HNC mature students.

You have recently developed The Financial Game App – can you tell us more about this?

I have created the Financial Game App which teaches financial literacy to non-financial people. The app does this in an intuitive way by turning the learning process into a game that imparts the essentials of accounting. It is a subliminal learning process using familiar environments and work processes to implant financial understanding; fear of numbers and convoluted accounting terminology are removed. The app is based on a tried and tested education programme over 10 years resulting in increased levels of financial understanding.

Over time I recognised that there is a dramatic lack of financial awareness not only in the younger generation and school children but in many employees, managers and directors in all sectors of industry and commerce. In fact the National Numeracy Charity say that £20bn a year is being lost in the UK each year because of lack of numeracy. I believe that these fundamentals should be a Life Skill for everyone.

I devised a game using Lego bricks that teaches the basics of accounts without using the words debit and credit. I have used it successfully in the Care Sector where at the beginning of the session delegates weren't sure of the difference between income and expenditure and one home saved over 30% of their admin costs through allocating costs more efficiently. A Social Enterprise running a supermarket who didn't understand margins and the relevance of stock, BTCV to young people up to the age of 21 who hadn't been in employment and Italian Students wanting to study accounts and had limited understanding of English and of course MBA and HNC students.

The real inspiration for the app came when I had dinner with Chi Onwurah in the Palace of Westminster when she was shadow innovation minister. I boasted that with the game children of 12 could talk intelligently about finance rather than regurgitating notes to pass exams at the age of 16 and 18. As a result I was given a space before lunch in the local secondary school with a group of mixed ability year 9s. They understood direct costs, indirect costs, margins, bottom line and were even able to produce simple P&L accounts in just 40 minutes. Being in no doubt that I had something very powerful that could revolutionise the understanding of finance while improving numeracy, not only in the UK but around the world, I ran about trying to turn the Lego bricks into a computer game. I had no idea whether this would cost £50k or £250k. I was invited to make a five-minute presentation at a meeting of ESTnet when Richard, who was less than half my age, approached me and understood immediately what was needed and the problems it will solve for people in business. Thanks to the skills and vision of members of his staff, one of whom is a third of my age, the first two apps are now available on Android and iPads.

The primary one teaches the fundamentals of Profit and Loss from sales income, direct costs, contribution to overheads and margins. The knowledge gained from this basic app will help knock chunks out of the £20bn a year being lost in the UK because of lack of numeracy. The Balance Sheet App provides higher level understanding and imparts the construction of Accounts as well as the important Financial Ratios in a fun way via experiential learning. Apps will be customised for any company in any sector using their own branded images and structure of accounts. Broadcasting corporate messages can be sent by using push notification features in the app. The benefits go way beyond increasing profitability through the understanding of figures. Team Work will be improved as a result of a common language and barriers to culture change will be reduced.

Bivek Sharma of KPMG, who is rolling out the £40m programme for SMEs, immediately saw the potential when I presented the app to him in Chester and I am also involved in conversations with Jayne Gadhia, CEO Virgin Money, and Stephen Kelly, CEO Sage.

I visited Baton Rouge earlier this year to carry out further research on the potential for the apps and I'm delighted to say there is great enthusiasm with members of the Louisiana State University Incubation Centre to commercialise it in the United States.

What would you say is your greatest professional accomplishment?
Refinancing CC after Hurricane Gilbert nearly wiped it out. They were well underinsured and had massively overspent on the rebuilding and refurbishment, the relationship with their bankers had fallen apart and there was no clear strategy about how they were going to survive. I didn't realise this was the challenge when the MD invited me back in 1990. I helped bring all this together and continued to carry out assignments for them until after the property was leased to Decameron in 2001.

Which three attributes have helped you achieve success?
Positive mental attitude which grew during my three-month trip round America in 1970.
As they say in the Shaolin Temple – get knocked down seven times get up eight.
Enjoying different cultures in work and travel and learning from those experiences.

What are your future plans?
I'm passionate about making the Financial Game App a success as my family, friends and target audiences will confirm.

I want to spend time with my family and grandchildren, skiing, golfing and becoming a better beekeeper and bell ringer. Following a full thickness tear of my distal biceps tendon playing rugby for the Golden Oldies in Edinburgh in 2008, my boots have been hung up for the last time.

On a voluntary basis as well as being treasurer of the local Christian Aid Branch I'm involved with Erlas

Victorian Walled Garden, which is both a charity and a place. The charity exists to promote the health, wellbeing and development of people with a variety of disabilities and challenges

I was instrumental in Hanson gifting their 70 acres land holdings at Fagl Lane Quarry, Hope in Flintshire, to the Park in the Past project. In all 120 acres of land have been acquired which will lead to the construction of a Roman Marching Fort, Iron Age farmstead, a facility for the community with special interest in wild life and biodiversity and a visitor centre. There is also a 35-acre lake for passive water sports.

I have recently been appointed independent examiner for the Bloom Appeal. This charity has been set up in the last 18 months to:

1. Support the care and wellbeing of patients with blood cancers.

2. Fund scientific research into treating and curing leukaemias, lymphomas and other blood cancers.

3. Enhance the education of patients, scientists and healthcare professionals in the field of blood cancers.

The reason I welcomed this opportunity to offer my services freely is because my son-in-law Mark has received excellent treatment in ward 7Y in Liverpool Royal Hospital since he was diagnosed with Acute Lymphoblastic Leukaemia last October, a few floors above A&E where my eldest daughter Emily works as a consultant.

Other things you didn't know about Tim:

Who or what inspires you?

The Rev. O J Hill, who was a Clerk in Holy Orders in the Church in Wales as well as being my father. He had so much love, wisdom and understanding of events and people, especially me. He and my mother Enid set me on the road to a happy and fulfilling life. Oliver was never afraid to fight an injustice or for a cause he believed in.

I wouldn't be where I am today without the Inspiration of Alan Pownall (senior partner Peat Marwick Mitchell

Liverpool) who employed and guided me. I wrote to him on the suggestion of the father of a school friend I was staying with in Cornwall who asked what I was going to do. I wasn't sure so he said Peat Marwick Mitchell were the auditors of the Hong Kong and Shanghai Bank in Singapore where he was the manager and intimated accounting might be an interesting profession.

Is your glass half empty or half full?
Half full.

Motivational phrase or quote that resonates with you
HH Dalai Lama – "If you want others to be happy, practice compassion. If you want to be happy, practice compassion."

AUTHOR PROFILE

Timothy Oliver was born 4 February 1949 in Smithdown Road, Liverpool. He had an enchanted childhood amongst the luscious green rolling hills and vales of Montgomeryshire, mid-Wales, thanks to the abundant love from his parents, the Rev Oliver and Enid Hill; Oliver was one of the most enlightened people ever to walk this earth. All this changed when this sensitive, romantic child went away to boarding school at the age of nine. He discovered resilience, survived and gained a degree in Economics from UCNW before qualifying as a chartered accountant with PMM/KPMG. He soon headed for South America before landing up as financial controller of Club Caribbean, Runaway Bay, Jamaica, the best address he's ever had. He is proud to have shed blood playing rugby for Jamaica when they became Caribbean champions in Barbados and went on to captain Miami University for a season and lead Florida to victory over the southern states of America. Family means everything to him, and with his wife, Sue, he has three wonderful children and six grandchildren.

***

WHAT DID YOU THINK OF LUCKY BASTARD?

A big thank you for purchasing this book. It means a lot that you chose this book specifically from such a wide range on offer. I do hope you enjoyed it.

Book reviews are incredibly important for an author. All feedback will help me improve my writing for the rest of this trilogy and for future projects. If you are able to spare a few minutes to post a review on Amazon, that would be much appreciated.

TESTIMONIALS

Still waters run deep. Mild mannered accountant with hidden talents invariably wearing a smile. Few of his many friends know the full extent of Tim's life or colourful history. Read this fascinating, warm story to find out more and feel the joy that a free spirit can bring.

Chris Peake, Kate's Godfather and Tim's golfing buddy

Lucky Bastard is a revealing insight into Tim's personality. We get an account of his formative years in Mid Wales giving us a hint of the future family man that we would come to know. At the end of the book the search for his true birth family leads us to the conclusion that both nature and nurture have an effect on who we are. Book One leaves us wanting more in anticipation of the follow up.

Carolyn Lord, international teacher and global traveller

COLOUR PHOTOS

Please go to **www.luckyb.life** to see the original photos in colour.

PUBLISHER INFORMATION

Rowanvale Books provides publishing services to independent authors, writers and poets all over the globe. We deliver a personal, honest and efficient service that allows authors to see their work published, while remaining in control of the process and retaining their creativity. By making publishing services available to authors in a cost-effective and ethical way, we at Rowanvale Books hope to ensure that the local, national and international community benefits from a steady stream of good quality literature.

For more information about us, our authors or our publications, please get in touch.

www.rowanvalebooks.com
info@rowanvalebooks.com

CPSIA information can be obtained
at www.ICGtesting.com
Printed in the USA
BVHW041516270121
598900BV00008B/455